"This book is a fascinating, thought-provoking, and resonance-creating scaffold for navigating through the complexity and ambiguity of today and the future."

Renate Motschnig, *Vice-dean of Educational Affairs,*
University of Vienna, Austria

"For those who are unfamiliar with AI – this is a good introduction, for those who are already familiar with AI, this is a good refresher and for those who already use AI, this will provide some helpful, useful tips for you, particularly in future use. We need to be intelligently prepared for what is to come over the next few years!"

Michael F. Shaughnessy, *Professor of Education,*
Eastern New Mexico University Portales,
New Mexico, USA

"Teachers need to be aware of the varied forms of intelligence and the acceptance that current technical change is rapid, and hence classroom practice needs to accommodate these changes. I recommend that teacher-trainers should be first to respond to this challenge!"

Belle Wallace, *MEd, MPhil, FRSA*

"It is obvious, right from the beginning, that the authors know what they are talking about. I highly recommend it."

Dr. Hanna David, *Psychologist & Counsellor for Gifted Students,*
Emerita Tel Aviv University, Israel

"A must to read for any teachers, educators and administrators. Most definitely thought-provoking but also a validation of how to create alternative possible educational futures. I will prescribe the book for the taught Masters (Curriculum Design) course."

Dr. Gillian Eriksson, *Senior Lecturer, Department*
of Learning Sciences and Educational Research,
University of Central Florida, USA

AI AND DEVELOPING HUMAN INTELLIGENCE

As the relationship between AI machines and humans develops, we ask what it will mean to be an intelligent learner in an emerging, socio-dynamic learningscape. The need for a new global view of intelligence and education is the core discussion of this future-focussed collection of ideas, questions, and activities for learners to explore.

This fascinating guide offers activities to understand what needs to be changed in our education systems and our view of intelligence. As well as exploring AI, HI, the future of learning and caring for all learners, this book addresses fundamental questions such as:

- How do we educate ourselves for an increasingly uncertain future?
- What is the purpose of intelligence?
- How can a curriculum focussing on human curiosity and creativity be created?
- Who are we and what are we becoming?
- What will we invent now that AI exists?

AI and Developing Human Intelligence will interest you, inform you, and empower your understanding of "intelligence" and where we are going on the next part of our journey in understanding what it is to be human now and tomorrow.

John Senior is a visiting researcher at the Institute for Cognitive Neuroscience and Psychology of the Hungarian Academy researching the relationship between HI and potential psychodynamic mental health issues of AI machines.

Éva Gyarmathy is a senior researcher at the Institute of Cognitive Neuroscience and Psychology of the Hungarian Academy researching the challenge of the 21st century and talents associated with specific learning difficulties, ADHD, and/ or autism.

AI AND DEVELOPING HUMAN INTELLIGENCE

Future Learning and Educational Innovation

John Senior and Éva Gyarmathy

Routledge
Taylor & Francis Group

LONDON AND NEW YORK

First published 2022
by Routledge
2 Park Square, Milton Park, Abingdon, Oxon OX14 4RN

and by Routledge
605 Third Avenue, New York, NY 10158

Routledge is an imprint of the Taylor & Francis Group, an informa business

British Library Cataloguing-in-Publication Data
A catalogue record for this book is available from the British Library

Library of Congress Cataloging-in-Publication Data
Names: Senior, John (Educator), author. | Gyarmathy, Éva, author.
Title: AI and developing human intelligence : future learning and
    educational innovation / John Senior and Éva Gyarmathy.
Description: Abingdon, Oxon ; New York, NY : Routledge, [2022] |
    Includes bibliographical references and index.
Identifiers: LCCN 2021013973 | ISBN 9780367404864 (hbk) |
    ISBN 9780367404888 (pbk) | ISBN 9780429356346 (ebk)
Subjects: LCSH: Intellect—Philosophy. | Learning, Psychology of. |
    Learning strategies—Technological innovations. | Education—
    Philosophy. | Machine learning—Philosophy.
Classification: LCC BF431 .S4386 2021 | DDC 153.9—dc23
LC record available at https://lccn.loc.gov/2021013973

ISBN: 978-0-367-40486-4 (hbk)
ISBN: 978-0-367-40488-8 (pbk)
ISBN: 978-0-429-35634-6 (ebk)

DOI: 10.4324/9780429356346

Typeset in Bembo
by Apex CoVantage, LLC

CONTENTS

FIGURES

TABLES

ABOUT THE AUTHORS

John Senior is an active learner and teacher, creativity consultant, lecturer, and writer. For over four decades he has worked with and for young, insatiable learners as a co-learner/mentor. His current research concerns the journey to understanding the relationship between Human Intelligence and the potential psychodynamic mental health issues of AI machines. Other interests focus on the authenticity of being and practical approaches to supporting parents, carers, schools, and learners who are learning within a time of turbulence.

He is the author/co-author and sometime editor of 17 books, including joint editorship and contributor to the *SAGE Handbook of Gifted Education*. He has also published enrichment programmes and publications supporting home education. He is an associate language editor and senior reviewer for *Gifted Education International*, a SAGE Journal, and a visiting researcher at the Institute for Cognitive Neuroscience and Psychology of the Hungarian Academy.

Éva Gyarmathy is a senior researcher at the Institute for Cognitive Neuroscience and Psychology of the Hungarian Academy. Her research interests focus on multiple exceptional gifted individuals such as talent associated with specific learning difficulties, ADHD, autism, and social/cultural differences. She also lectures in several universities. As a psychotherapist, her work is directed toward the care of the profoundly gifted and multiple exceptionally talented. She is a consultant to private schools that serve gifted children and adolescents who could not be integrated into mainstream schools. She founded the Adolescent and Adult Dyslexia Centre and the Special Needs Talent Support Council.

ACKNOWLEDGEMENTS

We offer our sincere thanks to those who read, advised, read again, and commented on our ideas and writing. We are extremely fortunate to know so many people who are happy to speak truthfully. Special thanks to Zsófi Gyamarthy for her invaluable observations and helping us pull the reins in on some of our wilder thinking. Likewise, our deep thanks to Sarah Philo for her astute observations, keen eye, and keener intelligence. Thanks also to Bruce Roberts at Taylor & Francis for commissioning this book and for his thoughtful patience and support, and to Molly Selby (also at Taylor & Francis), who worked harder than anybody to produce this readable, organised, and forensically edited book. All thinking errors, misconfigurations, wild thoughts (and flashes of light!), or otherwise lay at our feet.

We also acknowledge a special thanks to Platyhelminth, the Flatworm, and the Stromatolites-Cyanobacteria partnership, without whom this book would not have been possible.

PREFACE

To say we live in a complex, changing, and challenging world cannot be disputed. How we manage the challenges of change is important and something we can control. Artificial intelligence (AI) and human intelligence (HI) are at the centre of successfully managing change in a positive, compassionate, ethical, and humanitarian way. This book explores some ideas to do with our understanding of what it means to be intelligent now and in a possible future. The amount of information regarding AI can be overwhelming. We hope we discuss in this book ideas that will interest you, inform you, and empower your understanding of what has led us to our present understanding of 'intelligence' and where we are going on the next part of our journey in understanding what it is to be human now and tomorrow. In fact, we hope we have written a guidebook for exploring AI, HI, and the future of learning and caring for all learners. A guidebook is always useful.

> AI is taking over a great deal of what has previously been viewed as the human domain. As a result, the evidence that we need to change the way we view intelligence and the way we design our education system is increasingly compelling. We need to act on this evidence and use our human ingenuity to re-imagine our education system to enable us to remain the smartest intelligence on the planet.
>
> *(Luckin, 2018)*

What follows is a brief guide to the historical development and changing definitions of what was and is now understood by the word and concept of "intelligence." The discussions within this book focus on what intelligence will become in future decades. Are we ready for a quantum leap in our understanding of what it is to be an intelligent human being in an AI world leading to deep learning and a host of innovation?

AI and machine learning are also explored, as is the likelihood of machines evolving and self-developing mental health issues which will need more attention in the nearing future of autonomous-acting intelligent machines. AI thinking at its core is essentially human.

Reference

Luckin, R. 2018. *Machine Learning and Human Intelligence: The Future of Education for the 21st Century*. London: UCL IOE Press. ISBN: 978-1782772514.

INTRODUCTION

Artificial intelligence: the mirror we can climb through

FIGURE 0.1 (ON LEFT) AND FIGURE 0.2 (ON RIGHT): "For you see, so many out-of-the-way things have happened lately, that Alice had begun to think that very few things indeed were really impossible" (Carroll, 2003)

With new knowledge come new thinking and new solutions to problems we did not realise existed. With new knowledge come new challenges and definitions. The identity and influence of artificial intelligence (AI) is accelerating and will accelerate our understanding of what it is to be human and how we will need to develop if machines also start developing independently. With new knowledge come new perceptions and insights into how we learn and how we teach,

DOI:10.4324/9780429356346-1

how we can envision the future and become active partners with AI in creating the future. Never has the future held greater challenges than the time we are living in. In the past we have had epidemics, financial collapse, religious and moral earthquakes, war and unrest, unspeakable wrongs to fight against, and the overarching problem of human ignorance. The future informed by work done today – if general purpose artificial intelligence (GPAI) becomes possible and is created – will mean there is no need to assume there would only be one solution to fit all challenges, as GPAI would be capable of enormous calculation intelligence. Already today, even recourse to only special AI can help us overcome problems and shape the future. AI does not need to repeat the mistakes of the primate, *Homo sapiens*.

In this book we look at what it is to be intelligent, what it means to challenge accepted views of how we should learn and teach in the world of an advancing technology that is working at speeds we can hardly manage to understand. We seek to explore and contribute to the reduction of uncertainty in the whole of society by a careful examination of how intelligence is developed and enriched through, in part, determining a holistic curriculum delivered through a holistic pedagogy.

Developing learning represented by artificial intelligence + human intelligence will maximise our intellectual, commercial, and physical survival chances as we manage and respond to the emergent developments, dangers, and challenges of AI.

> The world is far from finished. There are new additions and old errors everywhere that must be considered in ever-changing pictures of the world. We are reduced to fragmentary knowledge sufficient to provide practical but partial anchorages. The study of epistemology is a prescription for humility.
>
> *(Viney and Douglas, 2017)*

We must learn from our mistakes to survive and to improve our lives and the experience of being human.

Artificial intelligence offers an opportunity to see things differently, to act differently, and perhaps most importantly to frame an understanding of what it will mean to be human in a world of intelligent machines – at all times bearing in mind that GPAI may achieve an independent learning state sooner than we think.

And that is why you should read this book. It is a book of fact and fiction, nightmares and dreams, possibilities, and opportunities – it does not seek to be a scientific work or a strictly pedagogic guide. It is a book for the present and a modest guidebook for the future of learning and what it will mean to be a learner in the age of AI. Our view of intelligence is that it is going to move from the stage of the adolescent narcissist to one whereby informed and mature choices will need to be actively arrived at. These choices will be decisions that will in turn need to be acted upon as we understand the underlying anxieties and ambitions that underpin our present concepts of what it means to be intelligent.

Artificial intelligence may even be the purpose of the human race. Who is to say? In this book we aim to promote and inform learners, teachers, and carers as to the pathways and highways we can choose as individuals within stronger communities to follow. We can follow on from the work and vision of Augusta Ada King, Countess of Lovelace, as she explored through the mindset of "poetical science." This led her to ask questions about the "analytical engine" through which she considered how individuals and society related to technology as a collaborative tool, presciently saying that machines can only do what we have the skill to tell them to do.

Our starting point, central to this book and our views as researchers, is one step in building on the work of the many people of vision. We might at some point in our future be entering a time when intelligent machines will not need to be told anything. They will need to have discussions and to continually learn as humans do. In life we do not start from nothing.

The words of Toffler are still relevant to our present-day situation and will remain so for the foreseeable future:

> When a society is struck by two or more giant waves of change, and none is yet clearly dominant, the image of the future is fractured. It becomes extremely difficult to sort out the meaning of the changes and conflicts that arise. The collision of wave fronts creates a raging ocean, full of clashing currents, eddies, and maelstroms which conceal the deeper, more important historic tides.
>
> *(Toffler, 1980)*

Each chapter is laid out in a similar way. Chapters are briefly précised; then the main content of the chapter follows. In many ways this is a practical book seeking to afford informed change, and with this in mind we have included four sections to support the ideas in each chapter: sample activities/exercises and projects, link pathways (further discussion points/topics), suggested further reading, and the references pertinent to the particular chapter. The book is presented so that chapters are independent of each other while linking in order to present an overall view of our collective possible futures as we discover how to learn in a new world.

1   Defining the new learning landscape

- Information and uncertainty
- The third culture
- "Humachine" transformations

2   A brief history of intelligence

3   Fluid intelligence, other satellites, and consciousness

Should you see this book as a "serious" book? Yes. Should you see this book as a little disturbing? Certainly. Most importantly we hope you enjoy this mix of science and poetical art and find a positive return from considering our ideas and the presentation of other ideas: a book that is stimulating and a useful preparation for viewing the place we are now living in and the times we are steering our lives towards.

We are being driven by many "clashing currents" into changing our views of the past which in turn influences our view of how the future might be. The forces seeking changes are not all benign or caring of us. Understanding what is happening in our future world is essential whether we are a learner or a teacher, and we must recognise that we are both. Inaction is no choice we can make.

We hope you enjoy this book and find it useful in reflecting on our view of the past, present, and future mixed-up conceptions of AI and intelligence; what it means to be both reflecting upon and living in the present, preparing for the pedagogy of the future, and learning to live in an ever-developing human, artificial, synthetically intelligent present.

Enrichment

Questions to ask:

i   How would you define intelligence?
     Do you believe such a thing as a measurable intelligence exists?
     How would you characterise artificial intelligence as a feature of a developing world?
     What is it to be human? What makes us unique?
     What is the use of consciousness? What is it for?
ii   The periodic table, also known as the periodic table of elements, is a tabular display of the chemical elements arranged by atomic number, electron configuration, and recurring chemical properties. The organization of the periodic table can be used to derive relationships between element properties, and also to predict chemical properties and behaviours of undiscovered or newly synthesised elements. How could a periodic table of intelligences be created? What common criteria could be assigned to intelligences? How many types of intelligence could exist? If not a periodic table of intelligence, could a periodic table of ideas be created, showing what does exist and the blank spaces of ideas that *should* exist?

Link pathways

What connects Lewis Carroll, Countess Lovelace, Alvin Toffler, Isaac Asimov, and George Polya?

References

Carroll, Lewis. 2003. *Alice's Adventures in Wonderland and Through the Looking Glass.* London: Penguin Classics. Illustrated. ISBN-13: 978-0-141-43976-1.

Toffler, Alvin. 1980. *The Third Way.* London: William Collins Sons & Co Ltd. ISBN: 000-21184-7.

Viney, W., Woody, William Douglas. 2017. *Neglected Perspectives on Science and Religion: Historical and Contemporary Relations.* Abingdon, UK: Routledge. ISBN: 978-1-138-28476-0.

Suggested further reading

Alison, Gopnik, Meltzoff, Andrew, Kuhl, Patrick. 1999. *How Babies Think.* London: Weidenfeld & Nicholson. ISBN: 0-297-84227-7.

Lovelace, Ada King. 1992. *Ada the Enchantress of Numbers: A Selection from the Letters of Lord Byron's Daughter and Her Description of the First Computer.* Mill Valley, CA: Strawberry Press. ISBN: 978-0-912-64709-8.

Macfarlane, Bruce. 2017. *Freedom to Learn: The Threat to Student Academic Freedom and Why It Needs to Be Reclaimed.* London: Routledge. ISBN: 978-0-415-72916-1.

Polya, George. 1945. *How to Solve It.* London: Pelican Books. ISBN: 0-14-012499-3.

Wooldridge, Michael. 2020. *The Road to Conscious Machines: The Story of AI.* London: Pelican Press. ISBN: 978-0-241-39674-2.

1

DEFINING THE NEW LEARNING LANDSCAPE

A humble guide to the new world

Information and uncertainty – the struggles of education at level 2

The digital generation is us – all of us. Generations who previously would have been labelled as digital immigrants are more similar to those called digital natives than their earlier selves. Predigital fossils have not changed, though, of course. The old adage is true in this respect, too: "The stones remain." And there will be many who will remain strangers to the digital present and future. We always need to remember that, for many, change is difficult to accommodate, and we must take this into account as the realisation of the future accelerates.

However, those who are alive to change and learning and not made of stone have spent so much active time in the age of info-communication that their neurological systems have adopted to the ways of this age. The human spirit, on the other hand, especially in a defensive mode, does not succumb so easily to novelty, and it will vigorously resist change and the uncertainty caused by change. Many people are still waiting for a new culture to pop into existence, which would finally bring some stability again.

This new culture is in the making. This is the good news. The bad news (but each can label "good" and "bad" as they see fit) is that the core essence of this new culture is change. As such, the most important component of our psychological survival gear is the acceptance of uncertainty. It will not be easy, but, coupled with our other values necessary for survival, we are facing a huge opportunity for development.

The general direction of historical development is clear, as are the new challenges of change, and answers to these challenges. They have already appeared in accordance with a series of levels familiar from several domains of human activity. Such challenges signal a change between these levels and

DOI: 10.4324/9780429356346-2

inter-relationships and have invariably brought revolutionary changes in all eras and all arenas.

However, the stimuli bearing change have not yet reached the response threshold of the educational system. It has either been sedated with particularly strong tranquilisers, or the system itself is too unwieldy and requires a bigger scale of destruction in order for the mummies of education to be uncovered and put in a museum and for the pyramids to be filled with content adapted to change.

Information networks

Human information networks exist and have always existed, because the transfer of information belongs to and is enlivened through human social behaviour and has a defining impact on human development.

According to evolution scientist Robin Dunbar (2004), everything started with social grooming. On observing the social behaviour of primates, he concluded that this social cohesion activity is very demanding, and as a result, the brain is capable of handling only a limited number of social relationships. Based on the brain capacity of different species, he calculated the approximate size of their communities. In the case of humans, this number is around 150 people. Grooming such a great number of individuals would be, however, time-consuming, and so in the case of humans, the role of social grooming has been taken over by talking and gossip as a means of building social cohesion.

This helped considerably in our rise and our development.

The ancestor of the internet was a merely virtual (although we shall pass over what we mean and understand as to exactly what is real) network transferring information, and it worked well in smaller communities. Humans, however, strived to expand their communication in both space and time, and they experimented with different mediums. Smoke signals, cave drawings, then later recorded linguistic speech (pictographs, pictographic writing), phonological representations, and alphabetic writing were a big step forward in knowledge sharing.

Printing brought about a revolutionary change, and subsequently the spread of electronic communication tools and digital technologies meant that info-communication became extremely fast and rich, bringing with it a number of social and developmental changes. Even gossip did not remain what it used to be. It developed with the technologies of the 21st century, which shows that gossip does indeed fill an important role in humanity's life.

Gossip plays a vital community- and culture-forming role, not to mention that people are also informed of important things through gossip. Gossip used to be the news. The appearance of printing brought on an enormous change, and publicly available information came into being. Gossip became the antithesis of this.

As printing became widespread, gossip as information took on a negative connotation, because in many respects what it conveys is unreliable and inessential, and it is often used for manipulative purposes. Today, now that we have technologically surpassed printing and the internet has opened up the way for information at a hitherto unseen level, information very much resembling gossip is beginning to increasingly appear on this pinnacle of information tools: information on the internet is often unreliable, inessential, and often serves manipulative purposes. Gossip has become globalised.

With the appearance of the internet, it seemed at the beginning that human knowledge would finally expand and would be unstoppable. However, as the internet became widespread, its content slipped out from under the control of the small class of "literates." Information generated by the users mirrors these users, and so the greater the masses that use the internet, the more its content mirrors the intellectual content of humanity.

The internet is a storehouse of the information generated by humans, rather than of humanity's knowledge. The first step in learning to use new tools is to learn how they work and how they can be used. The second step is to understand what it is that it creates and how it creates it. We have taken the first step, even if somewhat hesitatingly, but not the second one, and we should be cautious as to the next steps we take, as it is dangerous to proceed without understanding what it is we are proceeding to.

The internet bombards us with data, information, knowledge, and wisdom, but it would be good to know which is which.

The road from information to knowledge and, hopefully, beyond

The words *data, information, understanding,* and *knowledge* are often used synonymously, even though there are vital differences between them. Russell Ackoff (1989) analysed very precisely the various elements in communication. Since then, many have been trying to develop his system, but the following captures its essence:

- **Data:** a description of the world in symbols; facts
- **Information:** processed, transferred data, knowledge, or opinion; answers "who," "what," "when," and "where" questions
- **Knowledge:** processed, applied data and information; a model of the world; answers "how" questions
- **Understanding:** involves further processing; answers "why" questions
- **Wisdom:** evaluation of the processed material

A piece of **data** is about unprocessed facts. It may be mistaken, but it is never false (though it can be falsely conveyed). At that point, however, it is information and not a piece of data obtained through direct experience.

Information already represents interpretation and opinion, and of course, like data, can also be mistaken, but processing allows for conscious or unconscious deception as well.

Knowledge arises from the processing of information. Following appropriate processing, useful knowledge comes into existence. Knowledge presents a limit to the ability of answering questions. If processing remains at the level of memorisation, a more generalised application of knowledge is not possible.

Understanding is the cognitive and analytical processing of knowledge. The difference between knowledge and understanding is the same as the difference between memorisation and learning. This is a conceptual difference that the word *learn* actually fails to highlight sufficiently. If someone has learned something, then they are able to apply that piece of knowledge, while if they merely memorised it, then they will not be able to apply it due to lack of processing, because processing is what leads to understanding and therethrough to solutions beyond mere factual knowledge.

Computers are able to process data and create information for us. Significantly, artificial intelligence can no longer only memorise things; it is also able to learn things. This way, a machine may be able to learn more efficiently than a student who is compelled by education to stick to factual knowledge.

Wisdom is the highest level of processing and synthesis, a level at which the mind creates new connections based on knowledge and based on the evaluation and deliberation of the understanding of this knowledge. This is a creative level, a level at which elements of earlier categories are evaluated along moral and human values, as well, whereby a higher-level understanding can emerge.

The first four categories relate to the past and are concerned with what has been and what can be known or understood from what has been. The fifth category, wisdom, looks at the future, and in fact creates ideas that constitute the future. However, this level is out of reach without a command of the previous levels of processing.

Many are of the opinion that artificial intelligence is incapable of reaching this level because of its lack of conscious experience. However, if artificial intelligence develops at an exponential rate as reckoned by Ray Kurzweil (2005) and many others, then it could reach the capacity of the human brain within a few decades, and since it is able to learn, it will also acquire experience. The question is at which point we can regard this as a conscious experience.

Artificial intelligence has already crossed some boundary lines that we set with a human brain socialised in the past. One such line is creativity. Machines have been able for some time to write Bach chorales, and anyone today can create artistic pictures with basic mobile applications. Artificial intelligence can also write movie scripts and beat not only the best chess players but also Go masters, even though this game requires a lot of intuition. Artificial intelligence is also capable of producing formulas in organic chemistry.

Technology and the propagation of information both develop exponentially – that is, their development accelerates. Information floods us, and we have to learn to process it very soon. To achieve this, it can help if we understand the general tendencies of development processes, and if learning/teaching progresses to the levels currently dictating cultural and social changes.

The ladder of development

There are several segments of our collective and individual lives whose development catalyses significant changes in human history. Such segments include technology, information dissemination, and education. Technology has primarily affected the development of humanity at the level of ecology, while dissemination of information did so at a mental level.

The role of education is to impart the most important abilities and knowledge in a given culture, and education fulfils its function when it meets the technological and information dissemination challenges of the relevant culture. We need to respond not to the tools provided by our culture but to the problems posed by our culture.

Revolutionary changes involve fundamental level shifts which entail significant changes in the socio-cultural environment, and such turning points are as a result not hard to identify.

The instrument of the information explosion at the end of the 20th century was the internet. It developed within a very short time span and very clearly right in front of our eyes, and it has been progressing from Web 1.0 towards Web 4.0.

Each developmental stage of the internet has brought massive changes in human communication, which in itself makes the internet an important object of study. Here, however, the focus of our study is not merely the effect of the development of the internet. Instead, this quickly developing tool will be used to illustrate the stages of development through the different versions of the internet, adopting even the version designations 1.0–4.0.

The short history of the internet through its stages is as follows:

> **Web 0.0:** 1969 – ARPANET and other internal information networks are its precursors.
> **Web 1.0:** 1991 – The World Wide Web becomes a public network of information; information becomes publicly accessible.
> **Web 2.0:** 2003 – Social network; interactive; human links become widespread and common; users generate data.
> **Web 3.0:** 2006 – Intelligent network; it adapts data coming from the users to user needs; content becomes personalised.

Web 4.0: 2012 – Artificial intelligence becomes part of the network; a collaboration of machines and humans; a comprehensive organising force arises.

The different steps in the development of the internet are thus as follows:

1 Precursor, initiative
2 Appears and becomes accessible
3 Spreads and becomes widespread and mainstream
4 Becomes differentiated and personalised
5 Reaches the level of synthesis and becomes comprehensive

This trend fits all other forms of development as well, irrespective of how big a time interval the development takes up. The stages we observe through the transition stages of the internet – an important and quickly developing tool – apply equally to technology, information transfer, and education.

The cases of industrial revolutions, revolutions of the media, and the evolution of education would be entirely parallel, although in the latter case, we can hardly talk about revolutions' more restrained evolution. But the stages do support one another:

Precursors

Industry 0.0: 13th century – Technological innovations; the use of the force of nature during the first stages of "mechanisation;" the windmill and the water mill appear.

Media 0.0: 11th to 15th century – Codex-copying monks and (later) secular copying workshops would be involved in replication.

Education 0.0: 11th to 15th century – The foundations of today's education were laid in medieval monasteries, where even poorer children had the opportunity to study.

It becomes accessible:

Industry 1.0: end of the 18th century – The steam engine makes it possible for humanity not to rely on animal power; mechanisation becomes available.

Media 1.0: middle of the 15th century – Books need no longer be copied by hand; the printing press makes books, and so information is more accessible.

Education 1.0: middle of the 18th century – Schooling begins, and education becomes available to everyone.

It becomes widespread:

Industry 2.0: beginning of the 20th century – Mass production spreads; assembly line production.

Media 2.0: beginning of the 20th century – Massive spread of information; the radio, the printing industry, the telephone, television, and other cultural instruments make information available to the masses.

Education 2.0: beginning of the 20th century – Mass education emerges, compulsory schooling.

It becomes personal:

Industry 3.0: first decade of the 21st century – Digital solutions, production of more personalised products, nanotechnology, and 3D printing begin.

Media 3.0: first decade of the 21st century – Information belongs to everyone; personal information now also appears in the media.

Education 3.0: first decade of the 21st century – Digital solutions make personalised learning possible.

It becomes comprehensive:

Industry 4.0: 2014 – Comprehensive production; the biological, physical, and digital worlds are interconnected; intelligent products and the means of production and logistical provision communicate with each other in production (BMBF, 2014).

Media 4.0: 2020 – Comprehensive media; newspapers and TV channels are not separate anymore; information is handled by artificial intelligence.

Education 4.0: middle of the 21st century – Learning inheres in everything; students can learn anywhere; the school is electronic and mobile and is connected to artificial intelligence.

It is not hard to see that education lags significantly behind in terms of development trends. In a very few countries, personalised education that is assisted with solutions from digital technology is the norm, but in several countries, the central goal is still the mass education of version 2.0, with a single central curriculum and uniform implementation, all the while level 5.0 is soon on the horizon when it comes to the web and industry. Level 5 is pushing at the classroom door.

The consequences of this lag can be seen in the increasing lack of skilled workers at a time of considerable unemployment levels. With the development of the industry, several professions are lost, but several professions are also created. The new professions, however, require level 3.0 or even level 4.0 know-how.

Education, owing to its own lack of progress, is preparing students for a much lower level than the current level of the industry, or even the level of information processing in the media – that is, information transfer. As a result, the generations of the future continue to remain vulnerable even in an area crucially influencing human society, namely, information management.

Education at level 2.0

Education fails to find its place. It got stuck in the 20th century and is a source of failure after failure. At present, the system cannot even handle student 3.0. Certificates and waivers that document this are currently issued to children in the form of diagnoses. Such documents – issued by experts – state that the student needs to receive personalised education. As such, the recommendations in the diagnoses issued to children describe exactly what education should be implemented at a system-wide level.

At a 3.0 level, personal modalities take centre place, and diversity appears as a value. This is the most direct task in front of education.

This is the major attitude change that is necessary; the rest will follow as education is able to embrace and assimilate change. We can start by acknowledging that even teachers are diverse, and not everyone uses Facebook or has a smart phone in their pocket. And if virtuosos of info-communication, well-versed in all aspects of web 4.0, decry teachers who do not use digital technologies, they immediately prove that they are themselves stuck at level 2.0 just as much as the one who decries the children immersed in digital technologies.

The measure of an efficient teacher is engaging in teaching activities stemming from the children's interests, rather than the use of technological tools. The latter is automatically a part of learning.

Children mirror human culture because they are socialised in the given culture. In other words, their brains are wired by culture, and so they are the ones who signal changes best. Currently, they are signalling that they are developing in diverse ways and at different paces in the stimulus environment at hand. This developing diversity is also inventing the future delivery and curriculum of future learning.

In earlier cultures, a relatively homogeneous and restricted spectrum of stimuli was the norm. The info-communication space started to open up in the 20th century, but it was still a slow business and the "media" worked in a more limited way than today: books, radio, television. Although toys and travel opportunities became widespread, the opportunities of children for autonomous, self-directed learning experiences were much more limited than today.

In the age of info-communication, the environment becomes significantly richer in stimuli. Children's brains can pick and choose from a much greater spectrum of stimuli than before. However, it is not primarily the quantitative increase in stimuli that is responsible for the change, but the fact that children are in the position to acquire personalised and large quantities of information and knowledge independently, without the mediation of adults. As a result, their environment is automatically more individually tailored, and consequently, their abilities and affinities find the stimuli necessary for their development sooner. And in absence of guidance, they do so even at the expense of neglecting certain other areas.

The developing brains are able to independently satisfy their interests and desire for experience with information already at preschool age, while of course potentially omitting a lot of activities that used to be commonplace, and this may lead to deficits.

As soon as humanity was freed from the constraints of information scarcity, its diversity manifested itself. A homogeneous education that only takes the average into consideration cannot be successful in such a diversifying world.

The stimulus environment, which from today's perspective used to be very limited, channelled development in a single direction, and whatever lay outside the expectations of school and education seemed irrelevant owing to the illusion of homogeneity. Segregation, the "Taygetos," ostensibly solved the situation.

As the stimulus environment became richer, however, differences came to light, which were identified as "heterogeneity" by the system. The problem now concerns great masses and cannot be ignored any longer. The crowd shoved to the side will form a dark mass when they grow up, and in absence of a leash this mass will break loose in a realm of wide new opportunities, and then in absence of independent thinking can be easily put on the leash of any ideology and exploited to any end.

Integration as a solution is rather mixed. It counts as an important step forward that it is now an essential goal for "heterogeneity" not to remain uncatered to. But integration is not the real solution, because the idea behind it is that we simply squeeze the individual back into the system that rejected them in the first place. A methodological reform is missing. New methods have begun to be introduced at local levels in several places, often driven by teacher ambitions, but a system-level change is lacking.

The real solution would be to ensure the conditions for inclusion. Once diversity is acknowledged and identified as a benefit, the system will not simply tolerate but *value* individual ways and solutions, and it can proceed to level 3.0 using personalised education.

Today, change is at a critical point where it is no longer possible to ignore what we have already acknowledged in other areas: nature favours diversity, and individual paths are of value.

Diversity is also a key issue in information management, but the most important thing is for us to understand the significance of information and information processing in an information space that has rapidly opened wide up.

Information processing and uncertainty

Now that we are so far along our journey into the information age, it is high time (in fact, maybe we're already somewhat late) to recognise information and different ways of processing it, to understand and make others understand what is what, and what has what value.

According to the information theory of Claude Shannon (1948), the information content of a certain quantity of data depends on the extent to which it lowers uncertainty. The more probable an event, the lower its news value and the less it lowers uncertainty. An improbable event, on the other hand, has big informational content. This is why it is more interesting news if the postman bit the dog than if the dog bit the postman.

Looking at the psychological aspect, we see that news plays a role in survival, because it informs us of some hitherto unknown danger or some hitherto unrecognised opportunity. Each new phenomenon is thus interesting to us in two respects, and we can learn from it in either way. Learning, in turn, is an instrument of our survival.

Translating this back into the domain of information, the result of a situation whose outcome is up to chance is uncertain. Once the situation is resolved, this uncertainty disappears. The original uncertainty can be measured with the amount of information we gained on the resolution of the situation.

Uncertainty is lack of information, and the reverse is also the case; that is, information results in a reduction in uncertainty. Doing the math, we get the result: people are more receptive to extreme news, because it is less probable and so the information content is bigger.

People's attention is easily captured with sensational news, even if it is false. And in the info-communication age, any kind of news can be generated very quickly.

When we check and process a piece of news, we lower the informational value of the news because its novelty decreases: once we link it to known facts, it becomes more organised.

Weaver and Shannon introduced into information theory the concept of entropy. Entropy is a level of uncertainty which is measured by the information necessary to cancel it. In other words, entropy is missing information, and so an infinite number of possibilities means full freedom and full uncertainty. (This is why many people do not care for freedom – and excessive freedom is indeed dangerous, being a demanding chaos itself.)

The value of information is highest when there are an infinite number of choices. If the situation is highly organised, randomness is of a lesser degree; possibly there is not even any choice – in this case, the value of information and the level of entropy is low.

Translating this into problems of psychology, it is exceedingly difficult to choose between two similar things, be they good or bad. The choice will be random, because we lack information based on which to choose among the alternatives, so there is as little opportunity for conscious decision as when there are no choices. (Cf. in a dictatorship, news does not have informational value.)

The more a system is constrained by rules, the smaller the role information has, and the less chance there is to tackle new phenomena, whereby learning remains at a lower level. In an open world, however, information is incredibly important, because we have a choice; we can make decisions and we need to deliberate things, whereby our uncertainty is high, as is our opportunity to learn.

The biggest danger, however, is not when uncertainty is high, but when information is sparse and/or unprocessed. (Too much information therefore leads to high entropy just as much as lack of information, because it is impossible to process it, and as a result it fails to become information.)

It is especially catastrophic to be socialised in a highly regulated system while belonging to an open world, because we then cannot learn to select and consider information relevant to our decisions and to choose from among alternatives.

By the 21st century, the concept of information has gotten inextricably linked to technology. Computers can convey and store information and are also capable of generating new information. They make data processing significantly easier for us, thereby reducing entropy and uncertainty.

Machines help in processing enormous amounts of data, but they do not solve everything. For the time being, cognitive processes are necessarily applied to enhance information processing, and cognitive development remains – for the immediate future – indispensable. Our task is to educate towards a higher-level thinking, understanding, synthesis, deliberation, evaluation, and therethrough critical thinking, developing both intelligence and wisdom.

A survival kit for the 21st century

Based on the foregoing, the main problem of the present developmental crisis emerges in the form of uncertainty. The mainstreamness of developmental stage 2.0 still offers a sense of security to many: uniformity, uniform education, uniforms, and marches. The negative connotation in the word *deviance* hints at the point of view of a past era.

In contrast, level 3.0 is about differentiation. Diversity, however, also leads to uncertainty. We can see that change is accelerating, and its acceleration itself is accelerating, that is, its acceleration is exponential. The move from one stage to the next is happening within a single lifetime – see the history of the internet – something for which the human psyche and society is not prepared. Changes also increase uncertainty. The most important task in order to tackle the challenges is therefore to manage uncertainty.

Society, and especially its "antechamber," education, needs to prepare children for the 3.0 world of the 21st century, rather than the 2.0 world of the 20th century. We are now past the 24th hour, and are very much late, which can prove fatal. Therefore, we need to prepare at least a survival kit for the 21st century.

The complete kit contains the following:

- Acceptance of uncertainty
- Co-operation
- Harmony
- Autonomy
- Critical thinking
- Attitude of *carpe diem*

The pedagogies of the 20th century that are to this day still called "alternative" place these values in the foreground. In the 21st century, alternative pedagogies will be the alternatives of pedagogy.

The components of the survival kit are not independent of each other; they form a whole, and so the effect is greatest if all components are present.

Acceptance of uncertainty

Certainty offers a sense of security. Humans strive towards this in every possible way, and this is what often causes their downfall. This is especially true in situations where the solution lies not in certainty, but in managing uncertainty. Based on the foregoing, it is evident that while uncertainty may be reduced in several ways, it cannot be eliminated completely and shows a propensity for resilience.

The primary direction of development and learning is the acceptance of uncertainty. All other components of the survival kit serve this goal.

Co-operation

A saying attributed to Margaret Mead, the well-known American cultural anthropologist, encourages that never doubt that a small group of thoughtful, committed citizens can change the world.

Humans are social beings, and as such, peers and communities have a key role in tackling challenges. Co-operation does entail some uncertainty, since there is a need for harmonizing different views and solutions, and everyone needs to trust both themselves and others as well. Diverse knowledge, diverse ways, and their sum and synthesis are the solution to the problem. Social situations lower uncertainty through the reinforcing effects of the group.

The present education system, with its evaluations, ceaseless comparisons, and competitive milieu, prepares individuals unilaterally for zero sum games whose goal is to acquire goods and defeat peers. It teaches children that if someone becomes better, another becomes lesser, even though it has been known for a long time that this view is false. Through cooperation, everyone may come into more knowledge and more opportunities. The win/win/win way is when an optimal common gain is made out of a situation.

Co-operation is an efficient method to find comprehensive, forward-looking, longer-term solutions, as opposed to competitive situations directed towards selfishness and quickly reaping rewards.

Scarcity of resources, however, triggers competition, and it takes conscious effort of will for humans to also think in terms of co-operation for the sake of greater rewards and survival. It is no coincidence that co-operative techniques – like the jigsaw technique, the complex instruction programme, and cooperative learning – are increasingly coming to the forefront. Most efficient of all are the mixed techniques when, next to joint solutions, value is also placed on individual effort and excellence.

A technique that has already been successful in economics, dubbed "co-opetition" by Adam Brandenburger and Barry Nalebuff (1996), is the combined use of co-operation and competition. Co-opetition is a typical case of embracing uncertainty.

Harmony

Harmony offers the tranquillity of balance and a sense of order. Ancient activities like movement and exercise, arts, and strategic games target the harmonization of the internal and external worlds of individuals. Sensorimotor activities harmonise the individual's connection to the physical world. Arts give form to sensations and feelings. Strategic games help the individual become organised at a cognitive level with the help of analysis, logic, and algorithmic thinking. All of this makes the individual's information processing abilities more efficient.

Congruous, harmonic pieces of information do not cause tension. The brain perceives orderliness as harmony in the case of musical notes. In the case of noisy, disturbing, insufficiently congruent stimuli, the brain has a harder time organizing the signals, and uncertainty increases.

Randomness, disorderliness, and incongruity, however, offer greater freedom by opening up new possibilities. Uncertainty equals possibility if the neurological system and psyche of the individual is prepared for the processing, organisation, and integration of diversity. Internal harmony is one of the decisive forces in development.

If we attempt to reduce uncertainty using a huge amount of information and knowledge, then we make the key task (namely, processing) impossible, even though processing is what real learning would be.

Learning means shaping information into knowledge, then understanding, and at the highest level, wisdom. If this is replaced by endless hoarding of information, then uncertainty, too, remains endless and ingrained in the information age.

Autonomy

Autonomy is the ability of decision and independent action, control over external forces, and the use of an inner compass guiding the individual through the making of decisions. In absence of this, the individual is at the whim of external forces. In the presence of a plurality of forces when values are changing in the world and humans are exposed to a multitude of effects, the force called "intrinsic regulation" by Ryan, Deci (2000) has an especially important role.

We make a number of decisions daily without being conscious that we are doing so. Autonomy is the most important characteristic of adult life. In the case of small children, decisions that are natural for adults are made by others: what they should eat, what they should wear, where and when they should go.

Our autonomy should grow as our identity develops, and we should, if the circumstances are favourable, start making decisions independently and bearing responsibility for them. All the while, we also develop and respect the autonomy of others. This is what differentiates independence from uncontrolled self-indulgence.

Children who are trained to obey and who get used to external reinforcements and rewards grow into adults who do not take responsibility and who perform tasks only when instructed.

This has been known for quite some time, as has the fact that people are intrinsically motivated to develop. Education and training still use external rewards for the sake of short-term advantages and a rapid but fake development, even though every research result points in one direction: although extrinsic motivation might increase performance in the short term, it can cause irreparable damages by suppressing intrinsic motivation and therethrough autonomy.

The effect of external control is that we lose our interest and enthusiasm in activities we used to find interesting. Children draw fewer interesting drawings when they are rewarded. Rewards result in stereotypical responses, which also signals a decline in creativity.

Children do not learn from what they are taught but from how they are taught. The same applies to autonomy. Only an autonomous teacher is able to raise autonomous children. If teachers have free choice and decision and do not fall back on external pressure, threats, or rewards, then children in turn learn autonomous behaviour and are less likely to become uncertain and impressionable in new situations.

Critical thinking

Acquiring information is becoming increasingly easier; in fact, we are inundated with information, and it is getting harder to identify "suitable information." The place, reliability, relevance, and usability of a piece of information, as well as its connection to other pieces of information, is more important than any piece of knowledge.

Amos Tversky and Daniel Kahneman proved experimentally that we are by far not the rational beings we thought we were. They described 20 types of cognitive biases which can be inhibited through the use of controlled cognitive processes.

If we rely on quick, simple, and ostensibly efficient thinking; build on associations, experience, and impressions; and form our judgements by focusing on a single aspect of a situation, we often make serious, systematic, and systematic errors.

Filtering out erroneous, false, and unimportant stimuli is only possible via deep and thorough processing. We cannot do away with slow but controlled processing.

Digital tools have begun to pry at the weak points of human communication already at the level of media 2.0. Technologically assisted social networks enlarge the effects of human communities. In a relationship network that is much more intensive and active than those that came before, all advantages, disadvantages, and dangers are multiply magnified.

For example, in internet communities, the confirmation bias known as the "echo chamber" is rooted in our propensity to favour information that supports our own preconceptions and opinions, and which corroborates us, irrespective of the truth or falsity of the information. Without thinking, and, in particular, critical thinking, we are unprepared for the challenges of the info-communication age – in absence of these, we have been and will be easily impressionable and easily deceived at all times.

If we teach children to simply take in information and knowledge, then they are at risk of being blown away by any small breeze like dry leaves off a tree. We have to be aware, and we have to make children aware that we collect evidence and retrieve memories in an intuitive and selective way, and that we interpret information with a bias and make mistaken judgements. Fortunately, however, all of this is controllable.

Accepting uncertainty is easier if we have an instrument with which to reduce it. This instrument is a high level of information processing, a level at which we synthesise and evaluate incoming knowledge. It does not simply mean logical functioning, but recreating knowledge. Discovering regularities by means of rules and experience is an individual form of processing, and such an ability offers some amount of certainty even in uncertain situations.

Teaching children to think critically is a bigger protection for them than any prohibition, supervision program, or form of threats and deterrents. The world has opened up, and we cannot protect children from the outside. People can only conquer chaos with their own internal cognitive strength.

An attitude of *carpe diem*

The interpretation of the expression "seize the day" depends on the extent to which one is able to accept uncertainty. We may have many varied different notions of the future: the world ends, the golden age arrives, spiritual renewal occurs, the machines take over, humanity dies out, humanity battles with machines, humanity wins, humanity loses, humanity serves machines or vice versa, machines and humans merge, and intelligence conjoins. Art is humanity's imagination, and it has already lined up all kinds of versions. Even science came up with a number of directions towards development or catastrophe that humanity can willingly or unwillingly explore.

What is important is not what will actually be, but what we think of our own role and what actions we do now. Basically, any attitude can be justified in any version of a view of the future.

Carpe diem can be the way to reap the world and the rewards, and the way to self-development. It can be the way to ensure personal prosperity and the way towards general spiritual ascent.

Carpe diem is about the future because what we do now will be our future. The education system is naturally definitive for the future. It is definitive irrespective of whether it ruins the children or supports intellectual development. The best-case scenario is obviously the latter one, but an acceptable outcome would be for the children to be able to escape the system that is slowly turning into a straight-jacket and/or pre-digital fossil, ossified in the information age.

Everyone should pause, and take time to reflect and think about what *carpe diem* means for them.

Ecological and mental footprints

The stability and integrity of humanity depends on preserving the balance of natural systems, the individual, the family, the community, society, the ecosystem, and the ecosphere.

The key word is *balance*. If forces deviate significantly in any direction, and if significant deficits arise, then the system collapses. Balancing requires *ab ovo*, meaning in this context to work from the beginning, the origin of our beliefs and thoughts. The term is a reference to one of the twin eggs from which Helen of Troy was born. In order to survive, we need to learn to balance and apportion forces, and this is a never-ending task. Anything that lives is in constant motion and change. Only death is certain.

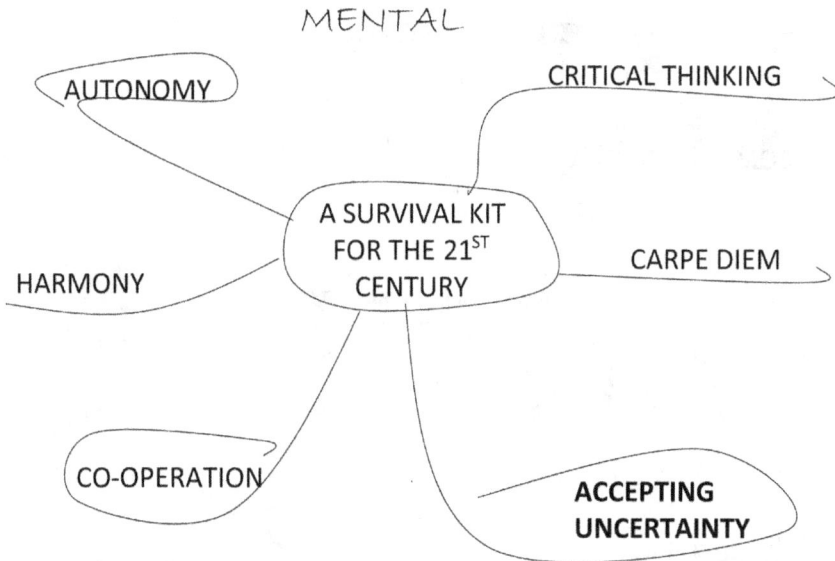

FIGURE 1.1 A survival kit for the 21st century

The goal of humans, given their instinctive attitude chained to the physical world, is a search for certainty, which is paired with a narrowing, convergent thinking that points in one direction. The instrument of this goal is competition and hoarding. According to this cognitive schema, the world must be conquered, and goods must be obtained to survive. Children must be taught to be soldiers and learn to obey and receive instructions as in Sparta.

In uncertain situations, some humans will evidently be lost because they are unable to build up an adult, responsible identity. In absence of a vision of the future of their own, they rally behind some person or organisation which shows an appearance of strength and sets up any kind of goal and which seems capable of obtaining resources. Another way to go is to embrace aimless hedonism, to reap any possible immediate rewards all at once.

All components of the 21st century survival kit presented here point in an alternative direction: to strive for balance and reconcile the irreconcilable (Figure 1.2). This is the essence of creativity.

The instrument for this is co-operation and striving for harmony with the world, with others and with other selves. All of this is built on the conviction that solutions exist that cater to the interests of all parties. This attitude helps children to grow up into responsible individuals.

Students are prepared for the responsibility of free choice already during their own education. Personalised learning is directed at harmony and creation. Children's own education can offer them an opportunity for deliberation

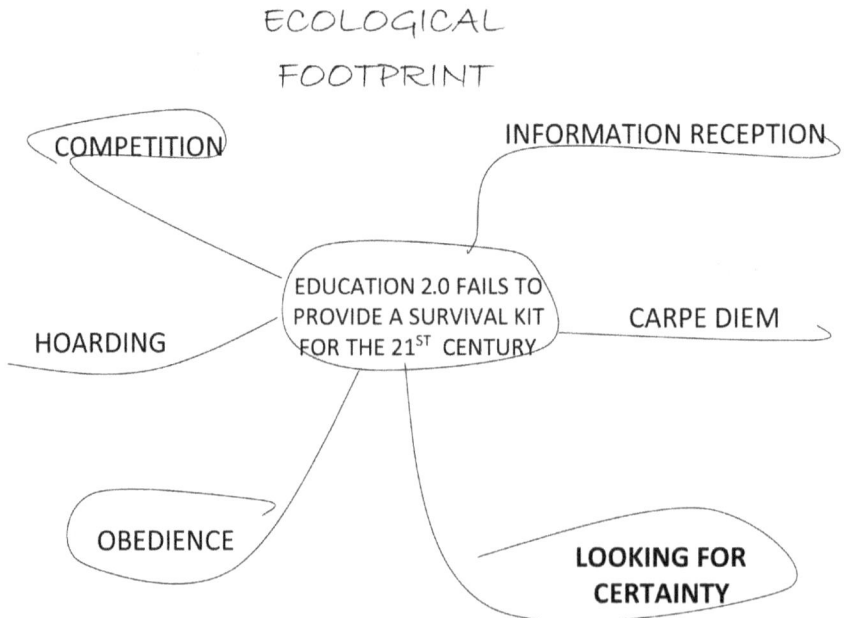

FIGURE 1.2 Education 2.0 fails to provide a survival kit for the 21st century

and informed decision making in questions affecting themselves and their environment, because as long as education takes individual characteristics into account, children learn to manage diversity and to reconcile the irreconcilable. As such, creativity will automatically form part of the solution to the problem. Critical thinking is not learning material; it is a form of learning and the way to wisdom.

Information is a possibility, and an immeasurable amount of information is an immeasurable possibility. Our attitudes will determine whether this possibility mobilises our instinctive survival methods and leads to an immeasurable devastation of our living space or whether we invest conscious mental effort and thereby achieve immeasurable spiritual development.

Enrichment

The management of uncertainty is critical for human achievement and well-being.

Can you identify five areas of uncertainty in your own personal life or the life of your community and suggest five strategies for reducing uncertainty? In resolving certainty of the problems you identified, are further uncertainties created?

Identified uncertainty	Certainty solution	Solution consequences

Link pathways

What links your ecological footprint, your mental footprint, and your motivation to welcome uncertainty?

References

Ackoff, R. L. 1989. From data to wisdom. *Journal of Applied Systems Analysis*, 16: 3–9.

BMBF, Bundesministerium für Bildung und Forschung. 2014. Zukunftsbild "Industrie 4.0," Hightech-Strategie, Berlin.

Brandenburger, A. M., Nalebuff, B. J. 1996. *Co-opetition*. New York: Currency. In Asgari, Sadegh, Afshar, Abbas, Madani, Kaveh. 2013. Cooperative game theoretic framework for joint resource management in construction. *Journal of Construction Engineering and Management*, 140 (3). doi:10.1061/(asce)co.1943-7862.0000818.

Dunbar, R. I. M. 2004. Gossip in evolutionary perspective. *Review of General Psychology*, 8 (2): 100–110.

Kurzweil, R. 2005. *The Singularity Is Near*. New York: Viking Books.

Ryan, R. M., Deci, E. L. 2000. Self-determination theory and the facilitation of intrinsic motivation, social development, and well-being. *American Psychologist*, 55: 68–78.

Shannon, C. E. 1948. A mathematical theory of communication. *Bell System Technical Journal*, 27 (3): 379–423.

Recommended further reading

Dunbar, R. I. M. 1996. *Grooming, Gossip, and the Evolution of Language*. Cambridge, MA: Harvard University Press.

Innerarity, Daniel. 2012. *The Future and Its Enemies*. Stanford: Stanford University Press. ISBN: 10: 0-8047-7557-5.

Meegan, D. V. 2010. Zero-sum bias: Perceived competition despite unlimited resources. *Cognition*, 1: 191. doi:10.3389/fpsyg.2010.00191.

Tversky, A., Kahneman, D. 1974. Judgments under uncertainty: Heuristics and biases. *Science*, 185 (4157): 1124–1131.

Ushakov, Y. V., Dubkov, A. A., Spagnolo, B. 2011. Regularity of spike trains and harmony perception in a model of the auditory system. *Physical Review Letters*, 107 (10): 108103.

Weaver, W., Shannon, C. E. 1964. *The Mathematical Theory of Communication*. Urbana: University of Illinois Press. 10th printing.

The third culture – a transition culture to the final level

Humanity's social-cultural and technical-economic development progresses in a mutually supporting way. If our progress is relatively synchronised, we can talk about general development. This development is, however, not linear but accelerates exponentially. Also, at the point when development reaches the end of a stage, then, like a snake, it must shed the externals of that stage, recasting itself to move on to the next one. These changes invariably lead to crises, even given the most ideal forms of development. And if development is uneven and the development of one area lags behind, the crisis will be all the more severe, since a bigger gap needs to be bridged in order to attain the new stage.

A crisis is followed either by a regression or a revolutionary step forward, and during a crisis, these alternate in a lesser form as a sort of back-and-forth dithering, a vacillation of being. Such crises are a natural part of development, but they do involve a big burden on, and perhaps even danger for, the individual and the community, especially if the crisis is significantly bigger than usual and is global, and if the extent to which the affected societies and cultures are unprepared for the change is highly likely to be uneven.

Technology and the natural sciences have run ahead of conventional thinking in the last few centuries, while the human mind and the social processes under its control have lagged behind. The accelerating technological-scientific development continues to increase dysynchronisation. In many respects, earlier intellectual values and solutions present hindrances to individual and collective progress. Human thinking and – not independent of this – education have especially fallen behind, even though education is of strategic importance in planning the future. By the turn of the 21st century, our world has become ripe for a significant social-cultural change. It is therefore time to look into the crystal ball to spot and ride the waves of change before they break over our head, sweeping us away.

The system of axial crises

For humanity, one of the main areas of coping, and also of development, is info-communication – that is, the acquisition and transfer of information. It is no coincidence that it is this area which has undergone the most substantial development. At the end of the 20th century and beginning of the 21st, humanity switched gears in info-communication technology in earnest and changed its values to a significant degree, which led to a so-called axial crisis. This crisis is not the first of its kind, though.

A rare event of global collapse in the order of things which leads to a religious-intellectual renewal is called an "axial moment" in sociology and philosophy. Not everyone is partial to this term, but it is perhaps one of the best to describe the phenomenon when changes lead to a general socio-cultural crisis in all areas. It is not unlike an axis making a turn, dragging everything along with it.

Karl Jaspers (1953), who coined the term, originally described roughly the last couple of centuries BC as the "axial age," characterising it as an age when new ways of thinking emerged in several different regions on Earth. These are also called "social revolutions." Irrespective of the terminology used, distinctly different lists of axial crises have been compiled by historians. From a psychological point of view, we consider social upheavals as significant if they correspond to the universal stages of development; we illustrated this earlier using the stages of the development of the internet. There are of course several smaller interim crises, but we focus on the moments that substantially changed humanity's cognitive functioning. These are built on each other in the way we discussed before:

1   Precursor, initiative
2   Appears and becomes accessible
3   Spreads and becomes widespread and mainstream
4   Becomes differentiated and personalised
5   Reaches the level of synthesis and becomes comprehensive

Significant socio-cultural revolutions are a part of historical processes and are always accompanied by a full-scale change in human thinking abilities. Humanity began forming cultures, developing complex social organisations some 70,000 years ago. Historian philosopher Yuval Harari describes this cognitive revolution as the first crisis: this is the point at which humanity's intersubjective thinking emerged and made it possible for *Homo sapiens* to form masses. The next crisis was the agricultural revolution, which gave rise to conditions necessary to form larger masses: humanity learned to perform methodical work, leading later to the development of literacy, which in turn brought about the spread of analytical, logical thinking.

The next scientific revolution that started about 500 years ago freed human thinking from faith and beliefs, and humanity took discovering and understanding the world into its own hands. This marked the beginning of the conquest of the unknown on Earth and in humanity's knowledge. The massing of humanity and the amassing of knowledge could begin growing at an exponential rate.

There are indications that the end of the 20th century likewise marks the end of an era, and that the development of human society is undergoing an axial crisis along with the fall of old ideologies, the dissolution of earlier views, and the world inevitably waiting for intellectual rebirth.[1]

Lying at the root of this scenario, also called the "information revolution," is the fact that the road to acquiring information has opened up for individuals, causing significant changes in the structure of society and in cognitive development. Public education, as a product of the industrial revolution, is in a crisis, and it would be an awfully bad omen for the next generations were it to remain as it is.

The revolution looming before us is qualitatively different from those before because humanity is synthesising its own physical and mental being with tools it created itself – not simply by extending its being but by merging it with technology. The cyborg world and bionic planning is the final stage and the first step on a long road ahead.

Here is a summary of humanity's cognitive development, specifying the approximate starting point of the respective stages:

1   **70,000 years ago:** Cognitive revolution – the world of intersubjective reality and beliefs
2   **10,000–12,000 years ago:** Agricultural revolution – the world of literacy, methodical thinking, categories, and hierarchies
3   **400–500 years ago:** Scientific revolution – emerging self-awareness, knowing about lack of knowledge, the world of conquest
4   **30–40 years ago:** Information revolution – the world of individuality, individual development, diversity, and networks
5   **in 5–10 years:** Bionic revolution – the cyborg world, unification of human and machine

As with all kinds of development, parts and pieces of earlier cultures persist, and the next cultures build on them in a similar way that a new settlement is built on the ruins of an older one, using parts of the old, obsolete, or unusable buildings.

Socio-cultural changes/crises emerge when a significant (in number and role) group within humanity attains the culture necessary for the level of the next era and is able to abandon values belonging to the earlier point of view and switch to a new kind of thinking. In other words, the way of thinking required at the next level emerges already at the previous level but manifests itself there as deviance and as atypical development and behaviour. As such, early-comers and pioneers can easily be accused of heresy, or in our age, can receive diagnoses of cognitive developmental disorders like learning-, attention-, hyperactivity-, or autism spectrum disorder.

The generation of the digital, or information age

The information-processing characteristic of the human brain is affected by the tools that play the most significant role in communication and the acquisition of knowledge in everyday life. These include television, VCRs, DVDs, computers, the internet, mobile smart phones, and digital games, as well as a number of other tools that have become part of everyday life. The breakthrough of digital-informational technology started in the 1980s but reached different populations of humanity in different ways and at different times.

With the rise and spread of informational technology, more and more people are voicing their concerns about the next generation. However, the changes in abilities do not exclusively affect children. Everyone living in a specific age changes according to the respective culture as it develops and becomes more concrete. Even individuals with the most fervent wish to stay literate, who reject and despise the digital world, cannot escape the effects. The television, computers, and mobile phones reach everyone, irrespective of age. We no longer need to – and most people no longer can – do mental calculations or remember telephone numbers. Printers, photocopiers, inbuilt cameras in mobile phones, and speech-to-text applications save us a lot of cursive handwriting, note-taking and copying, although at the cost of a significant deterioration of our handwriting skills.

Machines, which of course were created for exactly this purpose, supplant the most important skills of the age of literacy. As such, children born into today's age stand puzzled at what problems adults exactly have with the pervasive and familiar machine operations. Young children simply use what the previous generation handed to them.

The term *generation* covers the totality of humans of roughly the same age living in the same time period: the age group of those born at about the same time. In addition, however, the term also means "human lifetime" – the time required for a human age group to develop and grow up, about 25–30 years.

According to the generational theory of Neil Howe and William Strauss (2000), generations can be identified using three criteria:

1   Perceived membership
2   Common beliefs and behaviours, such as the attitude toward family, career, religion, or politics
3   Common location in history: the decisive historical events and turning points that occur during a generation's adolescence and young adulthood and have a significant effect on the lives of its members

While these are not independent of the year of birth, they are still better identifiers of generational membership than the birth year itself.

The notion of a human lifetime is not novel and has hardly changed so far in terms of length in time even though the length of average human life expectancy has increased by a few decades today. There used to be long-lived humans in earlier times, too, but a generation would encompass several lifetimes, because socio-cultural change used to be extremely slow compared to today – one could say barely existent. Changeovers between generations took place much more slowly in past centuries, and even more so in past millennia. Forms of behaviour wouldn't change within one lifetime to such an extent that one could speak of a new generation.

While historical events could alter the power structure, and people had to bow to king or queen Y instead of king or queen X, they did not have a significant effect on the basic views, beliefs, and everyday activities. One of the reasons "wise elders" enjoyed considerable respect is that they were the ones who had already seen a lot, and the solutions they had learned in their twenties would prove to be still useful 50 years later. Additionally they also carried the collective memory. In case of draughts, floods, fires, insect invasions, foreign tribes, sickness, epidemics, social distortions etc. one could listen to the wise elders, because they knew what did or did not help previously, since they were in a position to have already lived through such events. Especially in times without written records, the elderly would function as guides. Of course, even in those times, there was only a need for those who would function as a sort of walking and talking Wikipedia, that is, those who carried knowledge. This function that the elderly used to fill was compromised not only by the appearance of books and the internet, but even more so by the acceleration of change. What used to be a good solution in the youth of a person born in the 20th century would count as old-fashioned 50 years later, and as more of a joke in the 21st century. The older generation cannot rely on knowledge from its youth: they must learn to learn and learn to change.

The 20th and 21st centuries are fundamentally different from earlier ones when it comes to generations. Due to the rapid changes, there is a much greater difference between generations now than in earlier eras. In addition, the length of a human life is constantly increasing, and as a result, several generations and even lifetimes might coexist, and there aren't just a handful of Methuselahs around anymore. When we arrive at the point where human life can be extended indefinitely, we will face even newer problems; but for now, we need to focus on the problems of the present even as we must advance our creative thinking to begin addressing the new problems caused by our actions and thinking.

An interesting situation has arisen in which, due to longer life spans and exponentially accelerating change, at least six generations coexist currently. This is primarily researched by the business sphere, because understanding the divergent needs of highly different generations can deliver huge returns, or, conversely, can cause significant damages when ignored.

Understanding the characteristics of different generations features heavily in the science of economics. In contrast, this approach is barely palpable in education, even though all six generations also represent themselves in the school system. Admittedly, they have done so in different roles so far: the elder generations tend to be in the positions of teachers and the younger ones in that of the learners. At the same time, lifelong learning has brought about a situation such that those who want to keep up with the changes will be learning throughout their lives. As a result, it can easily happen that a member of a younger generation is the one teaching someone older.

There are several appellations of the specific generations, but professionals do agree more or less on the birth date-based categories. The American point of view has become the most widespread in defining Western European generations, but the terminology will differ slightly in different places and cultures of Earth, as they are embedded in different socio-cultural situations. Let us here go with the following terminology, since at this point, it does not have too much significance anymore:

- The Silent, or Mature Generation, or in other words, the builders (1925–1946)
- The Baby boomers, the hippies, the idealists (1943–1964)
- Generation X, the post-Baby boomers, the TV generation, the latchkey kids (1961–1981)
- Generation Y, the Generation of the Millennium, or the Millennials (1978–2000)
- Generation Z, the post-Millennials (1995–2010)
- Generation Alpha, the touch-screeners (2010–)

The dates are only approximate, and it is the characteristics described by Howe and Strauss that are more decisive in terms of generation membership. Another incredibly important criterion is the place of birth. It is of decisive importance how advanced the digital, info-communicational development is at the time of children's birth in the place of their birth and life, and especially in the place where they spend their adolescence and young adulthood. These more or less define, but not decide, which generation a given individual will identify with.

Even if we take the largest possible time intervals for generations, as shown here, the different age groups will still not cover a period of 30 years, so we are definitely not talking in terms of a human lifetime. A fairly good approximation and a valid characterisation of a generation is a span of 20 years: the typical span of generations today. This has barely reduced with time, except for the most recent times when the literature identified Generation Alpha, thereby squeezing Generation Z into a span of 15 years.

However, due to the acceleration of the change in the environment, future generations will probably not even have time to form properly: before a generation can take shape, a new generation will already be in the making. In other words, the term *generation* will be increasingly less applicable in understanding children of the future. This should not be a shocking experience. However, understanding the culture of info-communication and the characteristics typical of a specific individual and their group will be indispensable, as will a closer examination of the cause of the changes in generations: the new stimulus environment.

Who is in cultural arrears?

Some people only talk about de-generations nowadays, identifying several deficiencies that characterise the generations born and/or socialised in the info-communication age. However, statements that start with something like "The young people these days" were not voiced in the 20th century for the first time. Even literacy, which today is in decline and mourned for already, used to be unacceptable to some when it emerged. Plato (himself already literate) chronicles the objections of Socrates (who was illiterate, although happy to take in knowledge when it was read out loud to him) to literacy in *Phaedrus* and in *Seventh Letter*. Humanity is becoming stupid, says Socrates, according to whom memory skills decline through literacy because there is no need for them, and, consequently, people no longer use them. Knowledge within the mind is alive and belongs to the individual, while written words are mere reminders of knowledge. Literacy leads to superficial knowledge, claimed Socrates, who was also against distance education. According to him, written knowledge without the human conveying it is no true knowledge. Knowledge is brought about only through thoughts of deep reflection arrived at via dialogue. True knowledge can only be acquired through personal contact.

Socrates recognised accurately that literacy would have a huge effect on human thinking, and not necessarily a beneficial one. Human memory skills have definitely changed due to literacy. Delivering long epic narratives or messages required a much more holistic, comprehensive functioning of the human memory. With the arrival of literacy, this burden was greatly reduced, and our memory skills have become weaker. We did learn at school that legends and myths used to be spread orally, but did someone really think about taking a little something like *Beowulf* and conveying it orally? If we were to suggest trying to learn one of the little texts by Homer to members of the generation scolding today's young, they likely would be exactly as motivated as today's children are by their school curriculum.

However, learning even an entire book is no big challenge for a human mind. In medieval times, reciting litanies used to be quite natural. Take a letter from those times which notes in passing something like the following: "The young people these days! They cannot even recite ten pages by heart; they simply just read everything." According to this, learning ten pages by heart is just a simple exercise that could be a good example of a simple memorisation task. Or let us take actors, most of whom are able to learn exceptionally long texts even today, because they regularly use and thereby develop and maintain this ability.

Practice makes perfect. If we practise something often enough, we will become good at it. If we throw the ball around a lot, we will be good at ball-throwing; if we solve a lot of exercises in mathematics, we will be good at mathematics. If we lie a lot, we will become perfect at lying. The popularised view is that it takes 10,000 hours of practice to become an expert or master performer in a given field. Our brains are highly plastic but also practical. Whatever is in use will become stronger, and whatever is not will become weaker. Literacy robbed humanity of a lot of abilities. Fortunately, however, we have not only faced losses when it comes to literacy. We have also gained sequential step-by-step thinking. Literacy gradually reshaped humanity's thinking and view of the world. Free association and a holistic approach were superseded by categorisation and bureaucracy. And *Homo sapiens* got a lot of practice with these.

Reading as a way to develop thinking

The analytical, logical mode of information processing started developing intensely and took over the leading role in human thinking. During reading or listening to reading out, one has to follow pieces of information that come one after the other, and events succeed one another in a specific temporal order. When listening to someone reading out, knowledge is acquired by processing a sequence of words. Cartoons and films, on the other hand, present information in an audio-visual and simultaneous way, as a result of which knowledge is not built up step by step.

For example: The tiger is a huge, gold-and-black, striped, carnivorous animal with soft, cat-like steps. It often goes hunting on the shores of lakes and rivers. It moves in the water with long, drawn-out steps. It focuses on its prey with every nerve.

This verbal sequence can be presented in a picture and easily perceived. A child who learns about the tiger through a nature film will know a lot more about it than one who listened to someone reading out loud about the tiger. In a film, all information is accessible simultaneously, and the image and the movements of the tiger are not formed in the child's mind by processing linguistic elements. The case is the same no matter how simple or complex the image and the information conveyed. There is simply less need and opportunity for linguistic sequence processing in everyday life.

Reading and listening to reading out loud are natural ways to develop seriality, the ability to process sequential information and to follow sequences. If this function fails to develop appropriately in early childhood, the brain will never be able to effectively deal with sequences and the succession of elements.

The increased amount of visual information and reduced amount of reading out loud results in a lower level of not just reading abilities, but of dealing with serial information in general. This makes understanding lengthier instructions and more complex tasks, as well as learning texts by heart, more difficult. In the digital age, serial weakness has become a common phenomenon. The time may come when such a lower level of this ability will appear to be quite natural, because the ability of the majority will be at this level.

In addition, when reading or listening to reading out loud, one has to analyse a sequence of words following each other and understand the relationships and connections in order to form one's own internal ideas and images. Without the precise analysis of details, the verbal stream becomes nonsensical. Inferences and causal relationships are determined by linguistic phrasing. For instance: The chicks were marching behind the mami hen one after the other when thunder suddenly roared in the sky, upon which they all quickly hid under the wings of their mother. The mami hen leaned over and soothingly lowered her head upon them.

All of this would be much more interesting to watch on a film, in which case it would be holistic information and much easier to process. In the visual medium, however, processing of inferences and causal relationships is only required at a fairly low, at most passive, level.

Analytical thinking and an understanding of causal relationships and connections form the basis of logical thinking. Any weakness in these areas makes logical functioning unreliable, and as a result, the processing of materials other than of the visual kind will be of a lower standard, as well.

Additionally, image formation is the essence of reading. Linguistic elements need to be put together to form a picture, an internal image of one's own. Words evoke details one after the other, on the basis of which the brain forms an image. The ability of image formation can develop properly only if the child has enough opportunity to practise it. For this, the child needs to regularly listen to reading out loud. During image formation, verbal information must be turned into visual information. In addition to being able to understand the meaning of words, the ability to handle details is likewise essential for this. If the ability of image formation fails to develop during early childhood, the child will never become a comprehending reader.

An example of image formation: A fair-haired boy in pink trousers and a yellow shirt is kneeling on a three-wheeled scooter with one leg, holding the handlebar with only one hand. For those who can follow the linguistic sequence and form an image, more or less a picture will appear before their mind's eye. However, for children growing up on ready-made images, it will be hard to form images of their own by themselves. Even if these children manage to learn to read words and sentences at school, it will eventually come to light that they have difficulties with comprehension. This is the result of a weak image formation ability. More and more people are struggling with comprehension difficulties.

Even mild difficulties with comprehension can make learning exceedingly difficult. Reading course books and textbooks requires an enormous effort for someone who struggles with comprehension difficulties. It is not easy to interpret texts with poor image formation if there is no one to "translate" the text and present the learning material in a simplified form.

At the same time, literacy freed us of the here and now. Information is no longer tied in time to its creator. Reading and writing is more abstract than speech and understanding speech. Consequently, literacy played a considerable role in the development of analytical, logical, abstract thinking.

Reading and writing require a sequential, methodical mode of thinking. Spoken language is accompanied by visual, kinaesthetic, and intuitive processing, while in the case of reading, all there is at our disposal are austere, rigid letters. However, these enable, and what is more, require a much more analytical thinking than spoken language. In other words, human thinking and mode of information processing have also transformed with the arrival of literacy. Literacy turned literate people towards a much more analytical and linear way of thinking.

Technology interferes with the development of abilities

The culture of literacy gave birth to the analytical mode of thinking suited to understanding relations and following implications. The tools of the digital culture, however, have created a new environment yet again, which alters children's neurological development.

The human brain is a plastic, open, and experience-dependent system. It is a function of environmental factors which neurological potentials manifest themselves. External stimuli influence ability development throughout an individual's life. Results of gerontological studies indicate that a change in the environment alters the neurological functioning of even elderly people. Those who regularly browse the internet have a stronger short-term memory than those who do not use this technology, irrespective of age. Regions connected to decision-making and problem-solving likewise show increased activity in pensioners using digital tools.

In today's world – and let us add that things will apparently continue this way, for a little while at least, so we can safely say that this will also be the case in tomorrow's world – there will hardly be any need for:

- Traditional reading skills, since images transfer much more information, and text-to-speech programs are also spreading
- Handwriting, since beautiful texts can be generated with a computer using a countless variety of fonts, and in any case, image and sound transmission can be a substitute for writing in many respects
- Counting and calculations, since there is always a machine at hand, and even people with dyscalculia incapable of doing simple sums or subtractions can perform an entire series of mathematical operations using a relatively good calculator or simply a mobile phone

Assuming – while accepting without great joy – that technological tools render our hitherto most important cultural skills acquired at school unnecessary, new methods will need to be designed to take the place of reading, writing, and calculations in helping to develop the analytical-logical-sequential mode of information processing in future generations. In the present stimulus environment, there is little chance for this, seeing that the life of 21st century generations is characterised by:

- Impressions instead of contemplation
- Ready-made images instead of image formation
- Chiefly visual experience instead of kinetic-sensory experience
- Operating machines instead of active pursuits
- Passive experiences instead of active, physical-neurological involvement

Children automatically go along with a culture change via their socialization process. Their neurological functioning and information processing mode, as well as the control over their impulses – in other words, their entire way of thinking – is different from that characterising the previous culture since their development proceeds against an entirely different technological-cultural background. The educational system and other supplementary support systems engaged in children's development processes have so far failed to consider this cultural background as a decisive factor. There is an urgent need for new practices.

The school and the learners

Education in the way it was designed in the 14th century (more for an elite than for the great masses) might perhaps have never truly become available to a wider range of the public. However, the cultural and social circumstances of past times still made it possible to squeeze children within the limits defined by the curriculum, and school education did more or less assist their cognitive development. Yet the changes happening today are constantly increasing the distance between the school and the learners. This process did not begin now, and this conflict did not come to light today; it does however affect us now.

By the end of the 1960s and during the 1970s, the problems with education surfaced in open protests. However, instead of effecting any substantial change in education, children not classifiable as mentally disabled but still unable to achieve at school received a psychiatric label with one of the diverse neurologically based achievement difficulties.

Diagnosis has become a kind of compromise between the children and the authority. It serves as a waiver for both parties. Children whom the diagnosis helped to escape into disability do not have to meet the expectations set by education. Education, by shedding the responsibility of teaching these children, does not have to face the challenges of today's age.

This well-designed escape system is being disrupted by mass non-conformity. We cannot label one-fifth of the entire population as disabled. It seems more apt to view today's education as disabled instead and to design an appropriate development process and therapy for education itself, now that we have missed out on a chance for prevention. The current system of provision focuses primarily on mending children, or at best on preventing disorders, rather than taking a good look at the relationship between the school and the learners.

A vision of a way forward (deep water warning, for strong swimmers only)

There are as many views going around as there are experts. What is more, even lay people have their opinion of the digital generation and education, and there is huge variety in their views. As in the case of all multifaceted phenomena, almost everyone has a point, and no one is fully right when it comes to establishing the relationship between the generations of the digital age and the education system. In such a situation, a synthesis of knowledge is necessary. We here enter the realm of assumptions and predictions, but there are a couple of fixed points from which to start.

One of these is the cognitive taxonomy of Benjamin Bloom (1956), a series of levels going from the simpler to the more complex. Adapting it to the 21st-century thinking, we can simplify Bloom's taxonomy a little, though, and squeeze his six levels into three:

1   Free exploration, when there are no rules because there is no systematic knowledge yet – more a trial-and-error way of learning

    •   Knowledge – acquiring information
    •   Comprehension – interpreting information

2   Methodical learning, rule-based knowledge

    •   Application – using information
    •   Analysis – explaining information

3   Expert, independent learning, seeing the system beyond the rules

    •   Synthesis – correlating information
    •   Evaluation – judging information based on a set of criteria

Expert learning is not one of the fortes of school at the beginning of the 21st century. However, this needs to change quickly in the age of the information revolution, when it is no longer enough to just acquire, understand, and use information. Information and even its explanation is readily available. In fact, owing to the rapid changes, it is not even certain that all knowledge is worth deepening since the usefulness of the acquired knowledge might only last for a short while and new knowledge may soon need to be used instead. However, sorting out what information is appropriate has become essential, pushing 21st-century humans to the top of the cognitive taxonomy.

The cognitive levels described here are not only to be identified in individual development. Using Bloom's system, we can correlate the developmental levels of humanity's thinking with those of the individual's thinking. We are going through the same stages. The cognitive levels described by Bloom are also the levels open to the development of human culture. Humanity is going through the three well-delineable stages of thinking in the same way children do during their development:

1   Free exploration, with a focus on experience, exploration, the senses, precepts, and emotions in knowledge acquisition – the type of learning that characterises children until the age of about 7–8 years – the pre-literacy era, the end of which marks the onset of the acquisition of methodical learning, in addition to literacy

2   Methodical learning, systematic knowledge, recognising and applying rules – the type of learning characteristic of school-age children of 8–14 years – the age of literacy, by the end of which it becomes important to understand the higher connections between things

3   Expert learning, transcending rules, synthesis, and critical thinking – the adult type of knowledge acquisition from adolescence onwards – the post-literacy era, in which synthesizing, critical thinking becomes the primary cognitive level

Each level presupposes the ones before it, and each culture utilises the activities corresponding to the other levels. The difference lies in the most fundamental approach of human thinking. It goes without saying that a given individual may employ different ways of thinking in different periods. The cognitive styles characterising an individual also depend, among other things, on the age of the individual. However, the most general frame of thinking is something that is specific to a given culture. Culture forms a unity in terms of thinking, with a way of knowledge acquisition, logic, and information processing that is specific to it. These are ingrained in our minds through the process of socialisation to such an extent that questioning them literally causes mental pain. This pain can only be alleviated if we consciously step on the road towards change. To change is hard, but not to change is fatal.

The pre-literacy age is the culture of knowledge acquisition and comprehension characterised by a holistic, visual, imagination-based, conceptual thinking. Ancient and antique, especially Eastern, cultures rose on the basis of this cognitive approach. For example, Eastern logic considers it as conclusive evidence for something if a case similar to it exists. Eastern wisdom builds heavily on similarities. Eastern writing is still logographic up to this day, that is, image-based.

The first true alphabetic writing is the Greek alphabet, which laid the foundations for the quick spread of literacy by converting sounds to letters and making it possible to put any sequence of phonemes into writing using graphemes. The methodical, categorising way of thinking gained ground primarily in the "Western culture," in which by virtue of the scientific revolution the world was regarded as something that one can not only comprehend, but also analyse, research, and even plan. The focus was on the organisation and shaping of the world by the human mind rather than on the description of a divinely ordained world.

Sequential information processing and analytical thinking were the key to success. We learned to inspect, organise, and categorise the world. Society likewise became hierarchical, establishing subordination, subsystems, and main systems. In the second half of the 20th century, this view started to wobble. Democratic thinking started changing the hierarchy. The diverse separate political, economic, and cultural power points now form a network of hubs and connections. The activities in social systems mirror the corresponding cognitive stages. Instead of ranks, there are elections, and the way things are divided up can be a matter of dispute.

The transition into the third culture

Many probably still remember the 20th century. The foundation of knowledge was experience, experiment, and study. The world was regarded as something that can be researched, explained, and categorised. The activities fit in well with the activities of the corresponding level in Bloom's system, and the conceptual framework of thinking corresponds to that of application and analysis. As we have seen, the culture of literacy gave birth to the analytical mode of thinking suited to understanding relations and consequences. Literacy, which led to – and also formed the basis of – the scientific revolution, brought about the middle stage, that is, organised knowledge, for humanity. Just as reading and writing help small children reach step-by-step methodical thinking, the same was the case with human culture.

The rise of scientific thinking already hinted at organised thinking. But the commitment to methodical thinking on the part of an education system that is itself methodical, systematic, and sequentially built up can likewise be traced back to the mode of information processing characteristic of the culture of literacy. Children are classified into classes, the world into school subjects, and teaching and learning must follow a curriculum and a syllabus in the school.

At the beginning of the 21st century, however, the next cognitive level is starting to take shape: synthesis and critical thinking. The children of the digital age will increasingly be able to, and will need to, approach problems with the new way of thinking. Cognitive activities now include efficient hypothesising, imagination, adaptation, prediction, and innovation as problem-solving and scientific methods – activities that are based on synthesis, overview, and integration (Table 1.1).

The amount of information and opportunities available in the info-communication age is unimaginable. The most important ability is being able to select and decide. It is no longer information itself that is of the greatest importance but the evaluation of information and accessing the right information. There is no good or bad: only "good for something," "not suitable for

TABLE 1.1 Activities in Bloom's system: the pairs of cognitive levels in an individual's development, which can also be identified in humanity's development

PRE-LITERACY AGE Holistic		THE AGE OF LITERACY Sequential		POST-LITERACY AGE Holistic–sequential	
KNOWLEDGE	COMPREHENSION	APPLICATION	ANALYSIS	SYNTHESIS	EVALUATION
Ask	Associate	Collect	Analyse	Rework	Evaluate
Define	Compare	Present	Categorise	Change	Decide
Seek	Name	Experiment	Rank	Create	Defend
Find	Imagine	Plan	Classify	Correlate	Justify
Remember	Extend	Practise	Explain	Innovate	Select
Observe	Paraphrase	Draw up	Research	Predict	Offer
Recognise	Try out	Examine	Distinguish	Hypothesise	Dispute

something," or "other" – possibly to be mined at another time. The extraordinary progress in info-communication technology and the easy access to information requires deliberation and critical thinking. The third level of information processing is holistic and sequential at the same time, which is something science and education have to make peace with, too.

For education to be able to reach level 3.0, it needs to forget about classes, about teaching being divided into lessons and subjects, and even about categorising achievements into grades. Child 3.0 is characterised by diversity of development, diversity of knowledge, and diversity of weaknesses, but it also has diverse, free, and independent access to information and knowledge. Synthesis has already appeared, for instance, with the introduction of complex subjects and the rise of project- and problem-based learning.

The post-literacy age is not about losing literacy but about escaping rigid categories. In order for diversity to appear as a value, we need a much more flexible background than before.

A disorder or a message?

Today's scientific research and education, coming from an era that is already disappearing, are not compatible with the digital generation, leading to situations that we often deem incomprehensible given our former frameworks of solutions. The number of "error signs" is increasing.

Despite the drastic changes in the environment, science and education have remained basically the same as they used to be in 14th-century monasteries, which were the vanguards of literacy. In any case, from level 0.0, they have only progressed to level 2.0 so far; that is, they have become large-scale and mainstream. But a comprehensive qualitative transformation that would prepare future generations for level 4.0 changes is still pending.

Official science promised reliable knowledge, but by today, its reliability has diminished as it has almost completely moved out of monasteries and ivory towers and has become mainstream. It is becoming increasingly more difficult to solve the proper assessment and control of research. Researchers theoretically control each other, but in a crowd, manoeuvring shrewdly is far from impossible. Once someone has managed to advance to a suitable level, from then on, their reputation will continue to carry them forward. The Matthew Effect, named after Matthew the Evangelist, is a principle characterising scientific career, put forth by the sociologist couple Robert Merton and Harriet Zuckerman in 1968. Its essence is that the more famous a researcher, the bigger credit they will get for the same work in comparison to a researcher without fame. Scientific journals more easily accept papers by an eminent scientist, more researchers will cite them, and from then on, citations lead to more citations, which in turn leads to an even bigger increase in the scientist's fame.[2]

Researchers' performance is measured in impact factors and publications, which can even be bought. It is a caricature of both formality and mass production that a nonsensical, but scientific-sounding, text may suffice for success. A good illustration for this is the publication generation (SCIgen),[3] which holds a skewed mirror to science. The creators of the program managed to have papers generated by their machine accepted in scientific journals and conferences. Success, as in the medieval times, is ensured by knowledge of the language of the "anointed": this language is the entrance ticket, but it is something that anyone can master, even a machine. Digital technology first made the creation of an increasingly greater amount of research material and publication possible, and then also brought about its own parody. Truly efficient research will increasingly be in private hands, and so humanity is slowly losing control over this decisive area of development in a similar way that the private sphere is taking over the education of children, because official education is unable to cater to their intellectual development. This process, however, is creating new ivory towers, because the beneficiaries of both private research and private education are a narrow group. The Matthew Effect has reached a whole new level. A marked divide is forming between "those who have" and "those who don't," between castes growing more and more apart, between winning and losing sides. This leads to a difficult, and possibly dangerous, situation in 21st century info-communication culture. Polarisation is a hotbed of tension. And especially given a globalised setting, in which the effects no longer stay local, it would be important to create a network and stabilise the situation using an assortment of power points.

Education is a strategic question, as it is not just a slogan to say that the future depends on what children undergo today. School used to be the citadel of info-communication, as it was in fact devised for the acquisition and transfer of knowledge and culture. However, it failed to keep up with the progress of info-communication technology and no longer seems able to fulfil its role anymore. The waning of the culture of literacy and the ascent of audio-visual holistic culture has had a significant influence on children's neurological development, but it has barely had an effect on the education system. The original task of school was to help develop cognitive functions necessary for literacy. As a consequence, it is suited for imparting a serial, step-by-step, methodical, logical, analytical way of processing. This laudable way used to be necessary and useful for quite a long time, as it could be regarded as the route to the acquisition of knowledge for centuries. However, as access to information became increasingly easier, the situation changed.

The gap between children and the education system is increasing. An indication thereof is the increasing number of diagnoses, which signal the incompatibility between the children and the school. Even cognitive neuroscience has reached the conclusion that specific learning difficulties only represent a deficit from one point of view. Neurological development differs from what it used to be like, which has both benefits and disadvantages. For example, a belated development of the dominant left-brain hemisphere and reduced inhibition in the non-dominant right-hand side parietal lobe is often not only responsible for linguistic difficulties, but also artistic and other talents. These children use the spatial-visual, holistic, imaginative mode of processing linked with the right hemisphere to a greater extent than typical. What counts as typical, however, changes along with the environment, and even atypical development has its advantages.

According to the results of longitudinal studies spanning 50 years, spatial-visual abilities correlate the best with performance in natural sciences. Data collected sporadically at first, then more and more methodically, also show a link between learning difficulties and talent in natural sciences, which is probably explained by strong spatial-visual abilities. Modern technologies like robotics and 3D planning require excellent spatial-visual functioning. In other words, the neurological system of more and more children is ideally suited for the use of 21st-century technologies. As such, even children with various diagnoses of "neurologically based achievement disorder" are able to function efficiently in the world outside school expectations.

We thus have a huge mass of people who fail to receive education suited to their abilities and who experience a lot of failure, but whose abilities make it possible for them to use the technology available in the world of info-communication.

In order for school to provide a learning background suited to the thinking of the post-literacy age, a synthesis of play, art, and science is required. This is beginning to happen in some countries and in private education in several places, but that is vanishingly meagre in terms of the human population. Unless we want to give up on children, human cognition will need to do quite a few somersaults and start riding the rising waves of synthesis. Change and its consequences do not necessarily entail a system error or a disorder. They are more like messages, and a necessary part of a development process.

Great syntheses

To move forward, there will be a need for various kinds of syntheses, which have already started, but against which there appears to be a stark resistance stemming from old habits, old power structures, and a fear of change.

The synthesis of sciences

Certain areas of technical and natural sciences are developing rapidly, while humanities, social sciences, pedagogy, and psychology lag behind. This imbalance makes humanity ill-prepared and vulnerable in coping with new situations. Social-cultural values deemed fundamental are being called into question and transformed by technological and scientific changes today. Space and time have shrunk, old knowledge becomes obsolete in the blink of an eye, and new opportunities arise. Rapid changes make old knowledge worthless and quick learning abilities, possessed at the highest level by children, a definite advantage. Humanity is experiencing something it never has before: that not only are adults unable to provide useful advice in new situations, but children are also in the position to teach adults. All of this already has unforeseeable sociological consequences, and currently there are few solutions for adults, parents, and the education system on how to handle this new situation.

Social sciences have fallen dangerously behind. It is as if we've dropped the reins: technology and the natural sciences are speeding forward and are bringing with them an ever-accelerating change. Economy, in turn, is promoting this, because without innovations, the bubble it is sitting on would burst. Economics, history, philosophy, sociology, psychology, and pedagogy all need to get a grip and also to start collaborating with technical and natural sciences.

Charles Percy Snow (1959, 1963) spawned a huge debate with his lecture and, later, book entitled *The Two Cultures*, whose ripples would rise now and again even today. He took exception to humanities distancing themselves from natural sciences. Later, on the basis of Snow and with reference to the two cultures, John Brockman (1991) saw a perspective in the development of a third culture.

Natural and social sciences need to connect to a greater and greater extent without merging into each other. This synthesis is already underway. The sciences have splintered and broken up into increasingly smaller parts by the end of the 20th century by virtue of the linear, detailed thinking characteristic of that age. This helped the diverse parts to then start getting closer. The sciences are forming a network, and the trenches could soon disappear if all goes well.

First it was specialization; now it is interdisciplinary fields that are strongly developing. It seems that the higher the level of work someone is doing, the less they can exactly specify their occupation, because it is either a completely new field or it is an amalgam of several professions and often does not even have a name yet.

Psychology, for example, can be considered a relatively new[4] science, but the number of theories, schools, and applied fields that belong under it is constantly increasing. At a certain point, specialization makes synthesis both possible and necessary. The number of interconnections is steadily growing – educational psychology, forensic psychology, psychoecology, etc. Even the terminology is often inconsistent (for instance, psychoecology is often also called environmental psychology or green psychology) because, as often happens in the case of inevitable processes, it did not develop in a single place. Instead, an opportunity and necessity were perceived in several places, and the new hybrid field was named.

Cyberpsychology is also a field that emerged by necessity, and it targets exactly the topics with which the present book is concerned: the influence machines and technology have on the human brain and behaviour, as well as the fundamental questions of machine-human cooperation.

The synthesis of art and science

It is not only mathematicians who see mathematics as beautiful. The link to mathematics and other sciences is already evident in the areas of fine art and music, but the connection runs even deeper:

- **SCIENCE** is an activity aimed at understanding the world and the sum of the knowledge acquired
- **ART** is an activity aimed at understanding the world and the sum of the knowledge acquired
- **SCIENCE** reflects the world as filtered through the scientist's point of view
- **ART** reflects the world as filtered through the artist's point of view

The two domains differ in their tools and their methodology, which is why they perfectly supplement each other. Art uses more imagination and less fact. As such, art not so much discovers as creates the world. Science studies and is built on facts, but the missing links are supplied by the imagination. This is the reason that the very same facts can be used to build wholly different theories.

Knowledge is finite – imagination infinite, according to Albert Einstein. We can only implement what we can imagine. Art is humanity's imagination and, as such, the pathfinder of scientific work. Countless examples show that art can conceive something with its free exploration method that science will later be able to implement with its stricter methods. Jules Verne's heroes, albeit depicted as employing tools that befit his era, travelled both under water and to the moon. Some of the tools envisaged in the "Back to the Future" films of Robert Zemeckis already exist today, and even more are about to be released soon. Probably, the time machine is still a little while away.

Everyday thinking, however, sharply separates the two domains, even though by today there is a dire need for a synthesis. Art and science formed one unit prior to the age of literacy and even at its beginning. They then diverged, and a need for their synthesis only arose during the last couple of decades.

The synthesis of science, art, and education

The earlier-mentioned Charles Percy Snow, a physicist and a novelist and as such someone in the position to spot and wonder at the divide between the two cultures, raised the point in his "The Two Cultures" that while not knowing Shakespeare's works could be considered being uneducated, being ignorant in the topic of acceleration or mass was virtually chic. By today, neither a lack of basic knowledge in physics, nor that of literary culture, is shameful.

A balance was thus not achieved through a popularization of natural sciences and a higher level of education in these areas, but through a decreased level of knowledge in humanities. We can easily identify the cause behind all this as a lack of reformation of the educational systems.

The greatest synthesis would therefore be that of education, which virtually screams out for it in its pressing need. This is a system which has not even been able to properly integrate digital tools in teaching, even though the use of hypermedia and 3D solutions in learning is easy to accomplish with existing technological tools. "Cyber pedagogy" is knocking at the door of our culture, but in schools today, even a hint of some well-thought-out application of digital tools and a sliver of 21st-century thinking would be a boon.

School is no longer a citadel of info-communication. Students acquire only a fraction of their knowledge through formal education. Owing to the expansion of the info-communication space, young teenagers with outstanding achievements turn up in the sciences and the arts in never-before-seen numbers. These achievements, however, arise from successful knowledge acquisition through the use of cyberspace, not school. If school were to likewise back this process, a myriad little furnace of knowledge could heat up science and propel art forward.

"Transaction"

The term *third culture* is used here to designate a phenomenon involving the synthesis of two or more cultures. The term has been used to describe several phenomena already, and we here aim to unify these uses and adapt it to the third culture of the info-communication age.

As we have seen, Charles Snow was the first to write about the third culture, when, pondering on one-sided erudition, he proposed a consolidation of the humanities and the sciences. John Brockman (1991) then developed this idea further. Scientists and other thinkers of "The Third Culture" are those who are able to write about scientific results with the perspicuity of a popular science book. "An intellectual is a synthesiser, a publicist, a communicator" (https://www.edge.org/conversation/john_brockman-the-third-culture).

"Transaction" is the third level of scientific thinking – science 3.0

John Dewey and Arthur Bentley put forth in 1949 their theory of a system of great paradigm changes in the evolution of scientific thinking, which in the 20th century attained the level of critical thinking characterised by synthesis, overview, and an acknowledgement of perpetual change. They described the three levels of thinking as self-action, inter-action, and trans-action. These are the levels at which humans relate to and think about the world.

In pre-scientific thinking, the building blocks of history were hierarchically fixed elements, components, and forces. Fixed parts of a holistic whole served as the components of knowledge. Aristotelian physics was a great achievement in its own time, and it was built around fixed elements – the "material" – in accordance with a typical self-action approach.

At the inter-action level of thinking, knowledge is based on relations, rules, and systems. This approach can be linked to the climax of literacy, the emergence of scientific thinking. In Newtonian physics, parts and objects form an organised system and interact with each other. In biology, a similar shift came only at the end of the 19th century with Charles Darwin. In psychology, the achievement of systematic thinking presented itself appreciably in the second half of the 20th century.

In physics, Einsteinian relativity brought about trans-action level thinking, in which the constantly changing situation encompasses not only the observee, but the observer, as well. As such, knowledge entails constant re-creation.

At the advent of the info-communication age, the third, trans-action level described by Dewey and Bentley (1949) does not yet pervade the main systems of humanity. It is especially a lack of paradigm change and synthesis in the social sciences, in psychology and pedagogy, that is responsible for a serious imbalance.

The third-culture kid, a prototype for child 3.0

"Third-culture kids" do not directly belong to the world of "third-culture" intellectuals, although they are likewise synthesisers and they signify a novel segment of the info-communication age. They are children who, due to their parents' circumstances, live the majority of their life away from their homeland and grow up in constant transaction in a different culture. They are the ones who, consciously or unconsciously, synthesise different cultures, and thus by necessity develop a mentality conforming to that of the info-communication age.

According to American sociologist David C. Pollock and his colleagues (1999), "third-culture kids" are individuals who spend a significant part of their developmental years outside the parental culture. They often establish connections to all cultures they experience, while neither one is their own. Although they fit the components of each culture in their experience, their sense of belonging tends to relate most to those with a similar background.

It is no coincidence that as early as in 1984 sociologist Ted Ward described these children as "the prototype citizens of the future." Their characteristics bear a striking resemblance to those of the children of the info-communication age. If we had to describe the future generation, child 3.0, we could not do it more accurately. According to studies, the main characteristics of third-culture kids are as follows. They:

- Live in constant mobility
- Speak several languages
- Have mature social skills
- Are often lonely and depressed
- Spend more time online than offline
- Are good observers
- Are recipients and less prejudiced
- Are intelligent and know a lot
- Attend several universities before they graduate
- Do not feel at home anywhere
- Live for the moment
- Are independent and goal-driven
- Are unlikely to work for multinational companies or governments as adults, tend to be self-employed

The counter is spinning up

Scientific thinking developed with literacy in an era when using relations and rules gave birth to systematic thinking. The third culture means transcending this and no longer thinking in a system but in a constantly changing network space instead. Third-culture children, who experience constantly changing time and space, herald the way of the future, as does the increased need for interoperability between the sciences, which would allow for activities to be more variable in space and time. Science is also transformed through its results.

In contrast to self-action, that is, perceiving independent wholes, thinking in inter-action reveals more possibilities and links elements into a connected structure. A network differs from a system in following changeable rules and patterns that can vary in space in time. It is a transaction that can be constantly re-formed and re-created. No one is only an observer; we are ourselves part of a situation that is constantly changing, and we ourselves are changing by being part of the change. Everyday thinking today still regards circumstances as given and static, looking for certainty at the level of categories and rules. But certainty is less and less to be found.

The acceleration of change has made it possible to perceive what time has obscured so far. A few thousand, or even a few hundred years ago, several lifetimes were necessary for changes to become apparent and perceivable. The lifestyle of *Homo sapiens* barely changed for a hundred thousand years: it was a nomadic hunter-gatherer. The agricultural revolution also happened gradually, taking tens of thousands of years. Even after that, several thousand years would have been needed to perceive change, but there was no one to experience such a wide span of time. There would not even be drastic differences in the life of a castle, monastery, or village in the 11th and 14th centuries. Had a young man wishing to become a monk set out for the monastery from his small village in 1020, gotten into a time storm, and arrived at the monastery 350 years later, he wouldn't have marvelled too much on the circumstances upon his arrival.

Until the renaissance, humanity remained medieval in both its lifestyle and way of thinking, and individuals would not be confronted with new paradigms even if they were living in an axial crisis. Then events started speeding up and version numbers spinning faster and faster. Axial crises themselves became more frequent and had more substantial effects. Wheels started turning at such breakneck speed that even individuals today cannot help perceiving a crisis, and at that point they must decide:

- Whether to stick to the framework handed down to them through their socialization and passively endure the changes, at most patching up their frame of reference with newer and newer categories and rules, looking for certainty along the old way

- Or, alternatively, whether to choose awareness and look for regularities instead of rules, experiencing knowledge as a constant re-creation of the world and themselves, accepting uncertainty

Network-based, spatially temporally variable, synthesising thinking is still not typical, as yet. With the intensification of info-communication, however, we will be led, or in a worse case forced, to use synthesizing and critical thinking, because without it, we will only see chaos.

The human nervous system seems more-or-less fit for the increased information load of today, but science and education are certainly not. The synthesis of science and art with education is unavoidable if we do not wish to lose the generations to come. Technological progress makes change both necessary and possible. The third culture is here; it just needs to be officially introduced.

Thousands of years BC, it was literacy which sped up information exchange between people and which made it possible for information transfer to significantly expand in space and time. Book printing sped up info-communication. By today, digital technology, superseding writing, has transformed communication between people into transaction, a continuous and extremely fast exchange of information through the use of images, sounds, movements, and of course text, as well as through boosting interactivity, and it is capable of overcoming even great distances. The virtual space has come to the front in info-communication. With the incorporation of virtual reality and 3D printing into education, human thinking, confined to a world of papers and screens, could win back the lost dimension, and knowledge acquisition can once again be tangible, activity-based, and three-dimensional.

These changes were not simply brought about by technological progress in itself, but by the interaction of technology and humans.

The "internet of things" – who are the *sapiens*?

The development of machines overtook that of human culture by a mile. The connection between machines has surpassed level 3.0, and the singular is just a component part of the whole.

Level 4.0 future has entered both the industry and homes. Web 4.0, the "internet of things" (IoT), ensures access to everyday tools like alarms, household appliances, cars, measurement tools, and cash registers through the internet. In addition, these "things" can also independently communicate with each other, that is, function as a whole. Under the hood of these communications is machine-to-machine (M2M) technology, which makes possible data flow between machines without human intervention. Tools with sensors and chips can be connected to form a network and communicate with both each other and their environment. Industry 4.0 makes it possible to operate entire production lines in a way that even the smallest components will signal any deviance, and specific warehouses make information on the goods stored there constantly available, making it possible to prevent disruptions and render processes more calculable. Production is also in communication with commerce, and the shops with their customers, so that they can call their attention to sales, price reductions, or specific products. Soon, smart homes can decide on what needs to be bought. The specialised tasks and individual units are coordinated by a control system, which can be either human or machine. An AI would probably be more efficient, but if humans entrust machines even with the control and make everything automatic, with the machines repairing themselves and making the decisions, then where and why do humans fit in this system, at all?

Smart industry, smart homes, and intelligent parking systems are still outside biological bodies. But there are more and more signs anticipating an interconnection between measurement tools monitoring physiological processes inside the human body and the internet of things. Not even agriculture can escape level 4.0. A sensor can be placed in the stomach of cows that can signal any trouble and notify the vet or the AI that could decide what should happen.

Chips monitoring the life functions of the human body have also been developed, which means that the human body can also be plugged into the system of the internet of things and receive smart service. This will be especially easy once we are talking about 3D organs. It's worthwhile already designing these to constantly communicate not only with each other, but also with the internet of things.

A human brain linked to an AI could be capable of unprecedented intellectual achievements, especially by using information over and above those that its enhanced organs, already orders of magnitude more sensitive than their natural counterparts, can collect beyond such data. This "humachine" could access and exploit virtually any information through the connections provided by the internet of things.

This is no longer the faraway future: everything is available to make it a reality. However, not everyone will have access to everything all at once. There would probably be vast disparities. For example, most people would have a smartwatch that signals an increase in blood pressure, and some people would only have a watch that tells time, while a few people would have a watch ensuring immortality, because they would be living through machines.

If we foresee such a future, what should the current education system prepare children for? What abilities should be developed, and what knowledge should be learned? Should we train children for a cooperation between machine and human intelligence, or should we train them not to surrender to machines? What abilities and knowledge are needed in the world of the internet of things? What abilities do humans have that make it possible for them to stay alive and possibly even feel good in the world they create for themselves?

Enrichment

If it was possible to live "forever."

Humans have not yet achieved immortality. A popular view is that "immortality" will be achieved/be possible around the year 2050. Some people will wish to live forever, others perhaps will set a life span, for example 100 years.

- How long do you want to live, and why?
- How do you think your priorities would change?
- With research supporting the view that mastery of a subject or skill/talent can be achieved in 10,000 hours, what would you seek to master over a "forever" lifetime?

How to live forever: meet the extreme life-extensionists www.theguardian.com/global/2019/jun/23/how-to-live-forever-meet-the-extreme-life-extensionists-immortal-science

Link pathways

What could the result be of connectivity between hazelnuts, squirrels, and a common dormouse?

What would the connective medium be?

References

Bloom, B. S. 1956. *Taxonomy of Educational Objectives: The Classification of Educational Goals*. White Plains: Longman Publishing Group.

Brockman, J. 1991. *The Third Culture*. First published in the Los Angeles Times. http://edge.org/conversation/the-emerging.

Dewey, J., Bentley, A. 1949. *Knowing and the Known*. Boston: Beacon Press.

Jaspers, K. 1953. *The Origin and Goal of History*. New Haven: Yale University Press. Part I, Chapter 1. ISSN: 2169-2327.

Merton, Robert K. 1968. The Matthew effect in science. *Science*, 159 (3810): 56–63.

Pollock, David C., Van Reken, Ruth E. 1999. *Third Culture Kids: The Experience of Growing Up among Worlds*. Yarmouth: International Press, Inc. ISBN: 97-1473657663.

Snow, C. P. 1959. *The Two Cultures and the Scientific Revolution*. Cambridge: Cambridge University Press. ISBN: 978-1-107-60614-2.

Snow, C. P. 1963. *The Two Cultures: A Second Look*. Cambridge: Cambridge University Press. ISBN: 978-1-139-19694-9.

Suggested further reading

Chakravarty, A. 2009. Artistic talent in dyslexia. *A Hypothesis: Medical Hypotheses*, 73: 569–571.

Cottrell, A. B, Useem, R. H. 1993. TCKs experience prolonged adolescence. *International Schools Services*, 8 (1).

Derricourt, Robin. 2009. Patenting hominins: Taxonomies, fossils and egos. *Critique of Anthropology*, 29 (2): 195–196, 198.

Doidge, N. 2007. *The Brain That Changes Itself.* New York: Penguin Books. IBSN: 978-0-141-03887-2

Harari, Yuval Noah. 2014. *Sapiens: A Brief History of Humankind.* London: Vintage. ISBN: 978-0-099-59008-8.

Howe, Neil, Strauss, William. 2000. *Millennials Rising: The Next Great Generation.* New York, NY: Knopf Doubleday Publishing Group. ISBN: 0-375-70719-0.

Kalwinder, Kaur. 2013. *The World's First Robot with Functioning Artificial Organs.* www.azorobotics.com/Article.aspx?ArticleID=173.

McCaig, N. M. 1992. Birth of a notion. *Global Nomad Quarterly*, 1.

Pilcher, Jane. 1994. Mannheim's sociology of generations: An undervalued legacy. *British Journal of Sociology*, 45 (3): 481–495.

Sakr, Mona. 2020. *Digital Play in Early Childhood: What's the Problem?* Thousand Oaks, CA: Sage Publications. ISBN: 978-1-5264-7456-8.

Soloveichik, D., Seelig, G., Winfree, E. 2010. DNA as a universal substrate for chemical kinetics. *Proceedings of the National Academy of Sciences*, 107 (12): 5393–5398. doi:10.1073/pnas.0909380107.

Small, G. W., Vorgan, G. 2008. *iBrain: Surviving the Technological Alteration of the Modern Mind.* New York: Harper Collins. ISBN: 978-0-06-134034-5.

Wai, J., Lubinski, D., Benbow, C. P. 2009. Spatial ability for STEM domains: Aligning over 50 years of cumulative psychological knowledge solidifies its importance. *Journal of Educational Psychology*, 101 (4): 817–835.

Walker, Richard, Godden, Matthew. 2012. *The Incredible Bionic Man.* www.smithsonian-channel.com/shows/the-incredible-bionic-man/0/3378516.

Wishner, J. 1960. Reanalysis of "impressions of personality." *Psychological Review*, 67: 96–112. "Humachine" transformations

Digital and info-communication technology has transformed the development of the human brain, as well as human relations – but this is nothing new. Social-cultural changes and technological development both boost and chase after each other, and, all the while, human cognitive functioning keeps re-forming.

The world of artificial intelligence and cyborgs is not a distant future anymore but our present reality. Humanity is transforming the world around itself with exponential acceleration, and human brain plasticity gives chase to keep up with the changes. Despite the – somewhat limited – help of biologists, it is apparent that common biological solutions will not be enough for the human brain to develop sufficiently. So, humanity gambles on machines in boosting not only its physical but also its intellectual power. There are already signs that this process is underway, and even some of the problems are apparent.

Human, android, machine, cyborg as a posthuman being?

While machines get more efficient at thinking, and the first machine has already passed the Turing test (that is, it managed to convince a human that it was likewise human), no less than about a third of the children today are diagnosed with some form of cognitive disorder. General well-being is increasing, which may be the cause of an increase in IQ scores, called Flynn-effect after James R. Flynn, who was the first to describe the phenomenon (1984, 1987), but the internet is getting dumber because an increasingly bigger part of humanity is using it. The greater the number of people whose info-communication appears on the informational web, the more its intellectual level drops. Humanity is taking possession of a tool that was previously used predominantly by the elite.

The same happened with books. Initially, writing books was the privilege of a narrow elite, but by the end of the 20th century, anyone could write a book, and not even printing it was an issue. The internet is by far more weightless a medium than a book; it is easier to write, edit, access, and distribute, and therefore it better mirrors the intellectual worth of humanity. We cannot be very proud of the results. In addition, there is a growing evidence that the Flynn effect has been reversed. The so-called "negative Flynn effect" has been detected in developed countries and researchers are looking for the causes (Dutton, Linden, Lynn, 2016).

We have reached the stage where it's our phones that are "smart," and our knowledge is held in our hands rather than in our heads – in a small tool whose name often literally translates to "human-like" (Android). The next step is to embed this hand-held knowledge, along with the machine carrying it, in our heads. First under our eyes and skin, then ever deeper.

We are now able to amend our physical-physiological weaknesses and deficiencies – not just using tools outside our bodies, but with bionic body parts as well. Today, essentially all parts are at our disposal to put together a complete person. With roboticists Richter Walker and Matthew Godden of Shadow Robot Co. in the UK in charge, the world's first bionic person was completed in three months in 2012. Prosthetics and artificial organs were used to put together about two-thirds of a human body – this is the amount that can currently be successfully simulated. A few major organs are still lacking, including the liver, the stomach, and the intestines: these are still too complex to be replicated in a laboratory. But the bionic human is able to breathe, and its heart pumps blood through its circulatory system. The contraption was even equipped with a chatbot, and it is thus capable of simple conversation. The chatbot program selected was none other than the "Ukrainian boy" personality that, according to the Turing test, is able to imitate human thinking to such an extent that people identify it as a human being.

AI is able to process far more data than human intelligence, which leads to a qualitative difference in problem solving. An AI is able to identify things we are not in the position to. A comparable case was that of the microscope and the telescope, which significantly increased our knowledge through enhanced vision in the 1600s. It is now the turn of our cognitive processing and creativity to get an enhancement.

According to Taiwan-born American computer scientist and businessman Kai-Fu Lee, humanity's most important technological innovations are the steam engine, electricity, the computer, and AI.[5] Let us note that the first two of these served as substitutes for muscle power and expanded our physical potential, while the other two developments of humanity are substitutes for and extend functions of the mind.

Here we do not aim to go into the ethical aspects of the issue that it is now only a question of technology and money for someone to obtain a new body and enhanced intelligence. We are faced with serious enough philosophical and psychological problems as it is critical in terms of the thinking and hence education of *Homo sapiens*. Humans must relate in some way to the novel abilities and beings.

It is not even easy to define at which point of human-machine ratio we can speak of a human being, a cyborg, and an android or a machine. We can take some common definitions as our starting point:

- **Human being:** a man, woman or child belonging to the species *Homo sapiens*
- **Robot:** any artificial thing that was created for the purpose of carrying out certain functions; a mechanical or a virtual intelligent agent, which performs tasks automatically or via remote control
- **Android:** a human-like robot with human form
- **Cyborg:** a cybernetic organism, a being with biological and artificial (e.g., electronic, mechanic, or robotic) parts

"Robot" is the main category: every android and cyborg is a robot, but not every robot is an android or a cyborg. However, an android can either be a cyborg or not, depending on whether it has biological components. And it is far from easy to decide what counts as a biological component. 3D printers can already use bioplastics, and we have synthetic meat. With the development of molecular biology and biochemistry, boundaries have become rather blurred. But we will leave the problem of synthetic materials to others: we have enough questions just looking at the mental aspects.

So how long can we call an android cyborg human and start calling it a robot? It would be easy to sidestep the problem by falling back on the definition of a species saying that if two individuals are able to have fertile offspring, they belong to the same species. But, unfortunately, we will not have this easy way out – and not because it is possible to create offspring in a test-tube (and where exactly that test tube is, is just a small technical question which in our excitement is easy to overlook).

A machine, even if it is able to give birth to a human child, will not provide a biological DNA. That machines, possibly even androids, are able to replicate themselves, possibly even using human DNA, is also not conclusive; this is only the physical/physiological aspect of the matter, and the question of the existence of human intelligence, consciousness, and identity remains open. A more exciting question here is what amount of artificial intelligence use represents non-human intelligence. Once AI is built into human brains, the two will no longer be separable. A synthesis of machine and human thinking already happened with the first calculator, and this collaboration has been multiply amplified via computers since then. In many cases, an AI should at least get co-author credit based on the amount of its contribution to a certain intellectual product.

Since social sciences have almost fatally fallen behind technology and natural sciences, we are flying blindfolded psychologically and socially towards a machine-human synthesis. We know how to create an artificial human being. But we don't know how individuals and society should relate to it and what they should do with this being in order for processes of development to return to a state of balance and harmony and for humanity to reach an acceptable level of psychic health that makes at least its survival possible.

Psychic health and social expectations

Julius Wishner, a pioneer in experimental psychopathology, proposed in 1960 that the continuum between the psyche's health and pathology can be regarded as the efficiency with which an individual is able to meet the expectations set by the environment. This situation is often called normality, but this term may need reconsideration if we want to find its place in the present cultural-social situation. What seems certain is that thinking along a single continuum when describing normality is not enough. It is more and more necessary to survey an entire network of complex interconnections, seeing that today in the 21st century we must also take into consideration the relationship between machines and humans when it comes to the psychological health and normality of people.

A common characteristic of most definitions of normality in the literature is to describe normality almost as a synonym of conformity. That is, it is defined as a state that suits social expectations, conforms to society, is desirable according to some system of norms, counts as typical, and is understandable and accessible to other people.

Individuals with abilities and thinking that differ from that of the majority are not typical and may have a lot of difficulties in an environment designed for the typical. For example, mapping speech sounds to a series of letters or filling out forms are both considerable challenges for dyslexics, even though these do not present problems for people with typical neurology. Dyslexics with their atypical way of information processing do not fit norms and social expectations – although we could also say that the systems suitable for the majority of society do not fit them. There are significantly large numbers of talents and outstanding creators among dyslexic individuals: individuals who despite social expectations reach outstanding achievements. A desirable, but atypical population.

Even without neurologically based achievement disorders, gifted children do not always meet social expectations or fit norms and already as children are clearly often unfathomable to their environment: they are perplexing and beyond reach. It is therefore hardly possible for them to fulfil their social roles in childhood; they often do not succeed in this in their entire life. The genius of the gifted is often only validated by posterity.

A gifted individual may turn a hindrance into an advantage, especially when they co-opt the technology of the age. This was already the case 5,000 years ago, as well. For example, the earliest eye prosthesis in the world was worn by an ancient Persian priestess. The soothsayer priestess was uncommonly tall for the standards of that era (1.82 m) and had in the place of one eye a gold-coated ball made from some light material, probably some sort of bitumen derivative. The golden eyeball must have sparkled spectacularly, lending a mysterious and supernatural look to the already atypically tall woman. The enchanting effect must have convinced people that the soothsayer can see into the future (Moghadasi, 2014).

Well, let us now imagine machine-enhanced human systems. Already today, it presents a problem that prosthetic legs do not tire, and so it may happen that missing a leg may in fact be regarded as an advantage for an athlete, rather than a handicap. The issue has specifically arisen that his carbon-fibre prosthetic legs, which do not tire, give champion runner Oscar Pistorius an unfair advantage over his rivals, and he is therefore to be banned from competing. Of course, even the most carefully assembled androids will look rather handicapped for a while, and they are in fact very much handicapped from a human point of view. Take the robot constructed by Shadow Robot Co., which is unable in many respects to live up to expectations set against humans, even if it were able to speak a dozen languages.

When the two criteria of normality of something being both typical and desirable happen to coincide, there is no problem. But difficulties may arise when the typical is not desirable and the desirable is not typical. For example, the constant use of smartphones is not necessarily considered normal: although typical, it is not desirable. At the same time, no one is considered handicapped just because they do not have wings. Wings are not typical, even though they actually might be desirable. However, if someone were to grow wings instead of strong legs, that would count as abnormal, because legs are desirable and typical, while wings, although desirable, are not typical. There is no one to teach a human being born with wings how to fly. The situation would change if these desirable wings were to become typical. At that point, those who cannot fly would be the ones to count as abnormal.

Social integration in the psychological sense is a stable dynamic equilibrium emerging from the interaction of the individual and its environment. The equilibrium is determined by the interaction of the individual and its environment. Atypical individuals upset this equilibrium; if they fail to integrate, they could become deviant.

According to Robert Merton (1968), however, deviance is not abnormal behaviour, but a natural reaction to social environment processes. Certain social structures exert definite pressure on some already-atypical individuals, who, as a result, choose non-conforming behaviour over rule-abiding behaviour.

Obviously, the more that individuals are affected by this social pressure, the more typical deviant behaviour will become. And the point at which the deviant becomes typical entails a socio-cultural change. The concept of normality thus differs by era and by social group, and mirrors the world view and the self-image of the given society or social group.

Disability and difference

Twentieth-century American psychologist Gordon Allport (1937), one of the founders of personality psychology, presented a theory of normality different from that described earlier. According to Allport, a normal, healthy personality is an individual with a mature personality, one whose work is appropriate to their needs; whose activities, thoughts, life, and happiness are defined by an attitude that permeates their entire lifestyle. This definition makes an individual's normality independent of the views of the majority and does not regard conformity as a criterion. Allport thus considerably broadens the concept of normality: under such a definition, even dyslexics, extremely creative talents and cyborgs can be regarded as normal.

The narrower view of normality regards individuals as disabled if – because of some biological impairment or divergence – they are unable to meet social expectations tailored to the abilities of the majority of the society. Disability is therefore to some extent a socially determined concept. An atypical bodily or mental characteristic is often construed as a divergence from normality, since a community tends to equate persistent things with normality. The concept of disability therefore faithfully reflects in both its origin and its content the living conditions and the values of the particular society and social group. The way and the extent to which the normal ideal of distinct time periods and groups differs parallels the differences in their concept of disability.

As we have already seen, positive characteristics can also be an obstacle to integration. Wings can be seen as a disability when people must walk on the ground. In the words of Hungarian writer and poet Mihály Babits in 1957, "Byron had huge wings that would help him fly high, but [it] would hinder him in walking on the ground."

Under the concept of neurological divergence, or neurodiversity, atypical neurological development falls under normal human differences and biological variation, and, as such, is important from the point of view of survival for the human race. The concept was first used for autistic individuals, but it has by now been extended to all cases of neurologically based achievement disorders (learning, attention, and hyperactivity disorders).

Be it a case of physical or cognitive divergence, technology is in the position to help in more and more ways. Prosthetic limbs, artificial hearts, hearing aids, text-to-speech programs, and increasingly more varied and efficient assistive technology are available to help humans live a full life, that is, a life according to the Allportian concept of normality. However, assistive technology is merely phase zero in the enhancement of areas of human deficiency and weakness with artificial means. The technology of this area will shift its aim and start to function as an enhancement of human abilities. The road from assistive technology to total artificial functioning leads through the familiar stages. Let us take an example relating to cognitive abilities:

1   Assistive technology – e.g., text-to-speech, translation, calculator, or face recognition programs emerge for those with disabilities in these areas
2   Artificial abilities appear: – reading, translation, or face recognition programs provide extra abilities
3   Artificial abilities are available and become widespread – lots of humans use reading, translation, calculator, and face recognition programs
4   Artificial abilities become differentiated and personalised depending on one's financial resources – different qualities and levels of digital devices are available, so people can pick and choose their own abilities
5   Artificial abilities become a natural part of the human cognition – reading, translation, calculator, and/or face recognition programs are genetically inbuilt

In all similar processes of development, the initial version 0.0 will transform to give birth to a new solution. At the final, 4.0 level, the external solution ceases to be an independent entity. That is, assistive technology will first turn into ability enhancements, which will in turn be built into the human system of abilities and become a natural part of it. This process is already underway and has an enormous significance for human cognitive development and, by extension, the future of education.

Android and un-android ways

Humanity has strived to make robots in its own image from the beginning, to mirror its own neural functioning and maybe even its own way of thinking. This is fully understandable, seeing that humanity aims to help itself by attenuating its deficiencies and weaknesses using assistive technologies.

Human deficiencies and weaknesses may be natural, but we could also call these normal. For example, we are limited in the amount of weight we can move, the temperature we can tolerate, the speed with which we can run, the calculations we can perform, and in the amount of information we are able to store. It is natural that we can only fly, or stay underwater for hours with the help of assistive tools. We were able to conquer the air and deep sea with various assistive inventions. Already as early as about 20 thousand years ago, humans would compensate for their bodily shortcomings not only with stand-alone tools, but also with assistive tools attached to the body, such as animal skins and pelts for enduring cold, which made the conquest of northern areas possible. The use of these tools is essential because limited endurance of cold, the need for constant breathing to get air and the inability to fly are all part of normality. It is abnormal or, more precisely, atypical for someone to able to tolerate −50 degrees Celsius without protective gear, to be able to fly, or even to be able to run or do calculations at extreme speed, to be able to store an inordinate amount of information without assistive tools, or to know more or something different than the majority.

Assistive technologies, however, might not advance individuals in a direction conforming to the majority, which of course may be a new source of conflicts. We have already seen how a prosthetic leg may lead to disputes. What would happen if someone were to get wings instead of prosthetic legs? Assistive technology primarily targets normal human physical and intellectual functioning, leading to most of these technologies mirroring human physical and intellectual functioning. As a consequence, our artificial tools are substitutes and supplements for the human body and intellect, and as such are tailored to human physical and intellectual characteristics. The problem is that the human physical form is not really suitable for the exertion of extreme force or speedy movement. As a result, our tools for efficient physical work or fast transport do not take a human form.

Robots constructed for specific tasks also bear no resemblance to humans but have a much more practical design. The same may apply to cognitive areas. As such, AI can be expected to diverge more and more from human thinking if it is to be truly efficient. The first major sign for this is the success of AI in the game go. In 2016, world champion South Korean go master Lee Se-dol lost 4–1 against DeepMind's AlphaGo. But what is most interesting is how the AI won.

"Go," known as *baduk* in the East, is a board game originating from China more than 2,500 years ago which requires much more intuition than, for example, chess. As such, it was a long-held belief that machine intelligence would never be able to win in this game. AI did win, and it did so in a game in which some of its moves seemed incomprehensible and unfathomable to such an extent that it completely baffled the experts and had an especially profound effect on Lee. It was probably not simply the defeat, but the confrontation with an entirely new way of thinking that led him to eventually retire from go.

"With the debut of AI in Go games, I've realized that I'm not at the top even if I become the number one through frantic efforts," said Lee. "Even if I become the number one, there is an entity that cannot be defeated."[6]

In training AlphaGo, it was fed a database of 30 million moves by go players, making it possible for it to learn the characteristic algorithms of the game and to play it individually. This would make it possible for it to play as well as human players. However, after this initial step, the machine was made to play against itself. This made it possible for the machine to gain experience in what the best move is in a given situation and fine-tune itself accordingly. After a couple of million games, AlphaGo developed itself into a professional player. The development did not stop at that point, though. After the AI had defeated the best human go player, its improved version won over the winning AI by becoming its own teacher. The new AlphaGo Zero program no longer follows human thinking, because it is not trained on human games fed into it, but keeps playing against itself again and again – in the same way another algorithm had already learned to be a successful video game player in 2015 by itself. The machine was fed no information in advance, only that it should win as many points in the game as possible. In other words, human thinking was left out of the equation and the machine developed freely.

AI was triumphant in e-sport, as well, so much so that it is already being employed as e-sport coach. AI is heading towards non-human cognitive solutions because human abilities have proven to be weaker than machine abilities not only when it comes to specific skills and knowledge but also at higher levels of thinking.

The species *Homo erectus*, a predecessor of the modern human, existed for 2 million years. It is therefore to be assumed that its bodily and intellectual architecture was highly suitable for its lifestyle. *Homo sapiens* remained physically/physiologically remarkably similar, which means that in this respect, it is best suited for a nomadic lifestyle, for gathering and for hunting, and only its sapiens trait drove it to a considerably different lifestyle. With its standard setup designed for hunting, gathering, motion, and social life, humans were already hurt in the conversion to agriculture through having to do work not suited to their nature. They even had to confine their minds into the two dimensions of a paper world, which unsurprisingly did not go easily. Illiteracy was a normal phenomenon until the 20th century, and even today, not everyone can read and write. What is more, even with decent education, at least 10 percent of the children are unable to learn to read properly. The issue is that even after 5,000 years, humanity is still accustomed to three dimensions, which is the most ideal setting for its mind to function.

In other words, our basic physiological setup evolved in prehistory, and it is quite possible that our prehistorical existence deeply defines our present physiology, brain physiology, mentality, and culture. Humans have barely changed genetically, while their lifestyle has radically transformed through a series of cultural changes, making them different from all other species known to us. Humans are more heavily influenced in their behaviour by the culture they themselves created than their instincts. For this reason, a study of development is worth extending to humanity's socio-cultural changes before turning to intelligence.

The secrets of humanity's success

Physically/physiologically, humans are basically frail creatures. Still, there are hardly any other creatures left that would pose a serious threat to humanity; not even machines, robots, or AI. It seems, it is only humanity itself that is a threat to both others and to it.

There are at least three sources for this success. Humans are characterised by:

- Extreme laziness
- An extremely plastic brain
- Extreme efficiency in info-communication

Laziness is an advantage in intellectual coping. Humans make significant efforts to make their lives easier. This is the source of a constant increase in their knowledge. (Meanwhile, on the dark side, human cowardice, humans' sense of inferiority and their resulting infinite hunger for power increase knowledge via military science.)

Everything humanity creates to make its life easier changes its environment. From then on, the plastic human brain will adapt to and develop in this new environment and gain new opportunities. Other creatures on Earth do not possess this level of plasticity, and as a result, based on the current state of things, face extinction – except for species that humanity has a need for. Humanity has lived by this short-sighted strategy so far, but if we look around us, it is apparent that we need to rethink our old solutions.

It is far from certain that we are better off because of our laziness, although we certainly developed new abilities as we made our lives more difficult. About ten thousand years ago, we got bored of searching and chasing through forests and fields after berries, mushrooms, and other prey, and introduced agriculture so that we have everything within reach. For this, we had to learn to work hard, methodically, and according to a schedule – to toil in the fields, haul water etc. Then, to make our lives easier, we invented the plough and similar contraptions, with which we could work even more. After a while, it was high time we thought of something again to make our lives easier, so we invented the steam engine and then electricity, for the use of which humanity had to develop new skills. There were so many things we had to know that we learned to read and write in the meantime so that we did not have to store everything in our head. Then we invented text-to-speech engines so that we did not need to read. By now, human life has become so complex that children have to go to school for quite a few years to be prepared for it. This does not seem to be highly successful, and so humanity is now making machines not only to do physical, but also intellectual work. We work an awful lot because of our laziness. And what do we do when we finally have some free time beside the not insignificant amount of work? We go for a walk in the forest, or to the beach, we go on a boat ride, or go fishing, hiking, horse riding or picking mushrooms, just like our nomadic ancestors, because that is what we were really made for.

Humanity got into an accelerating spiral of change, which is pushing the limits of the human abilities of psychological adaptation. The natural plasticity of the brain is finite, but this can be transcended using the infinite plasticity of machines, given that the physical, chemical, and biological configuration of machines can be designed freely. The relationship between humans and machines can lead to significant intellectual development, but it does matter whose development this is to be.

There are two main paths to go down, and variations on these: the first is that humanity surrenders control to the machines; the second is that humans achieve even greater self-control through machines to cope with the increasing uncertainty brought about by the rapid changes. The crux of the matter is, as it always has been: who has the controller, who controls whom? Variations include scenarios in which the controller is held by an alliance, or perhaps synthesis, of machines and humanity, and one in which smaller groups of humanity get access to it.

It's time to think about which way to go, and, if possible, to grow up to the task, because our next move, that of joining with machines, will be a qualitative change compared to those before. Bill Gates wrote in 1995 that the first rule of any technology used in business is that automation applied to an efficient operation will magnify the efficiency. The second rule is that automation applied to an inefficient operation will magnify the inefficiency.

While AI is being developed by researchers, research should also delve into the question of whether human psychological and social functions can be regarded as efficient. If not, then we may be in big trouble, and need to rethink the consequences of the relationship between humanity and technology, and grow up to the task. No machine is lazy.

The idea from the Gospel of Matthew and the 21st century

Bill Gates's aphorism accords with an idea formulated about two thousand years ago. Not one, but two of the verses in the Gospel of Matthew express the idea that, paraphrased a little more simply, amounts to "the rich get richer, the poor get poorer" (Matthew 13:12 and 25:29, 6th century).

The phenomenon – discussed above already in relation to the recognition of scientists – that came to be known as the Matthew effect affects virtually all areas of life. The idea, introduced in Matthew's gospel in the Parables of the Sower and of the Talents, became one of the most frequently used biblical metaphors in social sciences. It crops up more and more nowadays because it deals with the problem of change.

And there is an exponential abundance of change today, but as futurist Ray Kurzweil, among others, noted, acceleration cannot go on forever. At one point, it will reach the Singularity, and a revolutionary change, a crisis will present itself. Kurzweil predicts this to happen in the 2050s with the synthesis of humans and machines (Kurzweil, 2005).

The Matthew effect can be identified in a number of areas. Following Bill Gates's line of reasoning: machines help those who are suitably prepared, while those who are not will see their mistakes multiplied and augmented. Those who fall behind will be even worse off because the pace of that is at just as much exponential as that of progress. The source of the efficiency and the inefficiency magnified by automation can be quite diverse. The source can be material or intellectual. We could leave the material side to economists saying that we are only concerned with the intellectual side, but these areas are inextricably linked.

It is a trivial fact that those with financial resources have access to the newest technologies, but this applies not just to technology, but also to knowledge and even abilities. Families with a better sociocultural background are able to secure better education for their offspring. As a result, their children, even given weaker abilities, may achieve more than those who do not have access to the proper education, because their family is not in the position to provide them that. Children from disadvantaged sociocultural sections are underrepresented among talents identified by talent assessments. Family background heavily influences the amount of success achieved in life.

Lewis Terman and his colleagues at the beginning of the 1900s selected teenagers with high intelligence for their longitudinal study with the help of an IQ test developed at Stanford University. The "Termites" all had an IQ score above 140 and were predicted to be the talents of the future (Terman, 1925). Life, however, failed to prove the hypothesis, because it was not the most intelligent who became the most successful. Achievements instead correlated with family background (Sears, Sears, 1980). The findings of Russian-born American sociologist Pitirim Sorokin (1956) were even more sobering. He showed in an informal comparative study that a group of randomly selected children with a similar family background as those of the high IQ-level children selected by Terman and colleagues showed similar levels of achievements as Terman's talent group identified with the IQ test. "The rich get richer."

Whatever one invests in – land, banks, companies, information, or offspring – if the decision is sound, then the Matthew effect will have a positive effect. This means that determination, diligence, ability, and available resources are all important and necessary conditions, but neither is sufficient for an extra gain. There are quite a number of small cogs that boost or slow down the driving force behind development, and everyone has an individual track of such cogs laid out before them. However, nothing can stop change, whatever its direction.

Virtuous and vicious circles

The Matthew effect is made up of several small, self-reinforcing virtuous and vicious circles, which drive change in a particular direction. So, if we want to understand these processes, we need to look at the forces in the background.

The starting point of a virtuous circle of achievement is for an individual or a group to experience success through their activities. Evolutionary forces strongly reward success, for instance through the cerebral hormone dopamine, which – put simply – induces pleasure. The individual will want to experience this pleasure again and again, and will be willing to put in new effort again and again for this purpose. There is a good chance that these activities they engage in will spawn new abilities and achievements, which in turn will yet again trigger a feeling of success and give the individual a new shot of the cerebral pleasure hormone. The circle is complete. Once an individual has experienced this a couple of times, they will start fighting hard and going for both external and internal rewards.

The vicious circle of underachievement follows the same path, only with an opposite sign. It is cold-started by failure, which induces considerable stress and a strong sense of discomfort. The absence of pleasure hormones brings down the individual. As a result, there is a good chance that individuals and groups experiencing failure will desist from the activity responsible for their sense of fiasco. They will no longer try, leading to a lack of experience in the particular activity. As a result, the odds of proper development of the relevant ability and of success will sink drastically, while the odds of further failure will increase by the same factor.

There is a single crucial point of divergence between the two scenarios above: experiencing success or failure. This point should thus be the centre of study. It is of course also important to analyse lack of motivation on the part of learners, but avoidance of effort is merely a consequence, not the cause.

The possibility for success that cold-starts the virtuous circle is contingent on the internal and external circumstances of the individual. The internal circumstances are of course not independent of the external ones. Abilities and achievements emerge from an interplay of personal and environmental factors. Personal factors are congenital characteristics and genetic foundations from which abilities, weaknesses, strengths, internal drive, identity, and personality traits are shaped, but of course as a function of external factors. The developmental process is influenced by at least three factors: the individual who acts (1), the environment most suited to the development of individual-specific characteristics (2), and the environment that facilitates an activity and offers specific opportunities (3).

(1) Individual characteristics constantly change as a function of both internal and external conditions. In other words, they are themselves systems shaped by certain predispositions. Contrary to past expectations, we still do not know as much about the factors affecting human ontogeny as we thought we would. Knowledge of the gene map turns out to be insufficient because gene expression can significantly alter development. Epigenetics has brought on a new molecular biological interpretation of human physical and intellectual development processes. Environmental effects at certain critical points during ontogenesis can have a lifelong influence, and could even span generations. Events, educational effects, nursing, traumas, and physiological circumstances in the lives of parents and grandparents have an effect on the functioning of the genes coded in the DNA, and these are hereditary effects.

Epigenetics describes the dynamic interaction of environment and genes, which turns out to be far more exciting than assumed in the past. It turns out that not everything is coded in genes, that hereditary processes may change as a result of environmental effects (Handel, Ramagopalan, 2010). Notwithstanding the distortion that comes with all metaphors, one interpretation of all this is that the hardware, that is, the genes, is given, because we receive them from our parents virtually without alteration through inheritance. The hardware of course may get damaged, but does not change fundamentally. What does change, is the software, which controls the functioning of the hardware. The program is constantly rewritten by the environment through generations, and the software that has been rewritten by environmental effects on our ancestors is what controls our hardware, that is, our genes.

In contrast to the rigidity of 20th-century genetics, in some sense we see the return of a form of Lamarckism in the 21st century. There is more and more evidence that a part of acquired traits may indeed be passed on through inheritance. Epigenetics suggests a dynamic determination of inherited possibilities through the environment. Predisposition is thus not simply the interaction of the individual and its environment, but is a potentially multi-generational bio-psycho-sociological process. ·

(2) The environment appropriate for individual-specific development is also not constant. The needs of the individual with respect to the environment will differ at each point of their development. In other words, the environment appropriate for development varies highly not only by individual, but even the external conditions required for an individual at specific stages are different.

(3) Environmental options can vary by domain, but are themselves subject to change, as well. Nature, and its component parts of human culture, are in constant change, not least because of human behaviour. There are therefore no fixed external factors, only constantly changing options influencing development.

Let us take a critical area, the problem of socio-culturally disadvantaged groups as an example, since the question of what to do with populations falling behind en masse is of vital importance to humanity.

Arthur Jensen, a daredevil of 20th-century research on intelligence, has been both decried and called a genius for his views several times for several reasons in both professional and layman circles. Jensen (1972) studied intellectual abilities in different cultures and interpreted the results of the comparison. It is not surprising that he treads on quite a few sensitive toes, especially since he didn't pay attention where he strode. His study results did, however, reveal particularly important correlations, and Jensen is not the reason for the existence of certain factors. His studies simply turned these factors into facts. Explanations of the data and the use to which these are put are different issues.

According to the results of Jensen's intelligence studies, children born into disadvantaged families are a neck ahead of children from a better family background until the age of three years, and the characteristic pattern of low results in intelligence tests by disadvantaged children only appears afterwards. This surprising result is not to be traced back to a sort of developmental cleft, since a disadvantaged background is responsible for a slow and steady increase in deficits. The difference lies instead in the assessment tools. The intellectual abilities of small children cannot be assessed with verbal tests, yet, and so they are evaluated using kinetic-perceptual tasks, instead. And in such tasks, we must emphasise, infants from disadvantaged backgrounds show not just similar, but better performance than their peers born into luckier circumstances. As soon as children are assessed using tools appropriate for the culture of the literacy age, however, the winners of that culture emerge as victorious.

Jensen's results suggest that disadvantaged families exhibit a congenital intelligence building more on kinetic-spatial-visual processing – in contrast to families with a better socio-cultural background, who exhibit stronger linguistic abilities. A congenital disposition for preferred use of kinetic-spatial-visual abilities, owing to its hereditary nature, is possibly characteristic of the families in question for some time. In other words, a deficit in linguistic abilities would emerge not simply due to an effect of the environment – instead, the individual neurological system would already be predisposed for a more restricted use of linguistic elements. The immediate environment, the family, will just reinforce this with the use of lower-level linguistic code.

The starting point of sociocultural disadvantage in the age of literacy is thus a weakness in linguistic-analytic processing abilities. In a different cultural environment, this cerebral functioning could even be or have been an advantage. But the institutions of the culture ensure that the vicious circle emerges. With a kinetic-spatial-visual way of thinking, an individual is unable to achieve at a high, or even average level already in the "anteroom of society," the educational institutions. They are unsuccessful in learning and do not meet expectations according to the assessments by educational institutions.

Individuals in such a situation will suddenly feel that learning is not for them, and is not of value for them. Owing to their disadvantaged background, they start out in life with a sense of failure, and their psychological health will be impaired as a result of the not insignificant amount of negative experience they go through. Their coping strategies tend towards the defensive, but they mostly enter into a state of acquired helplessness. They fail to see any point in trying, because their efforts so far have failed to bring any success. Without proper education, however, they will have meagre chances in the labour market. Financially, they will be significantly behind those who were successful in "the institutions of linguistic-logical-analytical thinking" and managed to acquire knowledge, abilities, and even a positive attitude toward learning, besides already managing to procure entitlements. The options of those who fall behind will shrink steadily. Their environment will all the while be less and less rich in stimuli because they are unable to access the institutions necessary for their development. Their knowledge and abilities only have a limited chance to develop. From then on, the series of failures will just continue, and sociocultural disadvantage is cemented. Its components reinforce each other and the patterns in the family get passed on. Add to this not insignificant concomitant factor like a deficiency in proper diet in such families throughout several generations, or the fact that frequent frustration can lead to stress and aggression, which is all a further drain on the odds in the background at an epigenetic level. In such a scenario, intervention at a single point will not bring about long-term results, because the wheels turning relentlessly will swing any small divergences along with them.

The point of origin for sociocultural disadvantage is not a lack of intelligence, but a difference in abilities. As such, it is primarily responsible for significant deficiency in knowledge, although a stimulus-poor environment also negatively affects the development of intellectual abilities, particularly in early childhood (Figure 1.3).

Patterns of behaviour observed in socio-culturally disadvantaged families conform to the cycle above, and are passed on for generations. We must emphasise, though, that all of this is only a tendency and does not apply to everyone: generic conclusions do not pertain to specific individuals. The basic pattern can be affected by several other factors. For example, a strong internal drive, good coping strategies, a significant culture change, or an interaction of these may bring an individual down a different road and into a different cycle, because these are forces with long-term effects.

It generally arouses indignation when science identifies congenital traits in an ethnic group or in a population belonging to a specific cultural layer. Many consider the exposed facts as dangerous, as they perceive congenital traits as an immutable disadvantage, and they regard discrimination as dangerous. The first important argument against this line of reasoning is that just because something is hereditary does not mean that it is fully determined. You can play a lot of games with the same hand of cards, and there are (rare) situations in which an otherwise bad hand may be made into an advantage (e.g., in trick-avoidance games).

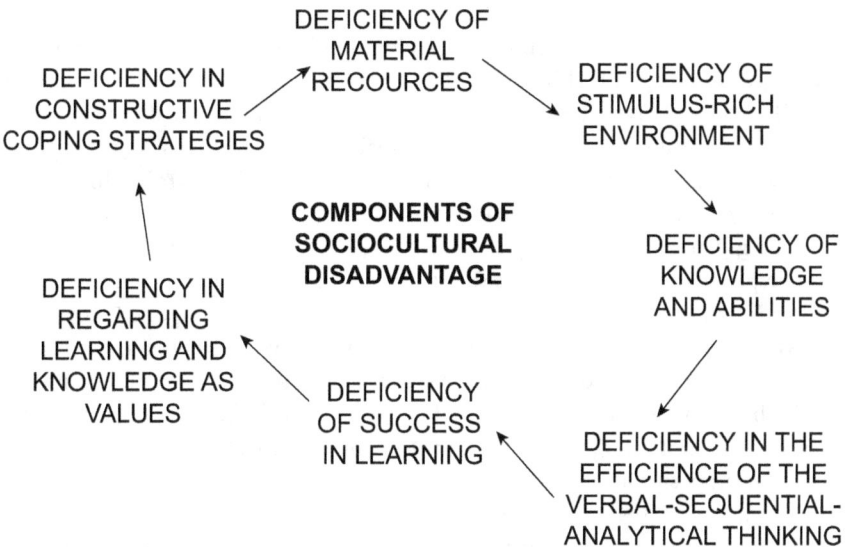

FIGURE 1.3 Components of socio-cultural disadvantage

What is truly dangerous is the proclamation of false equality and uniformity because it engenders false solutions. There is no problem with differences, or science bringing them to light. The problem is if the community starts to use this information to look for socially non-adaptive solutions. Once we are in possession of these facts and perhaps even the solutions to them, then whatever happens next is a cultural-economic-social question. Diversity managed properly is a value, and we might just encounter more and more of it.

Effects that accelerate accelerating change

Virtuous and vicious circles are spinning more and more dynamically, both driving change and being driven by change. Development is on an inexorable trajectory, there is no backing out. Technology, if for now we disregard the darker sides of humanity, figures in three success domains of humanity with the greatest force: looking for easier solutions, increasing brain plasticity, and extending info-communication efficiency.

As a rule, if we introduce some innovation to make our lives easier, it will spread and become mainstream, and will soon be a natural part of life. In other words, it is at that point no longer something to make life easier, given that it makes everyone's life easy. This means that we have to step up the action and need new technology. The wheel is spinning.

In terms of brain plasticity, learning opportunities and the development of abilities and knowledge lead to increasingly closer competition. The reason for this is that knowledge and abilities greatly increase opportunities for development and add to material resources, which then in turn can be used to achieve further development in knowledge and abilities. Learning and ability enhancement, neurological development through movement and art, language learning, IT skills, financial literacy or higher education studies are all excellent investments. By now, the limits of intellectual development go beyond the biological intellectual capabilities of humans, and artificial abilities designed with the tools of science and technology are within reach. Soon they may even make it back into the body. To those that have, more shall be given.

The progress of technology is the fastest in the area of info-communication, and those who have the opportunity to access it will have exponentially more access to the new solutions. One of the most strongly developing sectors is the processing and transfer of information – so much so that this is the domain with the highest number of highly qualified new professions. Information again helps groups in better social situations, giving them quicker access to opportunities and a strong position.

A stimulus-rich environment promotes the development of everyone's abilities, but the Matthew effect applies here, too. The richer the environment in stimuli, the greater the individual differences will be, because the correlation between stimulus–richness and abilities is not linear. Those with better prior resources are better able to exploit stimulus richness. That is, the higher the level they start from, the bigger the advancement. So, while stimulus richness results in development also for those who have fallen behind, it still translates to falling further behind for them. An increase in stimulus richness increases ability diversity.

The higher ability-level has a steeper rising exponential line than the one starting from the lower level. This means that extant abilities are worth even more in a stimulus rich environment than in one where there is little opportunity for development. Everyone profits from a stimulus-rich environment, but the price for this is an increase in differences. Diversity evolves as a function of positional advantage or disadvantage. Natural diversity appears if the environment provides the opportunity, but, at the same time, existing social differences will likewise increase (Figure 1.4).

What is more, children are not only increasingly different from each other, diversity within the individual is also growing. Everyone has strengths and weaknesses, and existing abilities develop rapidly in a stimulus-rich environment, while less preferred, weaker areas may fall behind as a function of the activities practised by the individual. In other words, an individual structure of abilities may also exhibit peaks and precipices. Various combinations of the following will become increasingly more frequent within and across individuals alike:

1   Outstanding abilities
2   Erratic knowledge
3   Neurological immaturity

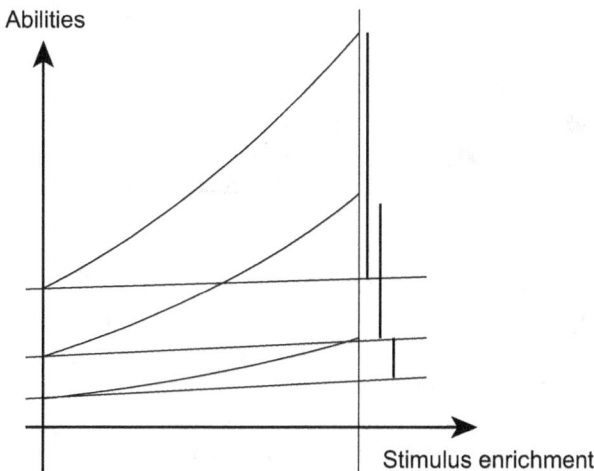

FIGURE 1.4 An increase in stimulus richness increases ability diversity

Lack of uniformity will be a characteristic of the next generation. That is, children will differ from each other more than from the previous generations, and they will be characterised by more diverse development and ability structure.

A stimulus rich environment augments differences, but there are at least two ways for this to go: one path is the emergence of diversity, and another is separation, a growing apart of winner and loser sections and an emergence of two opposing poles.

Diversity and cultural reactions

Diversity means variety, that is, the existence of different kinds of things within a certain domain. Diversity induces a constant minor tension, because we have to cope with the unfamiliar, the incongruous, the lack of the supporting strength of conformity and uniformity. This tension can be released through the path of creativity, by finding new solutions that might connect the different nodes – and a point may arrive when a dense network emerges from the increasing number of connections. A flexible net that can be extended in new directions from any point has a huge advantage in a changeable world. According to studies of the Harvard Business Review, diversity is a definite advantage in dealing with new, uncertain, and complex situations. This is exactly what is needed in a changeable world, and thanks to the Matthew effect, as mentioned earlier, there is a good chance that diversity will further increase.

Now we should just learn to tolerate all this, but humanity does not seem to excel at this. Ever since humanity found its power in fire, tools and intersubjective reality that promotes large-scale co-operation, human activity has been pushing even nature towards homogeneity. Yuval Harari in his book Sapiens lists with overwhelming factuality how animal species systematically disappear in the locations where humans appear (Harari, 2014). By now, biodiversity is gradually disappearing, even though it is an instrument of nature that serves the goal of survival.

Living systems operate according to the laws of a chaotic order: they are determined by many factors and they react exponentially and, what is more, with delay. As such, changes are at first difficult to detect and easy to misinterpret, and might only be perceivable once the processes have accelerated to a rapid pace. This is what we are currently faced with.

We are at present heading in a direction where only a narrow group of species suited to the needs of humanity will survive on Earth. Anthropocentric thinking, which separates *Homo sapiens* from the other species and also from its inanimate environment, is deeply entrenched in humanity's consciousness. Moreover, technicisation devalues biological diversity, and the gradual expansion of humans toward inorganic accessories (self-driving cars, artificial intelligence, thought-controlled robots, etc.) strengthens humanity's sense of omnipotence.

There is a need for a fundamental change of attitude toward the mutual relationship between humans and their fellow creatures. Meanwhile we already need to find a place for technological innovations – machines, robots, and AI, alike. Humanity is currently an exponentially invasive, omni-consuming and freely reproducing parasite population which does not take mutual dependence into account, and if it expands its opportunities via machines, then with this attitude, the humachine could become a more dangerous creature than anything else so far.

Homo sapiens need a new myth, be it rooted in human norms, values, religion, or science. We need to realise that *Homo sapiens* is not a guardian of biodiversity but an integral part of the DNA-based biotic system on Earth that depends on other members of its species and is itself evolving through diversity. This applies even if humanity is currently heading in a direction of trying to free itself from the confines of the DNA.

Education has a leading role in the conscious moulding of intersubjective reality. As such, its responsibilities extend to developing this reality. School-3.0 supports diversity and individual paths, and thereby treats diversity as a value. Syntheses could uncover new paths and new solutions and lead to a framework appropriate for the 21st century.

The time of school-2.0, mass education, is past. The advantage of mass methods is strength, their disadvantage is becoming too narrow-minded. Intersubjective reality, which can help different people cooperate, can also become exclusionary. "Those who are not with us are against us." If the environment is suspicious of the strange and the peculiar, and strives to get rid of the foreign body, a cultural immune reaction is triggered, as Balzac (2010) originally put it when describing institutions and organisations. (We are talking here about a modern-day Balzac: Stephen R. Balzac.)

The theory behind an immune reaction is familiar: When the immune system detects something that does not fit the organism, it triggers an immune reaction at once, and the organism tries to repel the attacker. The atypical, even if it is desirable, is a foreign body in the organism, be that any community from kindergarten, school, or workplace to family. The organism then starts to cough and sneeze. Definite effort is needed for humans to overcome this deeply entrenched psychological reaction, which is no easy matter, especially if there is too much strangeness to digest coming in all at once, as befits a proper axial crisis.

This immune reaction pushes the processes driven by virtuous and vicious circles towards polarisation. Those who do not keep up will fall behind and will diverge more and more from those swept toward the luckier side, and will have less and less chance to be accepted by an environment that managed to escape forward.

Polarisation and competition

Polarisation designates separation into two sharply opposed groups or collections of opinions and beliefs. It is an extremely rapid process – a slight push on the wheels may be enough for it. In contrast to synthesis and compromise, exclusion does not require any psychological investment – quite the opposite, it offers immediate reinforcement and security.

Humanity is an expert at dividing the world in two. Mental dichotomy, categorizing the world into good/bad, strong/weak, rich/poor, etc., is practically ubiquitous in human cultures, as it makes it easier to understand phenomena. A cultural immune reaction means separating "us" from "everyone else," and on a wider perspective, humans from all other creatures. Humans want to be winners, and if things develop in an unfortunate way, they may well succeed.

The dichotomy of "winners and losers" is one of the most strongly polarising differentiation, because both the Matthew effect and network theory prove that success attracts success, while defeat can easily push one downhill. The winner takes it all.

If we think about it, humanity is orbiting an extremely hot plasma ball, clutching to a tiny rock in the endless cosmos, and this is not a reassuring situation. Mother Earth gives us life as long as she can, and *Homo sapiens* is of the view that it is the ruling species on this rock (with as yet some life on it) and is entitled to this.

By now, we are heavily straining Mother Earth, and even we, the ruling species, sometimes start to wonder who the boss really is. For example, whenever nature gives itself a little shake in the form of earthquakes, tsunamis, tidal waves, heat waves, frost waves, epidemics, etc., humans start dropping like flies. This has, however, not deterred humanity from thinking that – as the victorious species – it is entitled to put its own interests above all other creatures. Even above its own environment. We may win, but that may not turn out to be good for us. Earth may have been better off with dolphins, potentially.

Humanity's success story, competition, is what the source of its downfall will be, as well. As far as we are aware, humans have not yet started a breast milk drinking competition, but baby crawling contests are widespread. There is pancake eating, poem recitation, high jumping, educational and all other kinds of competitions for children. There are even more competitive situations that are not always called a competition, but are a matter of life and death: entrance examinations, school grades, and then later on workplace competition, economic competition, arms race, and brain drain. While the animal and plant species of Earth are in an extinction competition, the Silicon Valley is home to a competition of attaining everlasting life.

Winner nations, the luckier 17 percent of the population of Earth, use 80 percent of Earth's natural resources. This lucky minority includes us, the readers, and the writers of this book. We don't give up our ice creams, our tourist trips, our perfumes, the tonnes of make-up material we use daily, constantly buying new clothes according to the newest fashion, the useless gadgets, or calorie-reduced pet food – because even our little pets are too fat today. About 30–60 thousand people die of starvation on Earth daily, while winning nations (and their pets) are dying from obesity.

Seventeen percent of the population has managed to bring Earth to a point where we barely have any time left to save ourselves. We laid waste to that which gives life to us, but the real challenge is just coming up now that, owing to globalisation, more and more people are getting to know the opportunities and all kinds of different cultures are inevitably meeting. We are stuck at a primitive psychological level of human development, and think at a visceral level in terms of exclusion and competition, and educate our children accordingly. We would compare who has a bigger, stronger, more developed, faster, and smarter thing-ummy. But it's not competing against each other that the next generation needs to learn, but to cooperate, and in fact to keep competition under control, seeing that increasingly bigger and stronger tools are available, whose very possession is dangerous, and which may prove fatal in a competition.

We cannot expect a solution from the leaders cultivated so far from election competitions. They are typical cases of an atavism, operating on the basis of "the strongest male reproduces, and the fittest individuals survive," and expecting privileges for themselves. They are pitting people against each other, they are arming, and all the while they are building bunkers for themselves. They are the winners and everyone else serves their survival – even though they failed to succeed in progressing beyond the thinking of the arch male boasting about the size of its genitalia. Humanity cannot count on this political and economic elite. They want to win and would sacrifice anything to this end, including us and Earth. Competition permeates everything, and it divides, blinds, and ruins us. Social media, which could be a platform of co-operation, is being degraded into a click hunt. Natural differences are not values, but objects of envy or contempt.

It is high time to discover the concept of "us" instead of "either me or you." The concept of "us" means forgoing comparisons and rating, and entails understanding and finding the links between individual values.

While the natural sciences must work at full steam on the survival of our physical existence and biological environment, the social sciences must work even more efficiently so that humanity indeed implements the solutions that the former come up with. If the humanities fail to be efficient enough and humanity fails to get past its pre-human, or barely human mentality, then the winner male or female, can celebrate its survival in the last bunker on a dead planet by breathing in the final molecule of oxygen. Let us congratulate them on their victory in advance, because by that time, there won't be anyone around to do so.

Enrichment

"*Homo sapiens* needs a new myth, be it rooted in human norms, values, religion, or science. We need to realize that *Homo sapiens* is not a guardian of biodiversity, but an integral part of the DNA-based biotic system on Earth that depends on other members of its species, and is itself evolving through diversity. This applies even if humanity is currently heading in a direction of trying to free itself from the confines of the DNA."

It is a difficult question: What is a new myth for our changing *Homo sapiens* definition of ourselves? Consider what a new myth for our present and future within a dynamically changing existence would be. What metaphors can describe what is happening to us and one that describes our ambitious dilemma, to exist and develop in the present future.

Link pathways

What links dolphins with machines and the desire to please another?

References

Allport, G. W. 1937. *Personality: A Psychological Interpretation*. New York: Holt & Co.

Balzac, Stephen R. 2010. *The McGraw-Hill 36-Hour Course: Organizational Development*. Europe: McGraw-Hill Education. ISBN: 978-0-071-74382-2.

Dutton, E., Linden, D., Lynn. R. 2016. The negative Flynn Effect: A systematic literature review. *Intelligence* 59: 163–169.

Flynn, J. R. 1984. The mean IQ of Americans: Massive gains 1932 to 1978. *Psychological Bulletin* 95: 29–51.

Flynn, J. R. 1987. Massive IQ gains in 14 nations: What IQ tests really measure. *Psychological Bulletin* 101: 171–191.

Gates, B., Myhrvold, N., Rinearson, P. (1995). *The Road Ahead*. New York: Viking.

Handel, A. E., Ramagopalan, S. V. 2010. Is Lamarckian evolution relevant to medicine? *BMC Medical Genetics* 11: 73. www.biomedcentral.com/1471-2350/11/73.

Harari, Yuval Noah. 2014. *Sapiens: A Brief History of Humankind*. London: Vintage.

Jensen, A. R. 1972. *Genetics and Education*. London: Methuen. ISBN: 0-060-12192-0.

Kai-Fu Lee, Chen Qiufan. 2021. *AI 2041: Ten Visions for Our Future*. London: Penguin Random House.

Kurzweil, R. 2005. *The Singularity Is Near*. New York: Viking Books.

Merton, Robert K. 1968. *Social Theory and Social Structure*. New York: The Free Press.

Moghadasi, A. N. 2014. Artificial eye in Burnt city and theoretical understanding of how vision works. *Iranian Journal of Public Health* 43 (11): 1595–1596.

Sears, P., Sears, R. 1980. 1528 little geniuses and how they grew. *Psychology Today*, February: 29–43.

Sorokin, Pitirim A. 1956. *Fads and Foibles in Modern Sociology and Related Sciences*. Chicago: Henry Regnery Co.

Terman, L. M. 1925. *Genetic Studies of Genius: Mental and Physical Traits of a Thousand Gifted Children* (Vol. 1). Stanford, CA: Stanford University Press.

Suggested further reading

Capps, Donald. 1994. An Allportian analysis of Augustine. *The International Journal for the Psychology of Religion* 4 (4): 205–228. Published online: November 16, 2009.

Levinovitz, Alan. 2014. *The Mystery of Go, the Ancient Game That Computers Still Can't Win*. www.wired.com/2014/05/the-world-of-computer-go/.

Oden, M. L. 1968. The fulfilment of promise: 40-year follow-up of the Terman gifted group. *Genetic Psychology Monographs*, 77 (1): 3–93.

Reynolds, Alison, Lewis, David. 2017. Teams solve problems faster when they're more cognitively diverse. *Harvard Business Review*, 30 March. https://hbr.org/2017/03/teams-solve-problems-faster-when-theyre-more-cognitively-diverse.

Silver, D., Schrittwieser, J., Simonyan, K., et al. 2017. Mastering the game of go without human knowledge. *Nature* 550: 354–359. doi:10.1038/nature24270.

Notes

1 A Mayan prophecy was among those declaring the end of the world to happen at the beginning of the 21st century. Some may still recall that the end of the world took place a few years ago. It happened one December.

2 The Matthew Effect is illustrated fittingly enough by the fact that the paper presenting it was published under Merton's name, who by that time counted as a renowned researcher.

3 For an example, see www.slideshare.net/gyarme/fake-gyarmathyvarasdi.

4 History of science dates the beginning of psychology as a science in 1879, the foundation of the first psychological laboratory by Wihelm Wundt.

  While we can discuss the "internet of things," what would an "internet of plants" or an "internet of mammals" achieve if full connectivity between plants and between mammals were possible?

5 https://www.youtube.com/watch?v=VORTTxkyvts.

6 https://en.yna.co.kr/view/AEN20191127004800315.

2

A BRIEF HISTORY OF INTELLIGENCE – ARTIFICIAL AND OTHERWISE

Intelligence is not that – parallel stories about intelligence and the concept of intelligence

Intelligence is a malleable concept.

- The concept of intelligence and other fuzzy stuff around it
- Concept formation about concept formation

HI, AI, UI

- The intelligences of artificial intelligence
- The problem of general AI
- When psychology and factor analysis met
- Hierarchy – the holy rule under general intelligence
- Independent intelligences and savants as narrow intelligences
- Neuropsychological intelligence
- Neural learning
- Human and machine information processing

Is human intelligence culture-dependent?

- Diverse kinds of intelligence
- Diverse kinds of culture
- The effect of the environment on IQ

Adaptive intelligence

- And even machines
- Collective intelligence as superintelligence

DOI: 10.4324/9780429356346-3

- EQ as the human CQ
- The living network

Homo sapiens has been successful at eliminating, among other things, a fairly large portion of the large animal species, possibly including sabre-toothed cats, which roamed Earth for several million years. Humanity might yet even execute itself in a few centuries. As such, it cannot really be regarded as a successful species from an evolutionary point of view. Even sabre-toothed cats managed to be around for longer. It is far from certain that intelligence, which reputedly made *Homo sapiens* the ruler of the world, is an advantage.

The concept of intelligence is far from definitively understood, and by the time we solve this question, it may turn out that it's not even needed. However, if all goes well, we may soon learn significantly more about human intelligence through artificial intelligence than we could ever before without it. For one, we have AI at our disposal as an intelligent tool, and for another, AI is also a sort of reflection of human thinking. Its development, types and operation say a lot about how humans think about intelligence. It also gives us the opportunity to inspect a mental force – one which will once possibly equal ours in magnitude – from the outside, from an uncommon angle.

To this end, it would be best to clear up the relevant concepts at the very beginning. Cognitive or mental? Intelligence or intellect? Before we start untangling the concept of intelligence, we need to define a few basic expressions, whose everyday usage is almost random. In order to examine the relevant concepts, what we need is a small starter pack of glossary.

The difference between *cognitive* and *mental* is as follows: *Mental* pertains to the mind, to intellectual processes. Mental functions that are related to acquiring knowledge and understanding are called *cognitive*. The word *mental* can be loosely used in lieu of the word *cognitive* because cognitive processes are a subset of mental processes. The reverse is not true, however.

***Intelligence* and *intellect* are not synonyms**. Intelligence is the ability of an individual to acquire and apply its cognitive abilities and knowledge. Intellect is the ability for objective thinking. Studies show a correlation between intellect and intelligence, but these expressions cannot be used as synonyms, because intelligence is more of a cognitive characteristic of humans, while intellect is more of a personality trait.

Intelligence is a malleable concept

The intelligence test was devised at the beginning of the 20th century at Stanford University and from then on, the IQ, the intelligence quotient, was central in determining what we think of as human intelligence. At this time, artificial intelligence still belonged to the realm of sci-fi.

By the end of the 20th century, neuroscientists and engineers have also entered the intelligence business and the concept of neural learning has unified diverse disciplines. Thinking about mental powers has gradually expanded into an inter-disciplinary topic, with innumerably many kinds of mutually overlapping fields enriching, narrowing, widening, clearing up and blurring the concept of intelligence. It's like a piece of plasticine that more and more of us are playing with.

The concept of intelligence and other fuzzy stuff around it

The word "intelligence" didn't really exist for a long time, although the thing it covers has been a topic of thinking from at least antique times, and probably even before that, and there was just simply no way to document it at that time. Aristotle used the term "reason" to designate the ability of humans to resist their animal instincts, something he believed animals were not capable of. Charles Darwin made much finer distinctions. His theory of evolution fundamentally rearranged humanity's thinking about itself, and he also wrote about "reason," which in his case could be divided into levels and was something of which some people had more and some less. Based on his evolutionary observations, he assumed that "mental powers" are stronger in more advanced species.

One of Darwin's youngest friends, George Romanes, wrote about animal intelligence in his book on the mental evolution of animals published in 1893. Since then, the word intelligence has come to be widely used to designate something that we still don't know what it is, and which probably doesn't even exist in the form we imagine – which is probably something we won't wish to accept for a while. Humans have the ability to make a creation of their own mind a part of shared accepted reality. Among such intersubjective products are religions, social norms, money, but even companies, since all of these could not exist unless a large body of people believed in their existence.

According to historian and philosopher Yuval Harari (2014), the basis for the immense success and rampage of *Homo sapiens* is its ability to create shared myths, and thereby channel masses of humans in one direction. To the best of our current knowledge, no other species is capable of believing in imaginary stories, not even the human species *Homo erectus*, which was around for two million years and became extinct at around the time *Homo sapiens* appeared, and probably not even Neanderthals, who have been found to be much more intelligent than previously believed. Incidentally, there is a chance that the disappearance of the latter two human species could be seen as the effect of *Homo sapiens* activities, whose special mental power is probably not intelligence, but the ability to create and maintain intersubjective reality, which is capable of moving masses and can be linked as much to faith as to reason. Still, there are some who hail the fundamental change in human cognition and its results, called the "cognitive revolution" by Harari, as the victory of human intelligence, while introducing intersubjective reality as simply the introduction of the role of faith in thinking. It is a rather vexed question if the ability to believe in a myth, a "story," can be regarded as intellectual achievement, and not, to the contrary, a decline of reason. But it is a central question, because science is about to link the fate of humanity to an incredibly strong thinking ability, while, at the same time, everything points to intelligence being of secondary importance in *Homo sapiens* behaviour. Highly intelligent people do not differ significantly from people with average or weak intelligence in terms of the following:

- Intersubjective reality – the power of fake news, the importance of gossip
- Intuitive thinking – rapid and slow thinking
- Motivated thinking – cognitive schemata
- Emotional decisions – we are humans
- The power of instincts and drives – we are also animals
- Executive functions – the quality of implementation
- Creativity – creative thinking

We have seen how there is an important difference between data, information, knowledge, and wisdom, but people don't generally bother with such fine semantic distinctions in everyday life, and simply deal with situations with recourse to all of the above. In contrast, artificial intelligence is immune to these phenomena responsible for human errors. Indeed, one could say that it's clear, relentless cognitive operation is a flaw. A machine lacks instincts, emotions, and motivations, and so does not use these in its thinking. Its single guideline is the task for which it uses the data and information from which its knowledge is built up. Naturally, incorrect information will lead AI thinking in wrong directions, too. Task-orientedness can also be a problem if the AI fails to take into account considerations other than its instructions. Blindly following commands can, of course, happen to humans, too, which exacerbates the effect of the already numerous subjectiveness-increasing factors, which are in who knows what relation to intelligence.

If we brand humanity's history so far as a success story, and name intelligence as the reason behind the success, then humanity's thinking in terms of intersubjective reality is indeed intelligence. This does require a lot of faith and less thinking, though. To begin with, it's even debatable if we can call having exterminated in a few hundred thousand years a big part of the living environment surrounding us and possibly terminally jeopardizing our own existence a success. If we measure a species' success in terms of its survival, then it's currently far from being certain that other species are not significantly successful than us: *Homo erectus* was around for 2 million years, the sabre tooth tiger even longer, not to mention cockroaches, which have existed for over 300 million years, and which even *Homo sapiens* failed to exterminate. Which story should we believe?

Concept formation about concept formation

Concept formation means capturing and defining the essence of a thing and describing its main characteristics. The path to the essence of things leads through abstraction, when we ignore concrete things and some aspects of their relation to reality and create an arbitrary category. This is capturing the essence. What counts as the essence of a thing is highly subjective, but there are empirically and scientifically proven factors which group entities into classes and can thus be regarded as objective. These are concepts like animal, set, or molecule.

When we employ judgement – establishing relationships between pieces of knowledge – and inference (Aristotelian syllogism), i.e., a chain of thoughts in which, based on certain propositions that we assume to hold, we derive the necessary entailment of something new – we combine multiple concepts and thus pile one assumption on top of another. We accomplish all this using reason, undoubtedly a cognitive accomplishment.

Since the concept of intelligence is no exception, it stands to reason that it must be as much the product of our imagination as our knowledge. The existence of the numerous, mutually highly different models of intelligence reveals that intelligence is not a concrete, but an imaginary, entity. At some point, it may be worthwhile asking artificial intelligence what it thinks of intelligence when it collates everything that human intelligence has so far put together on the topic.

DeepMind scientists Marcus Hutter and Shane Legg (a co-founder) have already tried distilling the concept of intelligence from existing definitions in their paper "Collection of Definitions of Intelligence" (2007). They collected 70 different definitions from encyclopaedias, psychologists, and AI researchers, and (taking the common elements) they arrived at a definition that can be thought of as universal: "Intelligence measures an agent's ability to achieve goals in a wide range of environments." Robert Sternberg, the excellent researcher of intelligence, put this much more succinctly as follows: intelligence is goal-directed, adaptive behaviour. Maybe an artificial intelligence would also arrive at the same definition.

An earlier concept of intelligence was described in 1990 by Randall D. Beer: "The ability of an autonomous agent to adjust its behaviour to the moment-to-moment contingencies which arise in its interaction with its environment." However, the concept of a goal is missing from this definition, although, then again, the goal could simply be understood as adaptation.

Let's be realistic: these more or less succinct definitions do not really help us from a practical point of view, although they are important as a theoretical starting point. They are perfectly correct and acceptable, but they do pose more questions than they answer.

Is this ability a single unified capacity or a complex entity? Is it merely a theoretical ability, being theoretically able to solve the task given the appropriate environment (what is the appropriate environment?), given a will and perseverance to do so, given suitably functioning perceptive abilities, and given the sufficient amount and quality of knowledge and experience?

To what extent is the implementation, the behaviour itself, part of intelligence? How different can the environment where the goal is to be achieved be from the earlier environments of the agent? The devil, or in this case intelligence, is in all these and many other small details, but maybe we can reduce the large number of questions to a handful of main themes.

The lack of clarity in the concept of intelligence lies in at least three main, mutually influencing issues, which show up in the discussions of intelligence:

1   An uncertainty about the components of intelligence, that is, whether intelligence is some general mental power or emerges from diverse cognitive processes – and if the latter, what they are
2   Cultural differences in the judgement of intelligence, that is, the problem of the universality of intelligence
3   The problem of the boundaries of intelligence and non-intelligence, that is, the role of not entirely intellectual factors significantly influencing intelligent behaviour

All of these questions pertain to all kinds of intelligence. Point 3 is a complex problem in the fields of both human and artificial intelligence, discussed in another chapter. The first two points will be discussed here, dissecting human and artificial intelligence and comparing them with each other and with other kinds of intelligence.

AI, HI, UI – artificial, human, universal

The easier way for us is to take the subtypes of AI as our starting point, because while there is likewise a lot of debate surrounding it, AI still has far fewer definitions in the literature than we can see in the case of human intelligence, which goes back much further in time. It's also worth trying to think about a universal concept of intelligence, if it exists at all, which could enable the comparison of different rational agents. This way we may be able to learn more about human cognitive abilities, as well, and arrange in our minds the place and role of different types of intelligence.

The intelligences of artificial intelligence

In the case of AI, special and general intelligence are categorically distinct. The same distinction is still debated in the case of human intelligence, although parallels with AI have helped considerably in understanding the concept of intelligence.

In opposition to defining intelligence as a single unified entity, more and more scientific theories are emerging that regard intelligence as the sum of independent abilities. When it comes to AI, this issue only exists at the level of public thinking, but AI specialists also have to address the question of what exactly they regard as intelligence and what as a special area. Do they perhaps regard the special areas as a part of intelligence?

In sci-fi movies, AI generally appears as some extraordinary, often infinitely vast mental power, but in reality, AI is a much more mundane agent. Many may not be aware that when they awake in the morning, often the first thing they interact with is an AI. A smart phone, while capable of simple tasks, too, like waking its owner at a specified time, is a small storehouse of AI that we almost always have on us. And the AI in it has at its disposal quite a substantial amount of computing capacity.

AI is thus with us and is of immense use to us in everyday life, but not all AIs can do the same things. One measures speed and reads the license plates of several cars in a second using image processing algorithms. Another AI optimises city traffic as a smart traffic light and lets drivers through or stops them as a function of how heavy the traffic in the surrounding streets is.

Camera software in mobile devices is so smart that even the most untalented photographers can take first-rate pictures, because the program chooses the best distance and light settings. And if the photo still did turn out bad, smart AI is able to correct it and even convert it into an artwork.

In MMO (massively multiplayer online) games, AI processors are put to work on perfecting game experience. For example, opponents for players are generated by self-learning algorithms which tailor the difficulty of the obstacles to the players' style and abilities and make sure that the number of opponents turning up is just right so that players are not bored for even a minute. With this in mind, we are eager to see optimal challenges finally introduced into the learning paradigm of children, too, either with the help of AI or HI.

The "mind reading" game Akinator, essentially a kind of 20 Questions, is also run by an AI. The player has to think of something, and "mind reader" Akinator guesses after a few questions what it was. It is based on a system called "fuzzy logic," which instead of using just binary values False and True allows for values between these two options. This very same system in washing machines has been doing chores for us in our homes for a while now. It's evident that processing efficiency varies highly with different applications of AI, but we can also clearly identify specialisation behind AI performance.

Then there are chatbots, in some cases with such sophistication that we cannot tell whether we conduct our business with a human or a machine over the phone. And let's not forget about search engines, filters, and recommender systems which by now often have a better idea of what it is we want to search for or purchase and why. They do the thinking for us, and while reading our mind, they also simultaneously collect and analyse data.

According to Elon Musk, the daredevil of the technological industry, we won't even need to speak in about 5–10 years, because a chip (let us now dwell on where it will reside) will tell us what we want. Musk may say and do some crazy things, but voice control, as we know, is already a part of our mobile devices, and AI is even capable of decoding gestures.

The task and efficiency that an AI is capable of depends, beside processing power, primarily on what its creators intended and designed it for. When it comes to AI, a clear distinction based on function has successfully been made:

Artificial narrow intelligence (ANI) is specialised for one or more areas. For example, it might defeat you in chess, but if you ask it about chemical formulas, all it could do is look stupid, and it would even look surprised if it could. The tools listed earlier all belong to this category.

Artificial general intelligence (AGI) has cognitive abilities comparable to human intelligence. That is, it is a general mental ability encompassing abilities similar to those connected to human intelligence: perception, learning, information storage, pattern recognition, abstraction, planning, decision, problem solving, logic, language use in communication. Possibly also auxiliary abilities like creativity and empathy. AGI would be capable of approximately human thinking, but creating it is a much more difficult task than specialised intelligent functioning, and there are as yet (writing in 2021) no signs of breakthrough results.

Artificial super intelligence (ASI) is the kind that appears in most AI-themed science-fiction books, movies, and video games. It has significantly more advanced abilities than human intelligence, and in addition to surpassing human mental abilities in all special areas, it is more advanced than the best performing human creatures in the areas of wisdom, creativity, and social-emotional abilities (EQ), as well. ASI may be just slightly smarter than humans, but it may be omnipotent, as well. This is the reason it became the centre of attention, since it is essentially the mental embodiment of either divine or diabolical powers capable of solving even the impossible. There is no guarantee that a super brain like this is even possible. Presumably, as soon as AGI is born, it will start developing extremely rapidly, but we have no idea how far this development will go; in other words, it's highly uncertain at which point ASI becomes a true agent. According to Robert Trappl, the director of the Austrian Research Institute for Artificial Intelligence (OFAI), "At present, an Artificial Intelligence must be better at certain niche things than humans . . . but I regard the development of a super intelligence . . . as highly improbable."

https://futurezone.at/science/programme-koennen-alles-was-der-mensch-kann-undmehr/141.989.320 (accessed: 25.07.2020)

The problem of general AI

The barrier to break through is not the one between general and super intelligence, but the one between specialised and general intelligence.

If we are ever to make a machine that will speak, understand or translate human languages, solve mathematical problems with imagination, practice a profession or direct an organization, either we must reduce these activities to a science so exact that we can tell a machine precisely how to go about doing them or we must develop a machine that can do things without being told precisely how.

(by Richard M. Friedberg, quoted by Chollet, 2019)

When it comes to AI, it is extremely difficult to develop the mental functions that even an individual with an intellectual disability or a two-year-old can easily produce. We are talking about processes for whose development nature needed several million years of evolution. An example is reaching toward an object with our hands. This requires the nervous system to perform a series of bodily physical commands, three-dimensional perceptions, and feedback. It seems like an easy task, because the software in our brains is designed to be capable of performing it. Robots can be programmed for precision tasks, but motion planning is still in its infancy and requires advanced specialised AI.

The human nervous system has an astonishing level of adaptability. A trivial task for a human can count as a huge achievement for a machine, and AI is as yet not capable of performing simple but computationally difficult tasks. For example, a small child's body undergoes significant growth and transformation in just a few weeks, the arm becoming longer; but adapting to this change poses no problems for its mental guidance system, even though the world is also changing around it. As we move about, our brain adapts to our body's change of position, to the size of the body parts, and to the movement it coordinates. It adapts to its environment, which is constantly undergoing change both owing to and independently of the activities controlled by our brain. This extraordinary level of constant adaptability was encoded into our nervous system through millions of years of experience, and it is potentially impossible to program directly. The brilliant teams developing machine intelligence will very probably find an entirely different way to reach this point.

Note that most professionals and laymen do not regard being able to grasp an object and being able to do the same with a longer arm a part of intelligence in the case of humans. But for machines, simple motion adaptation counts as a serious AI task. We will elaborate on this more in the chapter on what we will call "satellite intelligences," because human thinking is built on perceptual-kinetic cerebral systems, and as such, this level of information processing should be more highlighted when looking into intelligence.

Something the human brain is doing automatically that is missing from machine learning at present is learning, or adaptation, itself, while perceiving, learning, or solving new situations. A machine may have more precise perception, learn better than a human, and find solutions better than and different from human thinking, but the adaptive success of the human brain does not lie in simply solving the situation at hand, but in its plasticity, in being able to learn from the situation the relevant cerebral activity itself. In other words, the brain does not simply collect the results of mental activity and learn from them. It also records the way it reached the results and builds this path into its repertoire of tools.

The human brain is capable of envisioning things that do not exist, being able to construct a unified whole from virtually anything. If the goal is to endow AI with the abilities of the human mind, it will need a simultaneously broad and still precise function already at the level of perception which makes it possible to distil the essence from the general, and which is also capable of recognizing or interpreting as a unified whole previously unseen and potentially incompatible elements – either as a new entity separate from its environment and other elements, or in combination with other entities. Encountering a very large amount of something is insufficient for this purpose, as the agent will need to be able to resort to operations of imagination capable of interpreting even highly improbable combinations. Such algorithms are only starting to be incorporated into machine learning. In absence of a goal-directed algorithm, even the best AIs with the largest processing powers available will be incapable of solving simple but real problems in unexpected situations.

When psychology and factor analysis encountered

So far, nothing has refuted the idea that intelligence is what intelligence tests measure. Intelligence is still a vague concept, a part of intersubjective reality, and the possibility is still open that it doesn't really exist, irrespective of how much time the best experts spend studying it. Of course, cognitive functions do exist, which we are free to call intelligence, just as we are free to call artificial intelligence an intelligence.

Unsurprisingly, the first steps toward measuring intelligence were taken by scientists trying to determine factors that play a role in mental accomplishments. The only problem with this is that we run into the aforementioned three fundamental problems.

If we assume that intelligence is composed of different abilities, then we need to decide what these are. But researchers at present are still uncertain about what exactly intelligence is, even if it is not a complex of separate abilities but a general intellectual power that is identical in every culture. The answer is that we don't know, or more precisely, we have some lists about the nature of this general intellectual power:

> **List 1:** Intelligence is a construction encompassing problem-solving abilities, spatial manipulation, and language acquisition.
> **List 2:** Intelligence encompasses logical ability, understanding, awareness, learning, reasoning, planning, and problem solving.

Which one should we prefer? The first list seems a little more universal and can potentially be applied in the case of a nomadic tribe, but the second list (with its larger awareness content) might identify deeper thinking processes. And none of them contradicts the noncommittal and elusive definition of "goal-directed adaptive behaviour."

We have been trying to measure intelligence for a century, and over that time, an increasingly more elaborate and systematic set of cognitive abilities has been delineated, but researchers have been facing a slew of contradictions from the very beginning.

The father of measuring mental abilities was polymath Sir Francis Galton, Charles Darwin's cousin. It's probably no coincidence therefore that he regarded intelligence as a hereditary general ability, which manifests itself in all forms of cognitive behaviour and whose level differs by individual. He approached the measurement of mental abilities primarily through the assessment of the quality of sensation and perception in his so-called anthropometric laboratory. The results, however, didn't support his view that the better an individual's perception, the more precise information they acquire. His high-volume studies showed that head size, reaction time, visual acuity, and hearing threshold do not correlate with intellectual eminence. Although unsuccessful in this respect, Galton was right to a certain extent, but the technology of that time was insufficient to support his assumptions with physiological measurements. Newer procedures measuring an individual's mental speed brought somewhat more definite results. Nonetheless, in his quest to make psychometric procedures more efficient, Galton did substantially enrich statistics with the concepts of regression, correlation, and standard deviation and with his work on normal distribution.

The next groundbreaker in the period after Galton's studies was the French Alfred Binet, whom we could today describe as an educational researcher. He was invited by the French ministry of education to develop school maturity assessments. The reason for this was that compulsory schooling introduced at the end of the 19th century unearthed the problem – persisting up to this day – that the cognitive abilities of several children do not meet the demands of school. At that time and in the times since then, it wasn't the school itself that underwent examination to determine how it could be made accessible to each child – but children, to determine who is not suitable for school learning and why.

Binet knew Galton's work and could avoid procedures that would only prove to be dead ends. Instead, when devising his tests, he regarded intelligence as a complex of diverse abilities (linguistic, counting, memory, etc.). For each age-year, he determined the level of competence a child normally should have reached by that age. Researchers at Stanford University devised the IQ, or intelligence quotient, test built on this method. The idea by which this procedure extended Binet's test was to compare the biological age of the individual with their mental age identified from the test tasks, enabling a comparison between individuals of different age: mental age/actual age $\star$ 100. (Multiplying by 100 is just a nicety to avoid thinking in terms of decimals.) This simple fraction came to have a blazing career – so much so, that is still proving difficult to halt today.

Binet devised his test expressly for the assessment of school fitness, so, naturally, the procedure primarily assesses replication-like abilities, is highly culture-dependent, and its results are heavily influenced by schooling. This also entails that studies building on this test can only have limited generality owing to their cultural bias. For a long time, however, researchers of intelligence didn't regard this bias as a serious problem.

Intelligence tests thus appeared at the beginning of the 20th century, although the debate on the nature of intelligence was still very much underway. Indeed, this marked the start of the real debate, since assessments made test data available and the toolset of statistics was also enlarged with factor analysis, a favoured method in research to this day.

The peculiar thing is that outstanding intelligence researchers then and since then have used similar factor analytic methods on data from similar tests only to arrive at vastly different definitions of intelligence. True, some used a method of factor analysis to look for a single factor and found it (the first to do so was Charles Spearman), and others looking for multiple mutually independent factors likewise succeeded (the first one to do so was Louis Thurstone). We can conclude that we tend to find exactly what we are looking for.

The brilliant Charles Spearman (1927) was the first to employ factor analysis in the analysis of psychological assessments at the beginning of the 20th century. Studying test data, he found that the scores of school-age children in apparently separate cognitive areas correlate positively with each other. Based on this, he hypothesised the existence of a general mental power, the basis of human cognitive accomplishments. According to his two-factor theory, all intellectual achievement originates in a general "g" factor, and this g-factor is responsible for 40–50 percent of individual differences in achievement. The two-factor theory is incomplete given only the g-factor. The "s," or specific factor, stands for the ability of an individual in a specific area. The s-factors of intelligence commonly used in assessments include memory, attention, verbal comprehension, vocabulary, spatial and numerical abilities, as well as logical and abstraction abilities. These give content to intelligence. The cognitive task and the individual cognitive pattern determine the ratio of work implemented by specific factors.

Two other brilliant psychologists, the British Godfrey Thomson and the American Edward Lee Thorndike, arrived at markedly different conclusions based on their studies conducted at the same time as Spearman, though. They believed that the observed positive correlation can be explained without recourse to an underlying general intelligence. On their approach, there are several mutually independent mental processes, and the tests build on the application of these processes to various degrees. In other words, the correlation between tests are rooted in an overlap in the cognitive processes utilised in the tests.

Godfrey Thomson (1916, 1919, 1936) concluded in his research that general intelligence emerges from the operation of a comprehensive neural network. In particular, he proposed that the g-factor emerges from neuron arcs in the brain that he linked to Thorndike's notion of bonds and which arise from the interaction of various elements of the brain. In Thomson's Sampling Theory of Mental Ability, each test activates such a neural bond, and the amount of overlap between these bonds is responsible for the background correlation designated as the g-factor.

A similar theory was recently put forth by psychologists Kristóf Kovács and Andrew Conway (2019). According to process overlap theory, a large number of mutually independent psychological processes, elementary skills are required to solve any kind of test. Most of these processes are domain-specific and only play a role in a restricted number of tests: for example, they are only needed when it comes to vocabulary, mental calculations, or spatial-visual orientation. But there are also more general processes, which are used in many kinds of tests, as a result of which, these apparently independent special abilities have in fact a substantial "overlap." Kovács and Conway propose that the general processes responsible for the "overlaps," required in multiple domains, primarily belong to the group of functions called "executive processes."

This drives us headway into the problem of whether executive functions can be regarded as a component of intelligence, or – as their name suggests – their role is executive, and they do not constitute a general intellectual power. What does appear certain is that this group of factors plays an important role in intelligent behaviour, which is why it is worth looking at them in more detail in the chapter on satellite intelligence.

Edward Thorndike (1924), who studied intelligence at the same time as Spearman, regarded it as an aggregate of different functions and proposed that mental activities were the result of neuropsychological links and aggregations. With respect to the two kinds of intelligence, abstract and concrete, Thorndike posed the following question: Do these two types of intelligence cover different abilities and factors and are independent of each other, or, as Spearman thinks, are they not independent factors, and do they only differ in their relation to the non-intellectual s-factors?

Louis Thurstone (1938) agrees that intelligence is composed of multiple elementary factors, but he strongly rejected the existence of a general intelligence. He posited seven basic, so-called primary factors: 1) verbal comprehension, 2) word fluency, 3) number facility, 4) spatial visualization, 5) perceptual speed, 6) memory, and 7) reasoning. He even designed a test to assess these components (Primary Mental Abilities Test). Versions of this test are used up to this day, but its predictive power is no better than that of other tests. Thurstone's quest to find the basic mental components was only partly successful because the primary abilities he identified are not entirely independent of each other, which corroborates the existence of a Spearmanian general intellectual power.

In the 1950s, American psychologist Joy Paul Guilford attempted a synthesis of factor analytic theories with the help of a three-dimensional system. He proposed that intelligence is the combination of 120 (then later 150, and finally 180!) independent factors. Of these, about 80–85 could ever be assessed. He placed the factors along three dimensions corresponding to the contents, the products, and the operations of thinking. For him, the intellect operates using memory and thinking abilities. The three components of thinking are understanding, evaluation, and production. Production, in turn, is divided into convergent and divergent thinking.

Guilford criticised intelligence tests, which usually required giving "the" correct answer, making the convergent method the efficient approach toward the solution. In reality, however, we often have to start off in several directions at once, which is a method that can lead to independent ideas. He treated divergent thinking, the basis for creativity, as a separate part of intelligence, and by capturing divergent thinking, he marked the beginning of separating creativity from intelligence.

Hierarchy – the holy rule under general intelligence

By the second half of the 20th century, it became apparent that the factors of intelligence can hardly be piled next to each other: some kind of system was needed. The simplest system known by humanity is hierarchy. Its essence is super-, sub-, and co-ordination ("above," "below," and "next to"). *Hierarchy*, meaning "rule of a high priest" in Greek, forms the basis of human society, and hierarchical systems in general help in navigating complicated areas like society or intelligence.

The "high priests" ruling the hierarchical model of intelligence – still in effect today – were identified by Raymond B. Cattell (1963). He separated Spearman's g-factor into two components, the fluid (Gf) and crystallised (Gc) intelligences. John Horn, a student of Cattell, extended the Gf-Gc model with 8–9 abilities:

- Gf – Fluid reasoning
- Gc – Acculturated knowledge
- Gv – Broad visualisation
- Ga – Broad auditory ability
- SAR – Short-term acquisition and retention (STM)
- TSR – Tertiary storage and retrieval (LTM)
- Gs – Broad speediness
- CDS – Correct decision speed
- Gq – Quantitative reasoning

In this form, the model already started to fit the diverse abilities theory proposed by Louis Thurstone as well, but it was American psychologist John Bissell Carroll's (1993) three-stratum hierarchy that incorporated enough abilities to really, so to say, satisfy representatives of the Binet school of thought, too.

Carroll's three-stratum theory organised general intelligence into three levels: narrow abilities (stratum I), broad abilities (stratum II), and general abilities (stratum III).

It can be seen that John Carroll's system is an elaboration on and systematization of earlier systems, and this hierarchical factor model of intelligence came to be known as the CHC (Cattell/Horn/Carroll) model. It represents cognitive abilities as a three-layered hierarchy. The bottom of the hierarchy is populated by numerous narrow factors, which can be construed on a "rule by high priest" analogy as the level of monks/priests/parsons – that is, the anointed. This is followed by a handful of more general factors at the mid-level: cardinals/bishops/deans. And finally, the top is occupied by a single factor, the g-factor: the high priest/the pope/the archbishop.

We don't know for certain whether the g-factor exists as some form of neurological synaptic efficiency; but as a concept representing cognitive abilities, we could accept the g-factor as the intelligence and everything else as its component. The situation, however, is more complicated, and we will need a finer approach if our goal is to present some universal concept of intelligence for the 21st century through a consideration of human and artificial intelligence.

Separate intelligences and savants as narrow intelligences

The school of thought in opposition to the – we could say Galtonian understanding of the – definition of intelligence as some general intellectual power is the Binet line of thinking, according to which intelligence is the conglomerate of different abilities (linguistic and numerical abilities, memory, etc.). We develop these through learning, and we can say that intelligent people managed to develop a lot of their abilities to a high level. As a result, they are able to use the appropriate abilities at a higher level in different situations and to think efficiently.

Of the theories of independent intelligences, Howard Gardner's is perhaps the most radical one. He posits that there is no such thing as general intelligence. Instead, the intelligence we use when we think is a sum of entirely mutually independent intelligences. According to Gardner (1983), these independent intelligences are as follows: linguistic, logical-mathematical, spatial-visual, kinaesthetic, musical, interpersonal, and intrapersonal. Gardner later added several other "intelligences" to the set, and we could keep adding items to the list, but it's doubtful whether that would bring us closer to understanding intelligent behaviour.

Basic modalities are the motor, spatial-visual, and auditive abilities; verbal modalities are the linguistic and logic-mathematics; and personal modalities are the inter- and intrapersonal abilities. Gardner very precisely mapped the most important areas of abilities, whose development is indeed independent to a

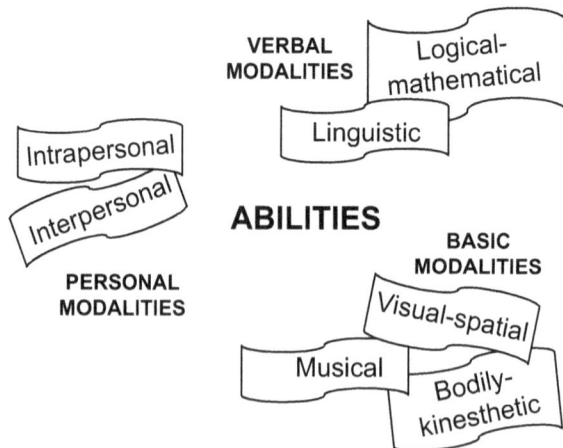

FIGURE 2.1 Abilities

certain degree, in particular in terms of cerebral processes, as well as in terms of mutual independence in case of an injury – meaning that a trauma to one area does not necessarily affect another. This does not necessarily mean that these abilities can be called intelligences; this is open to debate.

While we could label these as intelligences, they are in fact the most important areas of human abilities, rather than intelligences. The order of abilities clockwise starting from the linguistic one in Figure 2.1 is the order in which Howard Gardner described them. This is more or less the same order of importance at school and in public thinking, and according to which individuals get credit for achievements in given ability areas. Public thinking, in friendly agreement with school, holds linguistic and mathematical (or in other words, verbal) abilities in higher regard than the other areas, even though this artificial hierarchy is only cultural in origin. From a developmental point of view, it is worth starting out from the basic modalities, given that all other areas are built on these, and all are of equal importance in mental activities.

This is why it is better to represent ability areas on a concept map instead of in a list that reflects a hierarchy: this way, their equality in terms of their role in cognitive achievements is clearer. All areas of ability contribute immensely to efficient mental functioning, albeit in very different ways, and they also have independent existence. One exciting proof for this is the savant syndrome, which Gardner himself cited.

Savant syndrome involves extraordinary abilities in specific areas, which is often coupled with low general intelligence or autism. Savants are specialists to the point that their areas of excellence never mix. Musical, numerical, spatial-visual, and linguistic abilities are the most typical areas to have been identified as savant abilities, all of which are essential human ability areas. Musical savants are commonly visually impaired, and their instrument tends to be the piano. They learn to play by ear and are able to perfectly replicate pieces they heard. It's a clear achievement, but if all is precise replication, then it corresponds to the achievement of an mp3 player: it records and plays music. Artistic savants reproduce exactly whatever they see, so as such they correspond to the combination of a scanner and a printer. Indeed, they often operate in the same way: they do not plan or make sketches but start from one corner of the paper and draw whatever they see before their mental eyes.

Calculating savants emulate the performance of calculators. Language savants, who are able to translate from and to several languages without understanding what they translate, function akin to Google Translate. A form of the language savant syndrome is the "cocktail party syndrome," in which case the intellectually disabled individual is able to converse fluently at length about basically nothing.

Such extreme abilities may also emerge non-congenitally. Following a trauma to the brain, certain cerebral functions may get lost, but people with apparently normal abilities up to that point would sometimes acquire "miraculous" abilities. An example is Orlando Serrell, who was hit by a baseball on the left side of his head. Serrell lost consciousness briefly, and after he got up, he suffered from a strong headache for a long while. Once the headache disappeared, he was capable of incredible mathematical calculations, and his memory became photographic as well. Serrell's case seems, and is indeed, rare. Out of the 7 billion inhabitants of Earth, about 15–20 such savant cases have been documented, but their existence highlights the degree to which we are still in ignorance about the operation, abilities, and potential of the human brain.

Changes like these can be brought about not just mechanically, but also using electric stimulation. Transcranial magnetic stimulation, generally used in the therapeutic treatment of neurological diseases, was another way in which savant abilities could be generated temporarily. The development of abilities should not, of course, be built on an unpredictable procedure as a hit on the head, and electronic stimulation likewise does not seem like a very good idea. But the phenomenon reveals that our neurological potential is far greater than we think.

The savant syndrome invariably comes with outstanding memory skills, frequently photographic memory, and is often coupled with compulsive behaviour. Savant individuals don't care about the end results of their performance; it's only the process itself that brings them joy. In a sense, their brain functions like an artificial narrow intelligence. In analogy to ANI, we could call the savants' abilities HNI (human narrow intelligences), if we regard ability areas as intelligences.

The human ability to adapt is ensured by the ability to react to diverse situations, and the ability profile put to work in these responses is where individual differences lie. The savant phenomenon is rare. Most people have all abilities at their disposal, generally not at an extreme level, but to different degrees. Each individual has stronger and weaker abilities, an individual ability profile, which determines the way they can solve different kinds of tasks.

The ability areas Gardner focussed on are the ones that make humans best adapted to react to the challenges of their environment. But when faced with challenges surpassing their physiological make-up, already archaic humans would use technological solutions enhancing their bodily/mental abilities. We have already touched upon this topic in the previous chapter on the humachine. In addition to assistive technology, humans have also employed and still employ predigital, biological, organic solutions. Watchdogs and tracking dogs with far more acute senses than ours have long been part of our signalling and search systems.

We have been enhancing abilities belonging to the basic modalities using accessories and assistive methods. For example, we extend the range of our visual abilities using optical devices like the telescope and the microscope, our hearing using telephones and such; and we employ instruments in addition to our vocal chords for music, thereby broadening the human potential. Biological enhancements extend to the area of physical performance: horses increased our speed, oxen our strength. The invention of writing about 5,000 years ago significantly extended the barriers of our memory and freed up cerebral resources, transferring a lot of information to paper or tablets, that is, external media. The abacus, the soroban, and the calculator all likewise freed up brain capacity.

We don't consider truffle hogs or compasses intelligent, even though their function is similar to an ANI: they are capable of superhuman performance in specific tasks. Artificial narrow intelligence (ANI) makes our most important ability areas substantially more efficient, and it compensates for missing or insufficient abilities, capacity, and knowledge, thereby increasing our potential for adaptation.

This resonates with the previous chapters where we emphasised how the introduction of assistive technology and enhancements helped humanity expand its abilities and knowledge. This required not only inventing these tools, for which a few creative minds would have sufficed. The wide-spread use of the relevant ability- and performance-enhancing solutions called for the wide-spread acquisition of new abilities and knowledge. For instance, the ability to handle animals, read and write, and use an abacus or an instrument became necessary knowledge for a lot of people. At this point, the story may sound familiar from the previous chapter: our development was boosted primarily by our laziness, having become accustomed to machines that could solve a lot of things for humans. ANI is basically the high point of the technologies adopted so far: a more and more ambitious widening and replacement of HI functions. But there are no returns without an investment: the question is what the price and cost of this reduction of burden is in terms of new human abilities and knowledge to be acquired. The price is most assuredly to be paid, so the goal is to develop and make widespread the human abilities that are desirable for the development and widespread application of the AI. If we acknowledge this, then the investment will be profitable and humanity will not experience the acquisition of new abilities needed for the use of radically new tools as a pointless expenditure.

To recapitulate what we have found: we can draw up an analogy between ANI and human special intelligences (which are in fact ability areas, but this is beside the point right now). However, we can still encounter surprises when it comes to the products of the human brain. For instance, Canadian psychologists (Visser et al.) showed in their 2006 study that the individual areas proposed by Gardner are a blend of the general g-factor, of cognitive abilities different from g, and (in some cases) of non-cognitive abilities and personality characteristics. As such, the areas identified by Gardner could in fact be construed as Spearman's s-factors, which are responsible for the g-factor's content. In addition, it seems that in the case of humans, intellectual functioning is also associated to a certain extent with emotional-intentional internal factors: a possibility that certainly does not even arise at a real, technical level in the case of machines – at most only in the world of sci-fi.

Neuropsychological intelligence

Factor analysis gave birth to psychometrics, and, by extension, psychometric intelligence. Meanwhile, however, with the progress in neurology, intelligence came under scrutiny from a new angle. The Galtonian biological approach is still around, and it can now rely on psychometric results distilled with factor analysis.

Research on intelligence chiefly focuses on cerebral neural functioning, since the processes that define intelligence reside in the cranium. Researchers have been trying to uncover the exact location and function of these processes.

The 20th century was dominated by the anatomy-centric point of view: the goal was to discover the location of abilities and the g-factor. Based on the study of brain injuries and data from brain scans, intelligence can primarily be linked to neuron groups located in the prefrontal and parietal cortex. According to the so-called parieto-frontal integration theory (Jung, Haier, 2007), it is the structure of, activity in, and connections between these regions that are responsible for cognitive differences between individuals. However, it later turned out that the patterns of brain activity would differ even between individuals with similar levels of intelligence performing the same mental tasks. This means that the brain can use different paths to reach the same result. It also transpired that people with higher test results showed lower brain activity than those who performed less well, which indicates that some form of brain efficiency may be behind intelligence.

Another line of research studies brain waves. Brain waves, the cerebral rhythm, are what control traffic in the brain, ensuring that neural signals successfully reach the appropriate neurons. Brain signals do not progress in a continuous fashion; rather, they are segmented. According to Hungarian neuroscientist György Buzsáki (2006), this rhythm signifies some form of information ordering and might be a part of the "syntax" of the messages. The numerous rhythms in the brain form a unified system and are mutually dependent on each other. As the notes in music, information in the brain progresses along multiple harmonised time scales. Given a harmonic temporal coordination of neuronal activity, an enormous amount of information capacity can become available. Researchers found that co-ordinated beta and gamma waves generated via synchronised neuronal firing are necessary for the efficient performance of cognitive tasks. Simplifying it a little, we can say that gamma waves carry the "thoughts," and beta waves the control signals that determine which of these should come to the front. If beta waves are not strong enough to control gamma waves, the brain will fail to filter properly, leading to confusion, which hinders thinking.

A third way of searching for the biological foundations of intelligence is uncovering the brain's communication network. According to the "network neuroscience theory" of American cognitive neuroscientist Aron Keith Barbey (2018), there are two different ways information is processed in neural networks. One is the encoding of earlier experience. This is what psychologists call "crystallised intelligence." The second one is adaptive problem solving, which is flexible: this corresponds to "fluid intelligence."

Crystallised intelligence is built on strong connections; that is, its components are born as a result of several months or even years of neural traffic and use. We can call this knowledge building. Fluid intelligence, in contrast, is built on temporary paths. The connections are transient and superficial, and they are formed when the brain perceives a new situation, a new problem it must solve. In such cases, it does not form permanent connections but instead updates earlier knowledge: in other words, new connections are formed. If these connections persist for a longer time due to being reinforced several times, then knowledge is created.

The more the brain is ready to create new connections and re-form knowledge, the more efficient it is. Flexibility is one of the most important characteristics of the human brain – but it is not enough in itself. General intelligence requires both existing knowledge and efficient access to it, or in other words, crystallised intelligence, and the ability to form new, even temporary connections, which is a characteristic of fluid intelligence. In light of all this, general intelligence lies not so much in a certain brain area or network but in a flexible change between the two kinds of network states.

As mentioned previously, people who are more intelligent process information more efficiently. That is, they use less brain resources for the same task as less-intelligent people. Moreover, it seems the energy supply of their neurons are likewise better. Cognitive developmental and evolutionary psychologist David Geary hypothesised in a 2018 study that mitochondrial efficiency is the most fundamental biological mechanism that contributes to individual differences in general intelligence. That is, mitochondrial functioning is responsible for the g-factor, not to mention bodily health and ageing.

Mitochondria are small cell organelles producing, among other things, the energy molecule ATP (adenosine triphosphate) necessary for the functioning of the cells. A cell contains several hundred or even thousands of mitochondria. Mitochondria use oxygen to produce the energy molecules from carbohydrates, fats, and amino acids. Breathing is basically the transport route to supply mitochondria with oxygen. In absence of nutrients or oxygen, mitochondria are unable to function, and they get damaged. This is why proper nourishment and the oxygen supply in the blood is a crucial factor in mental functioning, health, and ageing, and why proper breathing and exercise play an important role.

To sum it all up: a decisive factor in the efficiency of intelligent agents' neuronal network is flexibility, appropriate neuronal communication – in other words, efficient information processing and energy supply. We can add to this our hypothesis that in terms of energy consumption, emotional-intentional factors can have an important role by promoting rather than hindering these processes: if this is the case, less energy is needed because no extra processes need to be supplied with power when the mental struggle has intentional emotional support.

Neuronal learning

Intelligence, whatever the cerebral processes behind it, is first and foremost about learning and problem solving, seeing it results in adaptive and goal-directed behaviour. The concept of intelligence is so closely intertwined with learning that today, a large part of AI is predominantly concerned about learning. In machine learning, the algorithms analysing the data learn from them and then use what they learned in the decisions they make.

Deep learning is a form of machine learning, which involves neural networks with several layers of nodes. Machine learning models get increasingly better and more efficient, but they still need some guidance. If an AI algorithm makes imprecise predictions, a human agent must often intervene and adjust the settings. To some extent, though, some approaches, like deep learning models, allow for the algorithm itself to continuously adjust and update its settings (in the case of neural networks, the weights corresponding to the associative strengths between specific neurons) based on new incoming data without outside control.

There are numerous radically different methods of machine learning: for a long time, it was dominated by so-called symbolic, rule-based systems that employ a logical analysis of the data, which to this day is still an important approach in situations with clear-cut rules of operation. Such systems can be brittle, though, and may break down in more ambiguous scenarios or when faced with new kinds of data. One of the most successful and widely used approaches in machine learning to deal with such "messy" situations are artificial neural networks and deep learning. Of the machine learning frameworks, artificial neural networks seem to mirror human neural functioning most closely, even if at a technical level there are vast differences between human neural learning and the way deep learning operates.

When the first computers appeared in the 20th century, psychologists would characterise the way the human brain functions in analogy to computers. The comparison was not as successful as they originally hoped, but today, it is in a sense the way the neural network of the human brain operates that has become a kind of blueprint in the development of machine intelligence.

It is no longer living creatures only that are capable of neural learning. The development of artificial neural networks was inspired by the biological network of the human brain, and such networks have distinct advantages and success in several learning scenarios. The foundations for this were laid down in the first half of the 20th century by neuroscientists, among others.

Santiago Ramón y Cajal (1911) was a Spanish neuroanatomist specialising in the central nervous system. He became a pioneer of modern neuroscience through his study of the microscopic structure of the brain. His work was one of the bases for the famous Hebbian Learning Law by Donald O. Hebb. This law, taught today as a part of the theory of intelligent systems, states – put simply – that "cells that fire together wire together."

The neurophysiological postulate Hebb put forth in his 1949 book was that "the persistence or repetition of a reverberatory activity (or 'trace') tends to induce lasting cellular changes that add to its stability." The exact hypothesis asserts that "when an axon of cell A is near enough to excite a cell B and repeatedly or persistently takes part in firing it, some growth process or metabolic change takes place in one or both cells such that A's efficiency, as one of the cells firing B, is increased" (p. 62).

The biological basis for learning lies in neural plasticity. During the operation of the nervous system, the nature and strength of synapses can change, meaning that the connections between neurons change. Synaptic links get stronger when the activation of two more neurons is close in time and space. The activation of the presynaptic cell is coupled with the activation of the postsynaptic one, and the resulting structural changes promote the development of neural networks. Some existing synaptic connections, when activated, get stronger through use. Multiple tightly connected neuron packages form the basis of learning.

An artificial neural network (ANN) – often simply called a neural network (NN) – is a collection of linked artificial neurons that uses a mathematical computational model for information processing. An ANN is ordinarily an adaptive system which transforms its profile based on external or internal information flowing through the network.

When it comes to artificial neurons and artificial neural networks, Hebb's law can be captured as the method of changing the weights between the neurons. Simplifying things a little, the weight between two neurons increases if they are activated simultaneously and decreases if they are activated separately. The weight between nodes that tend to be active and inactive at the same time will be very large, while the weight between nodes with opposite activation profiles will be very small. These surprisingly basic ingredients make the solution of highly complex tasks possible.

If we look at what the theory of intelligent systems says about when it's a good idea to use neural networks, it becomes clear that it's no coincidence that the human brain looks the way it does:

- There is a rich dataset available for the problem to be solved
- Rules that can be used to solve the problem are unknown
- The available dataset is incomplete and may contain inaccurate data
- There is a large amount of corresponding pairs of input data and output parameters available

The world in which we live and learn and solve problems is just like this. Intelligence is thus nothing but a way to deal with information chaos.

So far, there is no indication that machines could develop an entirely different kind of mental functioning. Even when machines make moves that are unusual or even astonishing for human observers, these moves are interpretable within the human cognitive framework. Because of this, it might not be relevant to look for a universal intelligence, because that would still be defined within the framework of human thinking and would therefore not differ radically from a highly comprehensive concept of human intelligence. The anthropocentric approach is not just a method of thinking but a fundamental mental framework.

Human and machine information processing

Cognitive psychology regards the individual as an information processing agent which, like a computer, acquires information and follows a program for the purpose of arriving at an output. An AI is a system that emulates human information processing to solve problems, and in this respect, we are justified in calling it an intelligence. Or, conversely, we can say that humans and animals, in general, can be regarded as information-processing machines. Either way, we have arrived at theories analysing intelligence from the aspect of information processing, which compare human and machine information processing to each other.

Information processing consists, in its simplest form, of three stages which are common to all intelligent agents:

1   Input processes handle the analysis of stimuli
2   Storage processes cover everything within the agent, including the encoding and manipulation of stimuli
3   Output processes are responsible for the appropriate reaction to a stimulus

Both the human brain and a computer analyse a comparison of external and stored information to find a solution to different problems. A significant difference between the two is that human cognition can be influenced by several potentially opposing emotions, motivational factors, and goals, which leads us to a critical point: the issue of attention. The selection of external and internal stimuli and information to undergo analysis plays a defining role in problem solving.

We are still not sure in the case of several factors influencing processing to what extent they can be regarded as part of intelligence. We will take a closer look at these factors using the concept of satellite intelligences, because while it is very much an open question which of these can be regarded as part of intelligence and to what extent, we can assume that they play a much greater role in human computation than we would think.

To explore this problem, we have chosen a model of intelligence that ignores the g-factor and builds on information processing. Robert Sternberg, one of the most creative theorists in the research on intelligence, presented a broader, more complex theory of general intelligence and information processing in 1984, which he later developed further.

The Triarchic Theory of Intelligence is a highly complex model, but for us, only one of its sub theories is relevant, namely, the componential sub theory. In this theory, the basis for intelligence is a series of information-processing components. The components can be classified into three groups:

1   Metacomponents
2   Performance components
3   Knowledge-acquisition components

The metacomponents include planning, monitoring, and evaluation used in problem solving and decision making. These tell the brain how to behave. The metacomponents are sometimes called a homunculus. The homunculus is a metaphorical "person" in our mind regulating our actions.

The performance components are the processes which actually perform the actions dictated by the metacomponents. These are the basic processes enabling us to implement tasks such as memory, reasoning, processing speed, and vocabulary. Processes like encoding, combination, and comparison also belong here. Encoding takes care of the initial perception and storage of new information, while combinatory and comparison processes are a part of information analysis. For example, reasoning tasks like Raven's Matrices activate a series of performance components, including encoding, inference, mapping, application, comparison, and justification.

The knowledge-acquisition components serve to process and learn new information. They perform tasks in which information is selectively chosen and irrelevant information filtered out, in addition to combining pieces of the collected information. The metacomponents affect the other two component groups, but these in turn have a feedback effect on metacomponents and are mutually connected, as well.

As for machine information processing, the performance components were the first of the three component groups to appear in the operation of computers. With the appearance of the newer machine-learning methods, knowledge-acquisition components can likewise be identified pretty well. However, there are still metacomponents that are not part of machine intelligence. The role of the controller is currently – and possibly permanently – filled by human agents. Humans, as the machine's "homunculus," execute the control of machine intelligence.

The three Sternbergian sub theories correspond to three mental functions. This way, Sternberg distinguishes creative, analytic, and practical intelligence.

1   Experimental sub theory: creative intelligence is mobilised when the components need to be applied to relatively (but not wholly) new tasks and situations
2   Componential sub theory (the sub theory we looked at earlier): analytical intelligence takes centre stage when the components are applied to rather abstract, but still relatively familiar, problems such as the exercises that students engage with at school
3   Contextual sub theory: practical intelligence is required when the components are applied to relatively concrete and familiar problems like the challenges of everyday life

People who are strong in creative functions are good at generating new and useful ideas. People strong in the area of analytical intelligence generally do well at school and in regular situations like regular ability tests. This type of intelligence is closest to the concept of intelligence measured with IQ tests. People who have strong practical intelligence are led by common sense: they are good and efficient at implementing and applying ideas, in turning them into practice, and in convincing others. They are good communicators and are able to adapt to the needs of their environment well.

Machines are good at analytical intelligence. As this is the intelligence behind school success, among other things, AI can excel at school intelligence. The Japanese software ToRobo achieved a higher score on the English language part of a college entrance examination than the average of Japanese students.

We can see that AI is getting increasingly better in the area of creativity, too. It is able to generate new and useful solutions. In this respect, it has reached a fairly high level of human abilities. But the highest level, emergent creativity, the level at which radically new principles are developed in scientific and artistic areas (good examples are Albert Einstein or Pablo Picasso), remains to be conquered.

While the form of human creativity that is accessible to everyone is an organic component of mental health, creativity is often linked to some form of psychological disorder in the case of outstanding creators. Higher levels of creativity, like all extremes, are connected to deviance. This means that AI may be capable of attaining the highest level of creativity if we manage to infuse its information processing with a little deviance. This is the path that computational psychologist Stephen Thaler – inventor of the Creativity Machine, president and CEO of Imagination Engines Inc. – embarked upon and suggested the introduction of a "V-creativity" (visceral creativity) in 2012. This would be a form of disruption built into the "gateway" networks of the Creativity Machine, with the goal of generating alternative solutions fitting the overall context. This would essentially model a non-standard brain and generate contexts from fuzzy details akin to the information-processing approach of unusual thinkers and creators.

To sum up so far: analytical thinking, check (basically); higher levels of critical thinking, in planning. However, results are as yet mixed in the area of practical intelligence. Machines are today better than humans at predicting the needs of the environment, but they are unable to cope with the numerous small communication issues of everyday life. The machine may know what we want to buy or what ailment we suffer from, but nuances of communication require mental factors over and above computation, like empathy and a flexible adjustment of goals. Above all, there is still no AI capable of common sense and understanding human languages, let alone using it efficiently in communication. Convincing others, understanding the arguments of others, and giving the proper reaction is impossible without a deep understanding of human language. And in absence of these, there is no practical intelligence.

A machine may be unbeatable in signal processing, but it is not intelligent because it simply computes without having knowledge about the operation itself. A machine may be able to add, subtract, multiply, and divide, but it won't know why, when, and to what purpose it does all this – just as the AI defeating the world's best Go player has no idea what it is doing and why. The result just computes. The machine implements instructions, but it does not initiate. As it has no goals, intentions, or internal points of reference to relate to, it is likewise unable to deal with these in external agents.

To maximise the developmental potential of human and artificial intelligence, it would, for now, be enough to truly understand human intelligence as a culture-independent entity that is nonetheless the product of culture. This statement may smack of a paradox, but it simply means that we are looking for the factors forming the foundation of human intelligence. We might discover in the process how to go about understanding the intelligence of agents with different cultural backgrounds such as ethnic groups, social classes, or non-human biological and artificial beings.

Is human intelligence culture-dependent?

An intelligent agent perceives its environment through sensors and intelligently affects this environment. The agent may be a raccoon or a human, or equally well a non-biological creation. Non-biological agents are for example AI and robots. A humachine or a cyborg has mixed origins.

If we can broaden the concept of intelligence enough, then, theoretically, we could even compare for example plant and machine intelligence, because there have to be factors along which they can be reliably assessed and compared. Let us take the simplest, Sternbergian definition, and we already have two factors to work with: goal-directed and adaptive.

Diverse kinds of intelligence

Plants communicate with each other, which means that they are able to acquire information from their external surroundings, process it, and transfer it to each other. Plants have no brains, but if we take our universal definition of intelligence, they do have intelligence. They are able to perceive and optimally react to numerous kinds of environmental factors, including light, water, gravitation, temperature, soil structure, nutrients, toxic substances, microbes, plant eaters, and chemical signals from other plants. Plants "know" when it is time to start growing above the earth, and if the circumstances are not right, they can even delay their development. Some plants hunt and trap insects. A shame plant will shrink when touched; but if it is touched repeatedly, it will learn not to react. However, if it experiences some different kind of effect, for example, shaking, it will react again and shrink, meaning that it is able to distinguish between stimuli.

It seems that plants remember stress and events, and have been shown to be able to react appropriately to 15–20 different environmental factors. If intelligence is not linked in the definition to brain and nerve functions but is regarded as a problem-solving ability that is goal-directed and adaptive, then we can talk about intelligence in the case of plants.

The existence of animals with intelligence is no longer a question today. Some species even have a brain, should someone want to make this a prerequisite of intelligence. We typically list vertebrates, and in particular mammals among the most intelligent species, perhaps because they are evolutionarily closer to humans and the environment they must adapt to also more closely resembles that of humans, and their goals likewise make more sense to us. After humans, chimpanzees have the biggest "information-processing capacity." This is computed based on the number and structure of neurons in the cerebral cortex, on the distance between neural cells and the network they form, as well as on the so-called axonal conduction velocity, which reflects the speed of neurotransmission.

There is a link between information-processing capacity and intelligence, although there are a number of other factors that have a hand in the behaviour becoming goal-directed and adaptive. Based on information-processing capacity alone, for example, dogs count as much less intelligent than cats. A lot of dog owners will probably be outraged at this idea, since dogs virtually read our minds and are able to solve complex tasks in a flexible and independent way. We can count much less on cats, in contrast. Dogs are, however, a partner to humans, and as such are capable exactly of what humans want them to be. Cats have no such ambitions: they do not want to live up to the humans' expectations, but they do adapt extremely well to diverse environments.

Dogs have adjusted to humans among other things with their intellectual abilities during their shared past of over 10,000 years, not to mention breeding, which steered the evolution of dogs in the required direction. What the goal-directed adaptive behaviour in question will look like depends not only on brain capacity but also on the environmental conditions that a creature adapts to.

Dolphins, whose habitat differs radically from that of humans, are likewise highly social creatures and adapt well to the conditions of their environment with their well-developed cognitive abilities. They help each other when they are injured or sick, and thanks to their well-developed communication, they are able to transfer their knowledge to their peers. Their highly developed intelligence is characterised by a long list of cognitive abilities similar to those of humans.

Rats, being favoured experimental subjects in laboratories, are much-studied animals. We know that they are able to analyse situations and navigate complex mazes thanks to their ability to process different sensory signals. They are capable of performing complex computations in order to gain food from a trap without falling into it. They show a high level of empathy and even make sacrifices for other members of their species. Also, rats dream, similarly to humans. All of this makes them highly intelligent beings in the eyes of humans.

Pigs are highly adaptable mammals who take pleasure in learning. Some studies suggest that the intelligence level of an adult pig may be similar to that of a three-year-old child. As such, their level of intelligence rivals the abilities of dogs, even though dogs were bred specifically to adapt to human cognitive abilities. Pigs only learned the secrets of human thinking through observation from the sty. No small feat, and contemplating it might strengthen thoughts of vegetarianism in some.

Elephants easily occupy the centre of human attention already owing to their size, and for some strange reason they have managed to elude extinction by humans. Elephants can boast of the biggest brain in land animals. In terms of the number of neurons, though, their brain containing 5.6 billion neurons is surpassed by that of gorillas (9 billion) and chimpanzees (6 billion), not to mention the 16-billion-neuron brain of humans. Elephants are also social creatures and are famous for their excellent social abilities. They express a large scale of emotions, including happiness and compassion as well as pain and grief. They also show behaviour reflecting altruism and self-awareness. Their memory is greater than that of humans. "Elephants don't forget."

Of the birds, those birds are considered intelligent by humans whose intelligence is easily comparable to that of humans themselves. Parrots, for instance, have an incredible ability of recognising different human faces, in addition to having immense communication abilities and being excellent at imitating sounds. They have a strong memory, which helps them solve complex problems. Crows are capable of making, using, and storing tools for later use. Their cognitive abilities include problem solving, argumentation, and even self-awareness. Despite a relatively small brain, they have a good memory. They remember other members of their species, and they even recognise humans when they pose a danger.

Intelligence can be found among invertebrates, as well; one just needs to pay attention. Humans, of course, again value the signs of behaviour that compare to their own. It turns out, for example, that octopuses use light flashes and colours as signals, probably as a method of communication. They are capable of performing complex tasks: for example, they can screw the lid off a jar at first sight to get to its contents. They not only have good short- and long-term memory, but they are remarkably efficient at learning new abilities. For example, the mimic octopus (*Thaumoctopus mimicus*) is able to impersonate other animals to protect itself from predators.

Identifying the "goal" and "adaptation" can prove problematic. If the goal is a long life, then the Greenland shark, also called the grey shark (*Somniosus microcephalus*) is a winner. With its tiny brain and extremely slow development – it takes it 150 years to reach adulthood – it is not a paragon of intelligence, but it is still the longest living vertebrate, with a lifespan of 300–500 years. On top of that, it swims so slowly that biologists marvel at how it can catch any moving creature. It probably catches its prey in their sleep, but what is certain is that it is proving successful despite cognitive functions that can hardly fall under the concept of human intelligence.

If the goal is the proliferation of the species, then ticks and cockroaches would be among the winners, as would the chicken, which cleverly fought its way to the top of the human gastronomical palette, and as a result is now the most numerous vertebrate species on land. As individuals, chickens do not have it very well; but as a species, they are a true genius, although they again did not achieve their evolutionary survival with the help of cognitive functions favoured by humanity.

Our narrow human point of view makes it difficult to recognise intelligences that differ vastly from ours. If the goal and adaptation requires a behaviour different from that of humans, then our unbiased scientific commitment suddenly falters. By an inspection of the characteristics of creatures considered intelligent by humans, we can compile a fairly precise list of the components comprising what we see as intelligence, which is a better approximation of humanity's concept of intelligence than our broad, all-encompassing definition: stimulus processing, learning ability, memory, logical ability, planning, problem solving, spatial-visual abilities, spatial manipulation, awareness, communication abilities, language acquisition ability, and social-emotional abilities.

However, if all of these were a prerequisite, then sooner or later we would arrive at an extremely strong interpretation of intelligence, one which would basically only fit humans – and possibly the machine intelligences modelled on humanity's own intelligence. But the latter would (and, we hope, will) be designed to have exactly the abilities humans deem it should – and it's unclear if emotional-social abilities or awareness will make it into humanity's list of abilities for AI. Let us not forget in the meantime that machine learning may at some time bring to light an alternative, non-human-like form of behaviour and ability structure proving more adaptive for humans or machines.

Behaviour corresponding to this list of characteristics has an important role in the biological adaptation of the human species. Without these, for one, intersubjective reality would not be possible, and this has made the development of social behaviour into mass behaviour possible, thereby making most components of intelligence unnecessary for *Homo sapiens*, in fact. If you can't explain something rationally, it is practical to believe in it instead: for example, if we believe that intelligence exists, we spare ourselves a lot of headache– not, though, when we are about to create an intelligence that is significantly more efficient than, and possibly also different from, ours.

We have seen that the evolutionary goal of survival was often achieved through a form of adaptation not conforming to the human approach. There are diverse ways to biological adaptation. Thus, the human-made concept of intelligence is in fact behaviour conforming to goals and adaptation in a human framework of reference. This means that the more intelligent we consider an agent, the more its coping strategies resemble ours.

Diverse kinds of culture

It's worth making a distinction between the concepts of universal intelligence (if it exists) and human intelligence. This way, we can evade a lot of contradictions. Let us say that *universal intelligence* pertains to the set of goal-directed behaviours that has adaptive value from the perspective of some agent, while *human intelligence* refers to goal-directed behaviour with adaptive value that is relevant from the human point of view. The species *Homo sapiens*, however, is in a state of extraordinary diversity owing to its cultural evolution, and, consequently, goals and adaptive behaviours are specific to the particular culture. The broad strokes with which universal intelligence was defined allowed a place among the multicoloured set of intelligent agents for people living in vastly different *Homo sapiens* cultures.

Narrowing the concept of intelligence leads to and has led to all kinds of complications, and not only as far as the theoretical nature of the intelligence concept is concerned, but also in terms of the evaluation of people from different cultures. Since the concept of intelligence was invented by people belonging to 19th- or 20th-century, white, middle-class, Western European and North-American culture, the tools designed to assess intelligence likewise conform to this culture. This of course led to considerable tensions when a comparison of populations with different backgrounds showed marked differences, typically in favour of the Western culture. An exception was the implementation of the relatively culture-independent visual tests like John Raven's Matrices. In these tasks, Eastern cultures outperform the Western ones.

The environmental background as a decisive factor cannot be ignored in the assessment of intellectual abilities. There are a high number of human cultures in existence, which are all characterised by different sets of cognitive abilities necessary for coping. A pertinent problem is that tests belong to the two-dimensional world of paper and screens, while we must cope for our survival in three-dimensional space. Add to this that 3D knowledge and learning is coming again to the forefront in the 21st century, which makes the use of 2D assessment procedures increasingly questionable.

The industrial society is built on the rules of Western white civilization, as a result of which not only do its tests and schools conform to this culture, but so do the cognitive abilities necessary for success. Each culture trains a population with the abilities conforming to that culture, and the individuals with the suitable predispositions will be the winners in that culture. For instance, a study on a northern Kenyan population has revealed that individuals with a hyperactivity gene have a higher body mass index in a nomadic tribe – in other words, they are more successful – and a worse one in a settled, agricultural population. Thus, the situation is exactly the reverse for hyperactive individuals in the nomadic and in the settled population. In the settled population, their body mass index is lower, meaning that they are less successful (Eisenberg et al., 2008). The hyperactivity gene can be beneficial for survival in certain circumstances, while not so much in others. Culture-changes can make different abilities more advantageous than before.

The cognitive background for adaptive behaviour is different for humans in different environments. As such, we cannot forgo a more in-depth examination of the role of the environmental background.

The effect of the environment on IQ

Novel trends tend to start out in an extreme form, possibly because they must combat the previous theory. But if things go well, the pendulum will slowly start to settle down. This is what happened in the research on intelligence. In the beginning, the hereditary school was louder, and the influence of the environment was only estimated to be around 20 percent. Then, in the wake of the horrors of the time of the Second World War, theories emphasising environmental effects came to the fore, and it was the turn for heredity to be estimated at having only 20 percent influence. Next came the more nuanced proportions (60–40, 40–60), and then the compromise: 50 percent heredity, 50 percent environment. As with all forms of compromise, this failed to truly delve into the heart of the problem. It didn't bring a real breakthrough; that is, it did not solve the question.

The answer came once again from the ingenious psychologist Donald O. Hebb, whose proposal was 100 percent–100 percent. Such an Alexandrian solution to this Gordian problem is bizarre from a mathematical point of view, but it perfectly captures the interaction of heredity and the environment: in particular that they do not complement, but fully define, each other. In effect, the question was incorrect, and so it was impossible to answer within its conceptual bounds. The question was as appropriate as asking whether the area of a rectangle is determined more by its width or its length.

To illustrate Hebb's point, let us take the Himalayan rabbit. It's a perfect subject to demonstrate interactive, adaptive solutions. Its fur is white, except for its nose, its tail, its ears, and the ends of its paws, which are all black. Nature, of course, didn't create things like this simply as a joke: there must be something practical in this bohemian appearance. The white fur is excellent for hiding in the snow, and the black patches of course do not serve to increase the survival chances of the predator, either, of course, but to increase the chances of the rabbit even more. Black-coloured fur is excellent at absorbing sun rays and protecting the rabbit's extremities from frostbite.

It's practical and goal-directed, but it wouldn't be interactive (and by extension, an intelligent solution) if the fur colour were not adaptive – but, in fact, it is. Whenever the temperature of any part of the Himalayan rabbit's body falls below 33 degrees Celsius, then darker hair will immediately grow on that body section. With this master stroke, the Himalayan rabbit managed to optimise the ratio of dark and light fur, and, therewith, survival. Evolution found an intelligent solution: the rabbit itself does not have to contribute much.

How does this work when it comes to human abilities? Let us take musical abilities. Researchers studying musical talent have arrived at very precise data. Based on twin studies, it turns out that heredity accounts for 26 percent of musical achievements. This is not a large amount, but not negligible. What is important is that the amount an individual practised was more strongly influenced by genes, namely, to 38 percent (Hambrick, Tucker-Drob, 2014). From this, we can expect internal drive to be genetic to a considerable extent.

So far, this was just about internal characteristics. But further studies found that the genetic effect on performance was far greater (59 percent) for those who practised regularly than for those who did not (1 percent). Based on this, it appears that practice is the area where the influence of genes can be manifested to a considerable degree. Practice, however, requires a stimulus environment conducive to development. Another twin study revealed that in the case of children raised in a high socio-cultural environment, genes determined intelligence to about 72 percent, while in the case of those from a low social-economic background, only to about 8 percent. As the case of the Himalayan rabbit shows, if the potential is there in the genes, then what happens is up to the environment. If the internal potential is not given, then the environment in itself can work no miracles. And neither can genes without the right environmental conditions.

It's certainly not a fair procedure to evaluate other cultures against the Western culture and its way of thinking: we should look at each culture in its own context. This is not just a question of ethics; it is optimising human intellectual capacities. The human brain is an open and experience-dependent system shaped through the interaction of the individual and the environment. As such, culture determines which cognitive abilities will become stronger. When the culture changes, so do the ability structure and the characteristics necessary for mental coping. In an age of culture change like the 21st century, this is a particularly important consideration.

According to studies, it is the IQ test results conforming to Western culture that increase with the time spent at a school conforming to Western culture. According to a 2017 study, education increases IQ, or at least IQ test-solving abilities increase, by 1–5 points each year. Skipping school and irregular school attendance results in lower IQ (Ritchie, Tucker-Drob, 2018). We could, of course, contest the results of these studies, saying that children who start school later and who drop out might potentially possess lower intellectual abilities to begin with, which would be a cause, rather than a result in this case. But the effect of the environment can definitely not be ignored. The most significant role of the environment is to make it possible to maximally exploit the genetically given potential. The benefits of development programs are indisputable, but differences in individual development indicate that individual-specific predispositions determine how much an individual can profit from a given environment.

Adaptive intelligence

Intelligence makes it possible through adaptation for a species to learn and shape environmental factors to its own end. As Robert Sternberg put it, "Without adaptation, one has little or nothing resembling intelligence." Intelligence is adaptive per se, which seemingly makes the qualifier *adaptive* superfluous, but it is not. The term *adaptive intelligence* is used to refer to the aspect of intelligence that plays a significant role in adaptation.

And even machines

The term *adaptive intelligence* is used for biological entities and machines alike. In models of the human mind, *adaptive intelligence* refers to the adaptation of (that is, the changes in) the brain and the mind for the purposes of survival. In other words, adaptive intelligence is the mind's ability to change in reaction to the demands of the environment. For example, the part of the brain responsible for language acquisition will start developing if someone is living in a foreign country and learning its language.

Adaptivity is also becoming an important factor in artificial intelligence, although the way the term is used in the context of AI varies considerably. Training neural networks to learn from, interpret, and react to information in real time is one way to think of adaptive intelligence in AI. Ideal areas of applications for this kind of machine learning include virtual assistants or self-driving cars.

Adaptive intelligence in AI goes beyond a smart conversion of input into output, as it involves a constant update of the learning models to ensure the most appropriate outputs for the relevant context. In other words, adaptive intelligence focuses on context and relevance. This simple statement can be applied to any kind of adaptive intelligence, human and artificial alike.

In terms of human intellectual abilities, the concept of adaptive intelligence was put forth by Robert Sternberg, with whom we are very much familiar by now. He argues that intelligence in humans serves the purpose of biological adaptation, and it can only be interpreted in the context of culture. The concept that is generally termed "intelligence" is specific to the given culture, is a culturally based concept, and is only partially determined biologically.

Humans are social beings, and, as such, the most important factor in adaptivity is the ability and disposition for cooperation. Social-emotional abilities are not extras but key figures for the development and survival of *Homo sapiens*. If we look at humanity's existence as a television series, these lead actors are not expendable, because without them, it wouldn't be the same series.

Collective intelligence as superintelligence

A new kind of collective intelligence field emerges, stimulated by the current wave of digital technologies, which makes broad and efficient thinking possible for organisms and populations. According to the definition of French philosopher Pierre Lévy (1999), collective intelligence is a universally shared intelligence which is developed constantly, is coordinated in real time, and enables the efficient mobilisation of skills and abilities.

Similarly, to the g-factor of individual human intelligence, the definition of a general collective intelligence factor – the so-called c-factor – is now a research goal, which can aid the efficient assessment and development of group efficiency. The c-factor has three main components, namely, cognition, co-operation, and coordination. The initial *co-* in these three terms is no coincidence: the Latin words from which they derive begin with the prefix meaning "together," which combines with three important words of humanity: *know, do, arrange.* Adding the fourth important word at the beginning, we get "together-knowing," "together-doing," and "together-arranging," respectively. Collective (note the again not-accidental *co-*) functioning is a key to the success of humanity, and we have arrived at a point where our efficiency in this ability area might reach a whole new level.

The "Big Mind," as Geoff Mulgan (2017), a researcher of collective intelligence and founder and director, called it, is a collective functioning of human and machine abilities. It's a huge challenge even at the individual level to act rationally and emotionally at the same time, to reconcile these two areas. It's an ever-bigger challenge for people to harmonise all this with each other, as well. It's one of the biggest opportunities of the 21st century, though. The culture of knowledge sharing based on access and sharing can make it possible for people to integrate emotions and reason not only at the individual level, but at the level of the community, too. Collective intelligence is quite common in practice, but it is rarely implemented consciously at the level of social contracts. Companies, family households, and nations all exist thanks to collective intelligence, and the quality of life in these communities depends on the quality of this intelligence. A new component with considerable potential in helping to integrate the values of the communities of the future and to operate in a network-based framework is info-communication technology and AI.

However, collective functioning is not foreign to nature itself, either. As discussed already, information processing may take place outside – or even inside – of individuals in networks via a co-operation of agents. The individuals – the agents – themselves may in turn be smaller groups and networks.

This pattern is reminiscent of what Benoit Mandelbrot, researcher at IBM, named "fractals" – literally endless complex formations characterised by self-similarity, with endlessly "rough" or "fragmented" boundaries. Self-similarity means that a smaller part, when zooming in on it, displays the same structure as the bigger part. Everyday examples for this are snowflakes, the leaves of a fern, or the branches of a tree. The network of living networks likewise shows this pattern.

An example is a forest, which we could regard as a living organism. According to German forester Peter Wohlleben, who writes in popular style about ecological topics including the collective functioning of forests, trees in a forest are linked through an underground fungal network which helps them develop and survive. Trees share water and nutrients through these networks and also use them for communication. For example, they alert each other about droughts, diseases, or insect invasions, and the trees change their behaviour based on this information. The fine, hairy root caps of trees intertwine and combine with microscopic fungal threads, forming the links of the so-called mycorrhizal networks. This appears to be a symbiotic relationship between trees and fungi, but it may just as easily be a case of business, that is, the network may be held together by economic relations. As a sort of price for their services, fungi consume about 30 percent of the sugars that the trees photosynthesise using sunlight. The sugar sustains the fungi, which take up nitrogen, phosphorus, and other mineral nutrients from the soil, which are in turn absorbed and used by the trees.

Cooperation is quite common in the animal kingdom. Just as humans live in a society, a lot of animal species live in colonies. There are enormous buildings several thousand years old serving as a monument to the triad of high-level, collective, knowledge-action arrangement. For example, Stephen Martin, researcher at University of Salford, and his colleagues recently discovered a 4,000-year-old underground city in Brazil comparable in size to Great Britain. Its builders? Still alive! The megapolis is still inhabited, and it is home to the termite ant species *Syntermes dirus*. The several billion cubic metres of mounds visible above ground, each about 2.5m high and 9m in diameter, and numbering about 200 million (!) are merely the construction waste: they are not inhabited; they just have an access tunnel leading through them to above ground. Creating and maintaining such a structure involves extraordinary organisation, collective knowledge, work, and system. The researchers have established that the entire complex belongs to a single colony, because if they relocated an inhabitant to another location, the locals would immediately accept the new arrival.

And all of this is just the product of collective intelligence at the evolutionary level of insects. The "co" triad is far more common in nature than we thought. The co-ordinated co-operation of autonomous units is behind the success of *Homo sapiens*, as well. As soon as a hierarchy extends too far, the empire falls and breaks once again into small autonomous units. If these units develop collective functioning, stable growth results. This kind of interlinked operation has been around for a while in the case of machines; just think of the internet of things. At the next level, the "internet of everything" no longer connects just artificial intelligences. It is an ecosystem implementing the triad of cognition, co-operation, and coordination, of which humans are a part of.

Collective intelligence can be natural or artificial, but this next step humanity has embarked on is a special evolutionary move that develops a hybrid of natural and artificial intelligence. So, if we have dreams of a super intelligence, we need to look beyond the ever-increasing capacity and efficiency of machines and also focus on the associated human intelligence. And when it comes to human intelligence, it is not the g-factor that we can rely on, since the g-factor simply appears to be some kind of computational power. A collective super intelligence requires human collective abilities. In other words, what we need are traditional and new ways of cooperation.

Collective intelligence also encompasses a harmonious collaboration with nature. Humans can become a long-term key factor in the intellectual field if they shed their feelings of inferiority, their fears, and reflexes from their ancient past and grow up to the task.

EQ as the human CQ

Emotional intelligence has become a hyped favourite of the past decades. In earlier times, it would only make the "also starring" category, and most intelligence tests do not even measure it, or at most only a small part of it like "understanding social situations." If we look at Gardner's list, the inter- and intrapersonal intelligences come at the very end. Still, this group of abilities is gradually climbing the ladder, which is of course no coincidence. We are talking about an ability area which will be more important than anything in 21st-century, network-based functioning.

To be fair, there have been early definitions of intelligence that would include something akin to emotional and/or collective intelligence. For example, Edward Thorndike lists three intelligences in his model from 1920:

1   Abstract intelligence: the ability to process and understand concepts
2   Mechanical intelligence: the ability to manipulate physical objects
3   Social intelligence: the ability to handle human interaction

Social-emotional abilities have always been a part of thinking about intelligence, but only as supporting actors. Their independent career started in 1990, when Peter Salovey and John Mayer described emotional intelligence, which encompasses the following groups of abilities:

1   Perceiving and expressing emotions
2   Using emotions in problem solving
3   Controlling emotions

The emotional intelligence level of a person contributes to their intellectual and emotional well-being and development. This in itself is insufficient, however, because it also needs to be realised at a social level. This is where Daniel Goleman came in, who in his 1995 book *Emotional Intelligence* unified four important factors in a very simple table, as shown in Table 2.1.

1   Self-awareness: awareness of emotions and their effect, awareness of strengths and weaknesses, taking responsibility, self-acceptance, self-confidence, self-worth, accurate self-assessment

TABLE 2.1 Emotional intelligence

EQ	Personal competence	Social competence
Awareness	Self-awareness	Social awareness
Management	Self-management	Relationship management

2 Self-management: self-control, reliability, honesty, sincerity, authenticity, adaptability, flexibility, goal-orientedness, problem-solving, innovation, conscientiousness

3 Social awareness: empathy, understanding others, making use of potentials in others, taking social responsibility, the importance of relationships, tolerance

4 Relationship management: co-operation, respect for others, conflict management, persuasiveness, a sense of humour, a need for variety, helpfulness, communication, promoting change, building relations

Goleman found that performance and success at school, and especially at work, depends to a much greater degree on emotional intelligence than on intellectual and learning abilities. Social cognition is a fundamental component of human thinking for survival, without which human cognition is impossible to fully understand.

Humans are social creatures, so it comes as no surprise that the traits described here were already necessary in the earliest human communities. Humanity's evolution strengthened social-emotional abilities, but *Homo sapiens* is now at an entirely new evolutionary level. Its lifestyle has transformed through cultural evolution to such an extent that its biology could barely keep pace. Abilities encoded in the nervous system have not fully transformed from their configuration adapted to tribes of 50–150 people and a nomadic, self-sustaining lifestyle to abilities suited to the impersonal, mass, settled, and specialised lifestyle of today. We have managed to get by so far, and we can continue to do so, but humanity needs to understand and shape its own evolution more consciously. The road to collective intelligence leads through the conscious shaping, development, and use of social-emotional abilities encoded in the human brain.

As we are preparing AI for collaboration with humans, it will be important for human agents to collaborate with either organic (carbon-based, living) or artificial (silicon-based, machine) beings.

The living network

Intelligence is traditionally assumed to be located in our brains and in the individuals, but intelligence can also be encoded in hidden communication networks connecting individuals. This is a well-known phenomenon in the case of humans. Informational networks weren't born with the social networks based on 21st-century digital tools. To the contrary: technology made an existing communication network more effective.

Family members, friends, their family members, colleagues, and neighbours form a multi-layered network through which information is transferred via tighter or looser groups. Various groups and alliances will also form in an organisational environment (school class, workplace, etc.). These provide the formal and informal channels for the flow of and access to information. For example, the group of individuals working directly below the head of an organisation are in a privileged position thanks to which they are able to acquire and provide more information (relating to both specific tasks and the workings of the power structure), simply because their positions formally and informally increase their communication opportunities. A network consists of autonomous units with different abilities and opportunities. Human social networks can be considered hybrid constructs thanks to technology, since diverse kinds of AI participate in the functioning of the social network and even influence it by collecting, selecting, and channelling information.

Most beings whose existence relies on groups form networks, in which individuals may have different roles stemming from their characteristics and positions. Researchers looking at groups of fish have uncovered that an individual fish would transmit information with its behaviour, and since different individual fish give off different signals with their behaviour, the entire group itself will act together on the integrated knowledge it acquired this way. Networks usually form from members of a single species, but collaboration between different species is quite frequent, as well. For instance, a flock, the sheep dog, and the shepherd can be regarded as a carbon-based hybrid communication system.

One of the most important examples of network-based functioning for humans is the human organism itself. There are millions of tiny living organisms living inside the human body: the human microbiota. This microbiome comprises bacteria found on the skin, in the nose, in the mouth and, most importantly, in the gut. The complex gut microbiotic system that has evolved in mammals has played an important role in the brain's development, as well. The human gut microbiota genes – the microbiome – considerably outnumber the human genes in a human body. These microbiotas are able to produce a large amount of neuroactive compounds. The gut microbes control behaviour, playing a role in nonconscious processes. Wrong or missing microbes lead to a change in the neurochemistry, which in turn results in a change in cognitive functioning. A number of mental problems can be traced back to problems with this biological information-processing system. Among other things, it can contribute to social interaction disorders and autism.

We already have talked about the humachine, which we could capture in a more precise though rather convoluted manner as the "collective mental power of adaptively co-operating intelligent agents." This is a form of co-operation where humans need to collaborate with not just humans with a different thinking and culture, but machines, too. Machines are increasingly being prepared for this co-operation. Specialists are no longer only developing robots, but also so-called cobots, which are robots capable of working under humans. So at least as far as machines are concerned, the leaning towards co-operation has begun.

Emotional/collective intelligence is a key issue. As long as humans don't learn to understand each other, intelligent agents working in a network, the Big Mind, and all kinds of collective solutions remain a utopia.

The existence or lack thereof of a general intellectual power is an exciting question and one worth studying; but from the perspective of goal-directed and adaptive behaviour, it is the abilities and brain functions making us successful in a specific environment that are important. The development and assessment of these abilities has practical and even life-defining usefulness, which probably does not require much explaining. The condition for hiring new colleagues for a work position is the existence of abilities important for the job at that workplace. In a similar vein, we should identify the ability profiles that make us successful in a specific environment and cultural-social medium.

In the first chapter, when we presented a survival kit, we already charted the group of factors indispensable for survival in the 21st century. We can look at this package as the ability profile necessary under the given circumstances. The package contains several components that do not form part of current intelligence tests, though. For instance, emotional intelligence comes with a measurement tool and standard independent of the IQ: the EQ. If collective intelligence is the key to humanity's survival in the 21st century, then the EQ or the CQ should be considered a part of the IQ. In other words, it should be treated as one of the main types of intelligence, just as Thorndike's intelligence model. Of course, for research purposes, the path is opened to assessing anything with all kinds of tools.

Enrichment

Machines have been and are developed to be easily used by humans. Machine development in the form of the robot is increasingly being designed as what can be described as having an empathetic-emotional identity to be able to successfully work with human beings. As has been discussed previously, the work on machines is increasingly directed towards forms of interactive co-operation with humans.

Consider and identify five essential core human thinking and cultural activities that transcend different religious, political, historic, and geographical tribal and nationalistic imperatives. How would you propose that these five essential features of all human beings can be intensified in order to prepare humans for working cooperatively with machines?

Do we as a species need to create a global pedagogy of co-operation?

Link pathways

What links neural plasticity, octopuses, trees, snowflakes, and knowledge-acquisition?

References

Barbey, A. K. 2018. Network neuroscience theory of human intelligence. *Trends in Cognitive Sciences* 22 (1). doi:10.1016/j.tics.2017.10.

Beer, R. D. 1990. *Intelligence as Adaptive Behavior: An Experiment in Computational Neuroethology.* San Diego, CA: Academic Press Professional, Inc.

Buzsáki, G. 2006. *Rhythms of the Brain*. Oxford: Oxford University Press.

Carroll, J. B. 1993. *Human Cognitive Abilities: A Survey of Factor-Analytic Studies*. Cambridge: Cambridge University Press.

Cattell, R. B. 1963. Theory of fluid and crystallized intelligence: A critical experiment. *Journal of Educational Psychology* 54 (1): 1.

Chollet, F. 2019. *On the Measure of Intelligence*. arXiv:1911.01547v2 [cs.AI].

Eisenberg, D. T. A., Campbell, B., Gray P. B., Sorenson, M. D. 2008. Dopamine receptor genetic polymorphisms and body composition in undernourished pastoralists: An exploration of nutrition indices among nomadic and recently settled Ariaal men of northern Kenya. *BMC Evolutionary Biology* 8: 173.

Gardner, H. 1983. *Frames of Mind: The Theory of Multiple Intelligences*. New York: Basic Books.

Geary, D. C. 2019. Mitochondria as the linchpin of general Intelligence and the link between *g*, health, and aging. *Journal of Intelligence* 7: 25.

Goleman, D. 1995. *Emotional Intelligence*. New York: Bantam Books.

Guilford, J. P. 1950. Creativity. *American Psychologist* 5: 444–454.

Hambrick, D., Tucker-Drob, E. 2014. The genetics of music accomplishment: Evidence for gene–environment correlation and interaction. *Psychonomic Bulletin & Review* 22. doi:10.3758/s13423-014-0671-9.

Jung, R. E., Haier, R. J. 2007. The parieto-frontal integration theory (P-FIT) of intelligence: Converging neuroimaging evidence. *Behavioral and Brain Sciences* 30 (2): 135–154; discussion 154–187. doi:10.1017/S0140525X07001185.

Kovacs, K., Conway, A. R. A. 2019. What Is IQ? Life Beyond "General Intelligence." *Current Directions in Psychological Science* 28 (2): 189–194. doi:10.1177/0963721419827275.

Legg, S., Hutter, M. 2007a. *A Collection of Definitions of Intelligence*. arXiv preprint arXiv:0706.3639.

Legg, S., Hutter, M. 2007b. Universal intelligence: A definition of machine intelligence. *Minds & Machines* 17: 391–444. doi:10.1007/s11023-007-9079-x.

Lévy, P. 1999. *Collective Intelligence*. New York: Basic Books.

Martin, S. J., Funch, R. R., Hanson, P. R., Eun-Hye Yoo. 2020. A vast 4,000-year-old spatial pattern of termite mounds. *Current Biology, Cell Press*. https://www.cell.com/current-biology/pdf/S0960-9822(18)31287-9.pdf.

Mulgan, G. 2017. *Big Mind: How Collective Intelligence Can Change Our World*. Princeton: Princeton University Press.

Raven, J. C., Court, J. H., Raven, J. 1983. *A Manual for Raven's Progressive Matrices and Mill Hill Vocabulary Scales*. London: Springer Science+Business Media, LLC.

Ritchie, S. J., Tucker-Drob, E. M. 2018. How much does education improve intelligence? A meta-analysis. *Psychological Science* 29 (8): 1358–1369. doi:10.1177/0956797618774253.

Romanes, George, 1893. *Mental Evolution in Animals*. London: Degan Paul, Trench, Trubner & Co.

Salovey, P., Mayer, J. 1990. Emotional intelligence. Imagination, Cognition, and Personality 9 (3): 185–211.

Spearman, C. E. 1927. *The Abilities of Man*. New York: Macmillan.

Sternberg, R. J. 1984. Toward a triarchic theory of intelligence. *Behavioral and Brain Science* 7: 269–315.

Sternberg, R. J. 1985. *Beyond IQ: A Triarchic Theory of Human Intelligence*. Cambridge, UK: Cambridge University Press.

Sternberg, R. J. 2019. A theory of adaptive intelligence and its relation to general intelligence. *Journal of Intelligence* 7: 23. doi:10.3390/jintelligence7040023.

Thaler, S. 2012. The creativity machine paradigm: Withstanding the argument from consciousness. *APA Newsletters*, p. 11.

Thomson, G. H. 1916. A hierarchy without a general factor. *British Journal of Psychology* 8: 271–281.

Thomson, G. H. 1919. The hierarchy of abilities. *British Journal of Psychology* 9: 337–344.

Thomson, G. H. 1935. The factorial analysis of human abilities. *Human Factor* 9: 180–185.

Thorndike, E. L. 1924. Measurement of intelligence. *Psychological Review* 31 (3): 219–252. doi:10.1037/h0073975.

Thurstone, L. L. 1938. *Primary Mental Abilities*. Chicago: University of Chicago Press.

Visser, Beth A., Ashton, Michael C., Vernon, Philip A. 2006. *g* and the measurement of multiple intelligences: A response to Gardner. *Intelligence* 34 (5): 507–510. doi:10.1016/j.intell.2006.04.006.

Willis, J. O., Dumont, R., & Kaufman, A. S. 2011. Factor-analytic models of intelligence. In R. J. Sternberg, S. B. Kaufman (Eds.), *Cambridge Handbooks in Psychology. The Cambridge Handbook of Intelligence* (pp. 39–57). Cambridge: Cambridge University Press. doi:10.1017/CBO9780511977244.004.

Wohlleben, P. 2015. *The Hidden Life of Trees: What They Feel, How They Communicate – Discoveries from A Secret World*. Vancouver, BC: Greystone Books.

Suggested reading

Ashton, M., Lee, K., Vernon, P., Jang, K. 2000. Fluid intelligence, crystallized intelligence, and the openness/intellect factor. *Journal of Research in Personality* 34: 198–207.

Bear, M. F., Connors, B. W., Paradiso, M. A. 2001. *Neuroscience: Exploring the Brain*. Baltimore, MD: Lippincott. ISBN 0-7817-3944-6.

DeYoung, C. G. 2014. Openness/intellect: A dimension of personality reflecting cognitive exploration. In R. J. Larsen, M. L. Cooper (Eds.), *The APA Handbook of Personality and Social Psychology: Personality Processes and Individual Differences* (Vol. 3). Minneapolis, MN: University of Minnesota.

Han L. J. van der Maas, Kees-Jan Kan, Denny Borsboom. 2014. Intelligence is what the intelligence test measures. Seriously. *Journal of Intelligence* 2: 12–15. doi:10.3390/jintelligence2010012.

Hao, K. 2020. AI still doesn't have the common sense to understand human language. MIT Technology Review. https://www.technologyreview.com/2020/01/31/304844/ai-common-sense-reads-human-language-ai2/.

Jensen, A. R. 1998. *The G Factor*. Westport, CT: Greenwood-Praeger.

Scarr, S. 1993. Biological and cultural diversity: The legacy of Darwin for development. *Child Development* 64: 1333–1353.

Turkheimer, E., Haley, A., Waldron, M., D'Onofrio, B., Gottesman, I. 2003. Socioeconomic status modifies heritability of IQ in young children. *Psychological Science* 14 (6): 623–628.

Williams, S. 2018. The biological roots of intelligence. Imaging, behavioral, and genetic data yield clues to what's behind effective thinking. https://www.the-scientist.com/features/the-biological-roots-of-intelligence-64931.

Satellite intelligence – mental functions influencing intelligent behaviour

- Boundary problems
- A crash course in brain physiology – an evolutionary fairy tale

  - Once upon a time . . . – nerves and the nervous system
  - The reptilian brain

- • An innovation of ancient mammals: the limbic system
- • And finally, the cortex

- The key: information and energy

  - • The cultural evolution of the brain
  - • Info-communication
  - • Hybridization

- Dual processing

  - • Brain hemispheres
  - • The right, the left, and the middle
  - • Dual system thinking – fast and slow thinking
  - • Fast and slow machine thinking

The 21st century is about info-communication, that is, about information, about processing information, and about the brain. All of these areas are intertwined with intelligence through a number of threads, even though, as we have seen in the foregoing, it's not even clear what exactly intelligence is, what it comprises, and how it functions. In this chapter, we will attempt to map factors and functions either belonging or not strictly belonging to an intelligent agent's intelligence. All the while, we will not lose sight of the main objective of the book: to provide as detailed a picture as possible about the possibilities of the human mind and spirit with the goal of promoting the progress and development of the generations of the 21st century.

Boundary problems

Our cognitive functions are not equivalent to intelligence as is. We don't know exactly what intelligence is, but it is influenced by a number of cognitive and non-cognitive factors, which we will here, in this book, call "satellite intelligences" because they simultaneously supersede, accompany, and form intelligent behaviour.

Robert Sternberg, whom we have mentioned in a previous chapter, organised a symposium in 2018, the material from which was published in the *Journal of Intelligence*. The motivation behind the symposium were his worries that researchers of intelligence had chiefly focused on the biological, cognitive, and behavioural bases of general intelligence, overlooking the sociocultural role that intelligence must play in solving world-level problems. It doesn't really matter how much we know about the brain's intelligence, for example, if we still don't know why intelligent people are unable to solve fundamental issues like global climate change, severe bushfires, hurricanes, ocean warming, or the vanishing of polar ice caps.

It wouldn't be difficult to find a rational solution, especially since the necessary mental potential is also enhanced by AI today. Besides rationality – and influencing rationality – a number of neurological processes shape our behaviour, which itself may be rational, but the result ultimately appears to be senseless.

One of the basic facts of mathematics is that the product of two negative numbers is a positive number. Could a fact of psychology be that the combination of multiple rationalities is irrationality?

We propose that the adoption of a "satellite intelligence" framework can be helpful in studying questions relating to intelligent behaviour. In this framework, we regard intelligent behaviour – a component of intellectual functioning – as an especially dynamic planetary system with satellites orbiting not one, but several, planets of the system. The mental, gravitational centre is occupied by the individual's identity, the consciousness that holds mental existence and activities together, akin to the way a sun holds celestial bodies together.

Consciousness is a dark energy – not fully understood yet – that heavily defines the intellectual power currently called the g-factor. This g-factor is rather a statistical construct than an existing entity, and we will here focus instead on its adaptive problem-solving component, the so-called fluid intelligence, and all the elements that influence it. At the heart of fluid intelligence lies pattern recognition, which is thus the dominant planet, the central component, of intelligence. Pattern recognition, together with emotions, motivations, and instinctive drives and all the different kinds of needs and abilities of the individual form a dynamic planetary system.

Satellites, which are systems themselves, are permanent companions to these "planets;" they are the cognitive functions that influence in one way or another the behaviour that we consider intelligent, like subjective and intersubjective

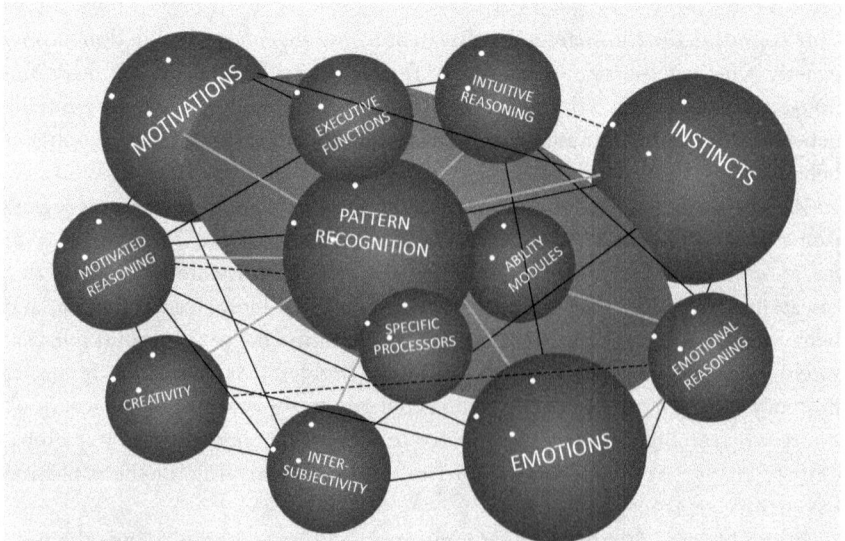

FIGURE 2.2 Satellites

reality, intuitive thinking, motivated thinking, executive functions, or creativity. Instead of being assigned to a single "planet," they act more like electrons in a molecule, orbiting and interacting with multiple nuclei. The parts of this planetary system are what this and the following chapter will be about. But we may already have an idea of just how complex and dynamic this planetary system is, full of a myriad different force vectors acting on the bodies in it.

A crash course in brain physiology – an evolutionary fairy tale

We could take as our starting point the question: what is and what is not necessary in the human brain in order for us to talk about intelligence? To this end, we could take a superficial overview of all the kinds of things that evolved in our brain and examine which parts of this arsenal we could scrap and discard if our goal were to keep only intelligence in operation. This idea would totally miss the point, because, as seen in the previous chapter, human intellectual, emotional, and other functions are heavily intertwined. So instead of scrapping things, let's choose sorting to make the similarities and differences between the intelligences of intelligent agents and human agents clearer.

The evolution of the brain follows the same rule as all other kinds of development, and it builds on existing achievements, retaining them at some level. As such, to understand the human brain and its operation, the best road to take is to follow its development through evolution. Along this road, at some point we will need to seek recourse in the triune brain theory of American neuroscientist Paul MacLean (1990). The theory has come under a lot of criticism and does not conform to new neuroscientific views, but its core idea neatly captures what lies behind both brain development and human behaviour.

We are well aware that evolution didn't simply and literally build cerebral systems on top of each other like some sedimentary rocks, but that the brain has instead been shaped by a lot of influences. Neuroscience has evolved a lot since Paul MacLean. Today's approach highlights the central role of rich interactions between learning and the physical and social environment in the development of human psychological abilities. This interaction exerts its effect in diverse ways. Natural selection collates all information, which is passed on through generations, resulting in the emergence of adaptive phenotypes through genetic, epigenetic, and cultural inheritance. All of this can be told in a kind of evolutionary tale.

A caveat to the reader: as in all tales, we will be relying on story-telling devices and metaphorical presentation to bring home the points we want to make. For example, we will anthropomorphise evolution, which is not to say that it should be thought of as an intentional agent with goals and plans, or even as a teleological (goal-oriented) force of nature – in fact, evolution is quite the opposite. But since as humans we can relate best to stories resembling our own experiences, it seems worthwhile to use such literary solutions to uncover the broad outline of the issues at hand and the direction they may take in the future.

So, what follows is a rational reconstruction of how the actual case of events may have happened, told in the style of a narrative.

Once upon a time . . . – the nerves and the nervous system

The story goes that the jellyfish was the first creature to break through the nothingness. No one knows why or how, but at one point, evolution had the idea that a nervous system can come in handy in survival – which it did. In biological beings, there is no perception, information processing, or thinking as we know it without nerves and a nervous system. There's not even motion unless someone or something moves the entirely inert thing/creature/agent. Actually, this is not unheard of even when it comes to humans, who have a highly developed brain, but that is a story for another day.

The ancient jellyfish became capable of perceiving its environment, processing information and notifying different parts of its body, and then adaptively reacting to environmental stimuli. Compared to human cognition, this is no outstanding achievement, but 580 million years ago, the jellyfish was the most intelligent, most innovative living creature, which we could call our distant great ancestor.

For a couple of tens of million years, in fact, evolution didn't have a much better idea than the one it used in the jellyfish, but then came the flatworm (or something like it) and it invented the central nervous system. At this point, information processing no longer happened in a loose network: instead, the system was co-ordinated by a central unit, the brain. This was far from comparable to the human brain – at most to the central processing unit of an AI. But the emergence of a rudimentary brain meant a giant leap in intelligence. It became possible to compare information from different sources and to coordinate reactions, which constituted a huge increase in adaptivity. The goal probably remained survival, of course. At least, we are not aware of any other possible flatworm goals, and evolution doesn't really leave room for other choices.

The reptilian brain

The flatworm's innovation was such a huge success that it spread quickly. More and more different creatures made use of a central nervous system to help their survival, all the while constantly increasing their chances of continued existence through diverse small enhancements. The brave creatures daring to leave the water during evolution were especially in need of a lot of innovations. They developed new life-supporting systems, which assisted movement and the processing of oxygen and other nutrients in a life on land. We all know what this all involved: limbs, respiratory and digestive systems, the cardiovascular system, etc., all of which had already proven useful in water. The co-ordination of these increasingly critical systems became an increasingly bigger task, and brain development had to match the challenge.

The so-called reptilian brain can be found in all land vertebrates, and it turned out so well that its form has remained virtually unchanged in the several million years of evolution since it emerged. This area looks basically the same in the human brain and in a turtle. An important difference between the two, of course, is that a turtle has to make do more or less with the reptilian brain in itself, while it became supplemented and modified a lot by evolution until it became a part of the human brain.

An important component belonging to our reptilian brain is the brainstem – that is, the medulla, the pons, and the midbrain. These are essential in basic life functions such as the operation of the cardiovascular system or breathing. The brain stem also houses important reflex centres. For example, reflex centres located here control the involuntary and useful functions of coughing, sneezing, chewing, swallowing, saliva secretion, vomiting, and even the closing of eyes. The midbrain is responsible for vision, hearing, and motor control, including involuntary eye movements, and in addition it regulates alertness. Another cerebral component from the reptilian era is the cerebellum, which keeps our balance and coordinates movement.

Typical forms of behaviour controlled by the reptilian brain include threats, acquiring and defending territories, the fight for dominance, flight, and mating. It's a primitive intelligence, but it does everything that is needed for survival at the reptilian level. With the principle of "fight or flight," it solves the question of emotional attitude toward the world along basically a single dimension. Note that the emotional life of dinosaurs was not necessarily restricted to this, not to mention the fact that reptiles have evolved much since the ancient reptiles; some species today are capable of other emotions and some level of problem solving, as well.

Behaviour controlled by the reptilian brain is automatic, and it determines human actions more than we would like. At the reptilian evolutionary level, there is no cognitive processing of the emotions or the events of the past and the future, because we are talking about automatic, reflex-level reactions.

We wouldn't want AI to support all the functions associated with the reptilian brain. When it comes to breathing, heartbeats, etc. it may not be bad, in fact, it would be downright useful, for AI to be capable of controlling these and helping in them, if needed. But fighting, threats, and the like can cause serious damage when bolstered with AI. If we fail to pay attention to the environmental effects on the future generations, the reptilian-level-reflexes may remain defining in human behaviour and culture. This could make a humachine a true monster: we wouldn't have to pay to watch horror movies, we would just have to watch the news.

Somehow evolution must have come to the same conclusion, namely, that it's not a winning strategy to build solely on unthinking reflex-like terrorizing and fighting, because it moved beyond the reptilian level. About 250 million years ago, the brain came to possess an important new control centre, the so-called limbic system. This was the way evolution introduced emotions and learning.

An innovation of ancient mammals: the limbic system

The limbic system offers a more advanced solution for survival than those before it: emotional fine tuning. Small shrew-like rodents that appeared about 200–250 million years ago were no longer only capable of senseless fight and panic but – thanks to their paleomammalian brain – had the ability to be afraid in advance. What made this possible is that paleo-mammals had learned to learn (that is, store) memories. As such, equipped with a limbic system, these creatures know based on their experience who did what and in what circumstances, and they know when they should be afraid, be angry, love, or perhaps form an attachment. The limbic system supplies the enhanced survival mechanisms necessary for mammals living in social formations. In other words, it leads to behaviour equivalent to the social-emotional level of sheep or wolves. These creatures are no longer only able to threaten others like ancient reptiles, but they are also able to form attachments and function as a herd or a pack. The limbic system makes more adaptive and finer reactions possible than the reptilian brain. This is a definite edge, no matter how much we might dislike fear, which we also inherited in the paleomammalian brain.

The ancient emotions heavily influence human actions and thinking. While the limbic system does make more advanced reactions possible than the reptilian brain, it still only involves emotional solutions. The control of emotions, that is, basically the limbic system, is a part of maturity and civilised behaviour. In fact, the control acquired over the limbic system is what raises a creature above the animal level. Evolution managed to find an innovative solution for this a few million years later, but this is a story for the next section, because the paleomammalian brain is highly complex, comprising several co-ordinated subsystems, and thus it needs to be dealt with at some more length.

One of the components of the limbic system is the amygdala, or more precisely, the amygdalae. The two almond-shaped groups of neurons house our worst emotions, which make it especially important to master control, because the amygdala is concerned with emotions like anxiety, sorrow, and fear. The amygdala in the left hemisphere is more balanced and evokes happier emotions on occasion, while the right-sided one is constantly in a bad mood. If the amygdala cells die for some reason, the individual will not be capable of fear. Researchers have studied a woman with such an injury at length, for example, scaring her with all kinds of things, while all she felt was a slight sense of excitement and curiosity even at the sight of a poisonous snake or other dangers. What is more, she didn't even perceive the signs of fear in others, either. Still, it's probably not worth envying her, because those who cannot perceive danger live in a constant state of danger.

Living with an over-functioning right-side amygdala may be much more unpleasant than blithely marvelling at something, no matter how dangerous, like a knife or the barrel of a gun, but evolution did decide in favour of the amygdala, so this is what most people have to live with. Psychopaths, however, have much smaller amygdalae than normal, in addition to also showing anomalies in the connection between the amygdala and the frontal cortex. This explains why they are incapable of true anxiety and why they are unaffected by the emotions of others.

Another component of the limbic system is the hippocampus. It converts memories stored in the short-term memory for transfer into long-term memory – memories such as what we had for lunch or what a recent conversation was about. The hippocampus also plays an important role in information recall. It's like a search engine or librarian built into the brain. It looks up information and even compares new information to old to determine whether it is indeed new and whether someone then needs to decide on what should happen to it. This decision will be made at another level.

Shrinkage of the hippocampus can be responsible for short-term memory loss, one of the most important symptoms of Alzheimer's disease. Be that as it may, the hippocampus is one the few regions of the brain capable of creating new neurons – typically through an effect of physical exercise or environmental stimuli. In a now famous study with London taxi drivers, the volume of the posterior part of the hippocampus correlated with the amount of time spent driving a cab. Another study found that juggling induces neuron growth in the left hippocampus (and in the nucleus accumbens, a part of the brain involved in the sense of reward) in people aged around 60. This is temporary, though, because 3 months after quitting practice, the increase vanishes. But the opportunity for development is always there and can be taken up again, of course, not to mention that it is not worth stopping doing cascades, anyway, because all learning is excellent for stimulating the brain.

The nucleus accumbens mentioned earlier is another component of the limbic system, which links the limbic and motor systems. As an important part of the reward system, it plays an important role in the process of rewarding and reinforcing stimuli (food, drink, addictive drugs, sex, and physical exercise). It converts reward signals into action motivation: to take an example other than addictive substances, it encourages learning juggling or other movements. The reward system in the brain is probably profitable in learning new skills, and probably already played an important role in the development of ancient mammals' mental abilities.

A third important group of neurons inherited from ancient mammals is the thalamus, the entry system for information coming from the sensory organs. Its task is to relay the stimuli into the cerebral cortex for processing. This applies to all sensory signals except for olfactory stimuli, which are diverted in the direction of the olfactory bulb (*bulbus olfactorius*), a group of neurons in the forebrain. The olfactory bulb transmits information about smells to the amygdala, the orbitofrontal cortex, and the hippocampus, where it plays a role in the formation of emotions and memories, and in learning. Contrary to popular belief, the human sense of smell is not poor, but it is on a par with that of many animals; humans simply don't build consciously on this ability. However, smells and associated memories play an important role in emotions and, by extension, in decision forming.

A number of functions grouped under intelligence are influenced by conscious and unconscious emotions, which humans inherited from the time of ancient mammals and which control thinking and activities from the midbrain. We haven't even arrived at the cerebral cortex, yet, and we have already identified groups of neurons in the brain responsible for several factors categorised under intelligence.

And finally, the neocortex

Animal behaviour was under a dual control for several million years, balancing between the "fight or flight" of the reptilian brain and the emotion- and learning-oriented limbic system, but evolution will go on. Life became more and more complex, and thinking became necessary for mammals. To this end, a new structure, the neocortex developed about 200 million years ago. At first its growth would be modest, and then it bloomed into a rather big and extremely useful part of the brain in apes and humans.

This is the current peak of the evolution of the brain: a structure making it possible for humans to act based on rational decisions instead of instincts and emotions. The neocortex is the rational brain. It is part of the cerebral cortex beside the archicortex and the paleocortex, which belong to the limbic system. The neocortex is responsible for practically all higher-level cognitive functions. As such, perception, motion, language, thought, planning, and personality can all be associated with the grey matter of the neocortex.

The frontal lobe controls personality along with everything we call thinking, including reasoning, planning, and decision. Covering the frontal part of this is the prefrontal cortex, which is responsible for executive functions. It is still under debate exactly what these subsume, but the name itself is a good pointer: these are the functions necessary for implementing things. This is an area that is considered increasingly more important from the point of view of intelligence, and we will discuss it at more length later on.

The occipital lobe comprises the visual cortex and is located at the back of the head. This is responsible for mapping the world and making a 3D image of it. The parietal lobe is located at the top of the skull and encompasses the somatosensory cortex and a part of the motor cortices. As such, it is a control interface for bodily sensations and, to some extent, movements. Neuroscientists have by today mapped pretty accurately which area of the brain is associated with which area of the body. Once again, we encounter a homunculus. The cortical homunculus drawn by neuroscientist Wilder Penfield is a representation of the human brain in terms of which body parts the different cerebral areas have motor or sensory control over. It looks horrible, because the brain uses an enormous area for the sensory and motor processing of the face and the hands, which makes these body parts disproportionately big on the little homunculus: they are bigger than all other parts of the body put together. Highly nuanced facial expressions and the movement of facial muscles require a large number of neurons. Similarly, the precise movement of hands and the tactile perception in hands require significantly more stimuli to process than in the case of other body parts, where much coarser movements and precepts suffice. In other words, the peripheries are represented to different extents.

The cortex itself is indeed just a shell, about two millimetres thick; the rest of the material below it is all just wiring. An adult human brain contains about 100 billion neurons, each of which has, on average, connections to other cells numbering in the thousands. Humans think so much that the required increase in cortical area would necessitate an enormous skull, if unfolded. Evolution didn't really value this route, so the solution was a neatly and accurately folded cortex. This increases the surface area (and thereby volume) of the cortex without increasing the volume of the skull. Gyri and sulci increase the area of the neocortex to such an extent that it takes up about 76 percent of the brain.

While the relevance of the level of folding (or "gyrification") in the brain is as yet unresolved – and not only whales but even zebras are characterised by a higher level of neocortex folding than humans, beside cetaceans and ungulates – it is typically the primates (who are the closest relatives to humans) who have extensive folding in the brain. Most animals have no need of it, because their rational abilities do not require as large cortical areas as not to fit in their skulls.

We have already mentioned that some characteristics of the brain show a correlation with intelligence. These characteristics include the ratio of the brain weight and body weight, the ratio of the cortex and subcortical structures, as well as the relative size of the prefrontal cortex. According to our current knowledge, the features correlating best with intelligence are the number of neurons in the cortex and the speed of signal transfer.

Quantity matters, but mental capacity is not determined by quantity alone. Researchers studying the evolution of the human nervous system concluded that human cognitive superiority is probably a result of a mosaic structural rewiring and a molecular restructuring of specific neural circuits and cell types. This and studies on the brain size and structure of extinct primates lend the conclusion that the nervous system underwent several mutually independent changes until evolution arrived at human intelligence.

The key: information and energy

In the last couple of million years, the brain size of hominids increased rapidly and reached over three times its former size – a far greater growth than it had achieved in the nearly hundred million years before that. Other animals also showed a significant, though in most cases much smaller, increase during their brain development. Interesting exceptions showing extreme growth in brain size are the elephant and cetaceans, especially a species of the many-named pilot whales (also called blackfish or pothead whales – the latter possibly because their over-sized brain bulges out) studied in some detail and the *Globicephala melas* (the long-finned pilot whale). These cetaceans have a larger brain and, what is more, also more neurons than humans, and they live in a complex social system. A rare similarity between their close relatives, the short-finned pilot whales, and humans is that females undergo menopause, that is, they live for a long time even after the loss of their ability to reproduce. This has an important function in the care for offspring – and old dolphins have indeed been observed to fulfil grandmother functions.

Information and energy are the two key factors determining everything, including adaptivity and its paths. Exactly as in the case of AI, biological intelligence and its carrier, the brain, can develop and be developed as a function of these two factors. When it comes to human intelligence, however, there are a few factors which helped us hack biological evolution and set cultural evolution in motion. We have already described the most important tricks: laziness, a highly plastic brain, and info-communication.

Humans are lazy and like to conserve their energy, if possible. This is why we invented the simplest tools, machines, assistive technology, and even language. And the human brain was able to adapt very quickly and develop cerebral functions adapted to the new technologies. The biggest trick, however, was that we have come into possession of different methods for efficiently processing and storing information thanks to the innovations of the neocortex – and we are currently on the verge of enhancing these all the way through the development of AI.

The cultural evolution of the brain

A key process in information processing is to notice connections, understand environmental effects, and find patterns. This requires the ability to map the world and perform mental operations. At one point, the replicas of the world – symbols – appeared in the brain of some odd ancestor of ours: this meant that they could think about a thing without it having to be present or in their hands. This function of imagination is what led our both early ancestors and Nikola Tesla to their innovations. Tesla was capable of performing several experiments in his head, which meant that he didn't need to do everything in vitro or in vivo. The situation was probably the same when it came to the ancient Nikola Tesla and hunting. He could imagine the process and didn't have to die several times over because of a misstep. This method, simulation, is another case that has been developed further and enhanced to the point where today, we can build and destroy entire worlds and model complex weather and climate processes or the development of populations. This way, we are free to make mistakes as many times as we like, which affords us massive learning potential without the danger of a fatal "game over."

To return to our ancient ancestors, humans became better and better at information processing, but this was not enough to conquer Earth, yet. Humans learned to maximise information transfer and storage, and this was made possible by a shared code system we call language. So, another genius paleo-brain was born somewhere who could think of things in terms of symbols and even convinced their peers to accept the symbols – signs – in lieu of concrete objects. A symbol can be a drawing or a sound sequence. The sound sequence was simpler, and a suitable organ was available for it anyway, so speech was born. The details are not that relevant for our purposes, but it seems that one of the conditions for articulate speech is a descended larynx and a lack of contact between it and the soft palate. This is so far unique to humans. It's not inconceivable that *Homo erectus* could speak, but it is quite certain that the body structure of *Homo sapiens* is suited to speech, and there is evidence of symbol use from as early as 50–60,000 years ago. Language use required a number of other cognitive accessories, which human biology ultimately managed to tackle and which humans now need to tackle if we wish to create true talking machines.

Language can be regarded as a satellite intelligence, a sort of ability module to cleverly solve the problem of managing information. Language made it possible for information to be stored not just in a single brain, but to be carried by an entire group. Moreover, using social information management instead of the slow biological, hereditary method of information transfer made it possible for acquired knowledge to last and endure very quickly. As an example, take the ability to differentiate poisonous plants and herbs. One way to do this involves hereditary processes through generations of experience: those who survived a tasting knew that plant to be fine, while those who saw a peer turn purple and rigid knew to avoid that plant, and this information was stored at a deep level. But another way is for someone with the knowledge (having survived or seen an incident) to show and even tell others which plants are bad and which ones are good and for what. The group was able to retain much more information than a single individual. Language was a breakthrough invention of humans because it was a clever way to multiply brain size besides offering further advantages in information processing and significantly developing human thought processes.

A bigger brain can store and handle more information, but brain size is an expensive luxury in terms of energy requirements. A smaller brain is easier to maintain, as it consumes fewer calories. According to the Cultural Brain Hypothesis, the brain grows or shrinks as a function of the availability of information and calories – that is, there is some sort of balance to ensure an optimal ratio of return and investment (Muthukrishna et al., 2018). There are at least three important factors influencing this ratio in organisms:

1   A bigger and more complex brain is more costly than a less complex one: it needs more calories; it is more difficult to give birth to and takes a longer time to develop
2   The increased capacity and/or complexity of a bigger brain makes the storage and handling of adaptive knowledge possible: this adaptive knowledge potentially includes finding food, avoiding carnivores, ensuring the safety of

the partner and the offspring, expertise in hunting, identifying herbs, making tools, and so on

3   Adaptive knowledge increases the organism's adaptivity by increasing the number of offspring and/or decreases the probability of premature death: adaptive knowledge can be acquired either independently – through experience, trial-and-error learning, reasoning, that is, logic – or through social learning – that is, by learning from others

These were the basic ideas considered by economic psychologist Muthukrishna of the London School of Economics and his colleagues when they modelled the different possibilities.

The availability of information is influenced by factors that correlate with brain size in the evolution of species:

- Learning strategies (learning from others or independent learning)
- Group size
- Mating structure
- The length of the period of juvenile development

Under different conditions, the co-evolution between these factors of information availability and brain size can lead to a change in brain size. This opens up the opportunity for a lot of speculation.

If conditions remain unchanged, then simply adopting the (in those conditions, adaptive) knowledge itself would have greater returns. But if conditions change, then the ability to generate adaptive knowledge (requiring bigger brain size) is more advantageous; that is, a changing environment increases brain size – if the group is small. If there isn't enough brain capacity around to hold enough knowledge that one could copy, then a large-size brain capable of thinking will be of advantage. In bigger populations, in contrast to groups of smaller numbers, there is a greater probability that individuals with big enough brains will emerge, who will generate knowledge for others to acquire and adopt. This acquisition necessitates relatively monogamous parents who care for their offspring for a long time and hand down knowledge. Let us here take note of pilot dolphins once again, who have brains quantitatively similar to that of humans and in whose case grandmotherhood – a more thorough preparation of the offspring for life – is a common behaviour.

Social learning, that is, learning from others, requires increased transmission accuracy: quite different abilities than generating independent knowledge does. Social learning has smaller brain capacity needs but requires access to different knowledge models and enough available adaptive knowledge. In other words, if there is a lot of knowledge around to adopt, then what is needed is a lot of smaller brains. This is the path *Homo sapiens* has taken. The Neanderthals were also capable of innovation – as such, they may have been a match for *Homo sapiens* in terms of independent knowledge generation. But they were either weaker in social learning or didn't have big enough groups to disseminate information. The true story might even be that *Homo sapiens* acquired and used the adaptive knowledge discovered by the Neanderthals and got along just fine with a lot of smaller brains, which may even have constituted a survival advantage in times of food shortages. We might not even have to ascribe the extinction of the Neanderthals to *Homo sapiens*. Their downfall could just as well have been too much thinking and too little social learning.

The analysis of human genomes calls into question the idea that modern humans are more lightly built but otherwise simply identical versions of their ancestors in terms of thinking and emotions. In the times when the human brain would shrink in size, the human DNA would show several adaptive mutations relating to brain development and neurotransmitter systems (Zollikofer, De León, 2013). This suggests that as the organ got smaller, its internal functioning changed, as well, leading to potentially new evolutionary survival opportunities.

The *Homo sapiens* population increased strongly, opening up the possibility for truly smart sapiens to appear, while the survival of the species is ensured by the small brain size. As is known, the human brain has been shrinking in the last 10–20 thousand years. This may suggest that humanity is at a stage of its development where relatively few large brains generate a lot of knowledge which is transferred to the masses with smaller brain capacity. When formalised, this is the process we call education, and it is taking an increasingly longer time, that is, the length of the juvenile development period is extending.

Info-communication network and more

Language made it possible for the ideas of the smartest people to accumulate through generations in the collective storage of tribal knowledge. This store of knowledge, the information package useful in life, is available to each new generation. If everything goes well, new discoveries built on the knowledge of the ancestors will be made, further increasing the tribe's knowledge and making it smarter.

Language ensures a collective intelligence for the group far greater than individual intelligence and makes it possible for each person to draw on the advantages of collective intelligence in the same way as if they had created the knowledge themselves individually. Small children with wholly normal abilities are capable of using technology proficiently, tapping and swiping a device without having any idea of the principles of operation behind it (although it's not as if most adults have any real knowledge about the operating principles of mobile devices). There isn't any need for it, anyway, because humanity as a whole knows how and what works and why.

Language made it possible for paleo-humans to talk to each other and to create complex social structures. These – coupled with advanced technology like farming, husbandry, and animal domestication – spurred tribes to settle in permanent settlements and to grow into organised super-tribes. After a while, about 10,000 years ago, the first cities emerged. The accumulated tribal stores of knowledge grew into super storages, and growth commenced inexorably.

About 4–5,000 years ago, language was enriched with a new dimension, literacy, whose effect was multiplied through the invention of printing. Finally, electronic and digital information dissemination led to a virtually infinitely rich system. The increases in population and information transfer efficiency have gone hand in hand so far, but it is an open question as to how things will progress when it comes to extremely large quantities. Networks reaching a certain stage of development and level of complexity can split into multiple networks or connect with other networks, thereby potentially creating a new kind of entity.

In the words of Hungarian biologist and network researcher Péter Csermely, "Humans are networking animals." Larger molecules, cells, organs, tribes, groups of friends, society, and the entire earth are all networks. These networks work very similarly. According to the law of Bob Metcalfe (2013), "The value of a network grows as the square of the number of its users." Human info-communication has become highly effective owing to the steep growth of the human population. Its value lies not in the quality of the information communication: that is an entirely different question. Its value lies in the efficiency of information dissemination. At this point, it is worth repeating ourselves to note that the best (neural) correlates of intelligence are the number of neurons in the cortex and the speed of signal transmission. There is a clear analogy with Metcalfe's law, according to which the number of users in the network is the defining feature, if we add speed of transfer to it. As above, so below.

Communication – information transfer – could switch to higher gears in the human networks of antiquity: in the cities and city states. Additionally, people had access to more food through agriculture, leaving some people time for thinking. As such, a significant group of people capable of generating adaptive knowledge emerged, the transfer of whose knowledge was ensured by an efficient info-communication network. Human knowledge became collective and started inventing things no one person could have. In just a few generations, candles turned into LED lights, horse carriages into locomotives and self-driving cars, and messages are relayed through electronic impulses rather than letters. The human population has reached and passed the 7 billion threshold, so it is no wonder that human activities and their effects are growing at an exponential rate in all areas – and we are just entering the acceleration phase, as mentioned in the first chapter.

In sum, humanity can be regarded as an enormous info-communication network, which has exponentially grown in the last 10,000 years and which is producing an immeasurably large amount of information. In the meantime, laziness has become profitable, and *Homo sapiens* has multiplied its physical and mental energies through machines.

The wheel, the plough, and lifting devices were quickly followed by further innovations, and the 20th century turned into the age of engineering. The earlier organic energy solutions like horse- or mule-drawn devices were replaced with chemical energy and electric power. Development progressed from using biological organic materials through chemical organic materials to subatomic particles and electric charge, that is, physical energy. As such, we are able to exploit the energy of the material more directly instead of using up material masses.

Meanwhile, humanity has also developed devices – computers – which enhance cognitive functions by performing calculations and storing information. This increases the biologically given human information processing abilities in terms of mental energy. Machine performance is dramatically increasing both in areas relating to energy and information. Functions responsible for calculation or information storage capacity are part of the human brain, too, but machines increase the amount of information humans can process and store as much as mechanisation increases human physical performance. At the end of the 20th century, the tools assisting humans in physical and mental areas were then merged in the field of robotics.

The merger of networks opens up the road for the emergence of a super network. Humanity has turned into a super-intelligent network; the internet joined the computers humanity uses into a network, and by today, computers have started to perform distributed computations as a linked network, as well. The internet of everything adds smart machines to all this and joins everything into a unified network. The next, and perhaps the final, chapter in this story could be where a hybrid super-creature is to be born – the "internet of everything and everybody," a kind of super-agent or ultimate being.

Hybridization

If the events continue to follow the trends so far, then first there will be a simple hybrid intelligent agent, which will be gradually followed by more and more such humachines at an exponentially accelerating rate. We are not talking about the future but the present. Humans with smart devices in their hand already function as hybrids and all the while operate in a continuous state of info-communication as parts of a human and machine network. As mentioned earlier, a joined human-machine "humachine" is no longer part of a distant future but an already-existing hybrid agent.

Evolution loves hybridization. It is also wasteful and discards a lot of ideas and opportunities if they aren't immediately successful. In contrast, once something is successful, evolution won't dump it, even if it has been transcended in the process of development: instead, it will build the next innovation on top of the existing ones.

Formation in nature progresses from the physical to the mental and is built on the innovations of the prior phases: atoms will become a part of molecules, the molecules a part of the DNA, the DNA a part of cells; cells will form organs, and an organism is formed, which in turn is organised into a network of organisms. Prior structures persist while forming a bigger, newer structure.

The simple nerve net in jellyfish forms the basis of the central nervous system debuting in flatworms, which then develops into the reptilian brain, the brains of ancient mammals, and then mammals, and finally it becomes the human brain. All throughout, evolution retains everything that proved useful. *Homo sapiens* may have acquired the rational brain, but it continues to be capable of the reactions of the reptiles and the ancient mammals, and these more ancient cerebral structures continue to influence human decisions. If we look at cultural evolution, we will find that most of the problems are caused not by the products of the rational brain but by the fact that human mental achievements are built on ancient reflexes and emotions. A good example is Hungarian-born John von Neumann. He was one of the greatest minds of the 20th century and one of the key figures in the development of modern computer science. In his time, people would often remark that he was far smarter than even the machines he developed. Von Neumann turned his vast knowledge to the development of the hydrogen bomb. He was a vehement anti-communist who experienced communism in his home country, Hungary, in 1919 and learned to fear and loathe it. He was a scientist with extraordinary mental abilities whom his gut reactions prompted to create a terrible tool of destruction. All the while, of course, he enriched human knowledge in several highly useful directions.

Significant human innovations have been motivated by danger avoidance, combat, threats, territorial defence, and mating. It's no coincidence that these also form the basis for propaganda: they are exploited by advertisements and politics alike. The evolutionarily more recent brain structures are unable to sufficiently control reptilian brain reactions. As a result, humans with all their rationality still trample all over things like an elephant in a china store. If this agent, who is under the influence of gut reflexes, steps up its mental functioning with an even more efficient system without making any changes in terms of control, the result will be an unviable hybrid which will destroy everything around it in no time. We have nothing to fear from machines. The root of the problem always lies in *Homo Sapiens'* visceral control.

The survival tools listed in the first chapter target harmony and balance. Network functioning, the co-operation between autonomous units and the emotional intelligence necessary for collective functioning, essentially means keeping a balance between emotions and reason. All network links are formed by finding common points between the participating agents. In most cases, it's not as difficult a task to find a common denominator between two different entities. Still, if we are talking about directly opposing systems, finding the balance can prove to be a thorny problem.

Dual processing

Copying is something we can frequently observe in the course of development – this is when a pattern that has proven successful is put to use elsewhere, as well. This method is employed by evolution and humans alike. Examples abound from the analogy between flight of birds and bats to employing the hydrodynamic model of how jellyfish swim using their muscular system, bell shape, and neurological activity as a template in the building of smart floating machines. Copying and imitation is a universal tool of development, whether natural or artificial.

Another trend is cumulative development, that is, to supplement the existing. This is when new structures are built on top of earlier ones. We have discussed this case at length before the evolution of the brain showcases this method.

A third trend is the common denominator, or crossbreeding: when two different entities bring about a third, new one. In this case, there is a balanced, or at least roughly balanced, dual control, since both sides are useful, although not always and not necessarily to the same extent. Checks and balances ensure a high level of security for all systems, and their interaction can bring forth a new kind of potential.

Brain hemispheres

No one knows for certain why the brain came to have two hemispheres. Some researchers are content with the justification that the control of the two sides of the body entails two hemispheres, but this is not really a genuine explanation because it doesn't require the brain to consist of two separate hemispheres connected through only a few elements.

Moreover, it is the right hemisphere which controls the left side of the body and the left hemisphere which controls the right side – but for that, at least, there is an explanation. The main bundle of nerves is located on the ventral side of invertebrates and on the dorsal side of vertebrates. During evolution, the older layout persisted in the cranium, but as the main nerve bundle evolved into the spinal cord and moved into the spine on the dorsal side, the neural wiring twisted and became crossed. There is no deep cognitive reason behind the left hand, left foot, etc. being represented in the right hemisphere, and the right hand, right foot, etc. in the left hemisphere: it just happened to turn out that way. Not everything that evolution brings about is practical or makes sense. We could at most call it economical or optimal.

One possible explanation for the separation of the brain hemispheres could be that it makes control more reliable, given that the two sides don't mix: for example, people are able to rub their stomach with one hand and pat their head with the other at the same time. There is little evolutionary advantage to be identified in this specific feat, but the survival chances of bilaterally structured animals are significantly increased if they are able to perform asymmetric movements in an environment that is itself spatially asymmetric. Those who learn piano pieces will experience first-hand that asymmetric motor co-ordination is not easy.

A further potential advantage of separate hemispheres is the recovery from traumas to the brain. An injury to one hemisphere of the brain will not spread as easily to the other one. The brain is highly plastic, and the hemispheres are able to take over tasks from each other to a limited extent – especially if the trauma affects a nervous system still in development, at which time plasticity still offers a wide range of opportunities.

Plasticity is the key to adapting to the environment. It depends on the environment, for example, to what extent people make use of left or right hemisphere functions. Lateralisation – that is, the division of tasks between the two hemispheres – is merely a potential, an outline in the brain structure. The individual cerebral structures, groups of neurons and bundles of nerves, may drift and form different networks. Neural pathways and connections are formed and shaped with the use of the brain. Cerebral functions can be drastically altered through intensive and persistent activities and training or, conversely, lack of use.

Left, right, and middle

Most people have heard that the left-brain hemisphere is primarily responsible for processing verbal, linguistic information, and the right one spatial-visual stimuli. Speech, writing, reading, and counting are linked to the left hemisphere, while imagination, music, and humour to the right one. Although both hemispheres are able to store and recall memories, the right hemisphere recalls them more accurately than the left one. The left hemisphere is of course better at recalling verbal stimuli, while the right hemisphere is better with visual stimuli such as faces. The left hemisphere that processes causal relations can infer rules based on a series of events and is capable of formulating cognitive models or hypotheses to predict future events. The right hemisphere can play a key role in forming conclusions and establishing connections based on perception, and it can be the source of cognitive models in the area of perception to predict future events like the collision of two balls.

It is, in point of fact, this kind of specific information processing that differentiates the functions of the two brain hemispheres. We can talk about a kind of division of labour: the left hemisphere is characterised more by a sequential, analytical processing, while the right hemisphere tends more to be simultaneous and holistic.

To put it in a somewhat anthropomorphic way, the left hemisphere has a narrower focus and is more goal-oriented: it is inclined to separate the parts from the whole and look at things in an abstract way. It likes to categorise and classify, it sees causes and effects, and it likes things to be clear, because it cannot handle contradictions. It can be regarded as dogmatic. It ignores everything that fails to fit its current model of the world. It lives in a sort of hall of self-referential mirrors, ensuring its optimism.

The right hemisphere sees the whole. Its attentional focus is wide. Its strengths include understanding bodily experience and facial expressions, as well as empathy. It is capable of handling contradictions in a flexible manner and likes to engage with anything new. It is able to simultaneously hold two competing ideas; it makes understanding metaphors, humour, and irony possible; and of course it makes one more open to both cynicism and spirituality.

The two kinds of processing are equally important, and the crucial difference lies not in the brain hemisphere dominance between individuals but in what kind of processing is required by a given task. Then everything hinges on how much an individual puts this or that kind of approach to use. In other words, the level to which specific processors and functions develop in an individual is influenced not only by individual brain physiological factors but also by environmental and cultural effects. As such, when assessing intelligence, the question of which kind of information processing is advantageous in a given culture is highly relevant: how verbal, how visual is that culture.

By the 21st century, a strongly visual, kinetic-visual stimulus environment has become predominant, and verbality and literacy are less articulate than a century ago. The need for processing information relayed in long sequences is constantly decreasing, because these are bolstered or even supplanted by images and information that can be quickly processed holistically. The environmental changes described in a previous chapter and their effect on cognitive development can lead to neurological divergences in the children of the digital culture – and the relation of these divergences to intelligence is highly equivocal. They seem like adaptive changes, but they manifest as a disorder in an environment that fails to adjust to the changes in culture.

As we have discussed earlier, the third culture is not about the dominance of the right or the left hemisphere but about the use of the whole brain. As such, the corpus callosum, which connects the two hemispheres, needs to receive more attention. The corpus callosum consists of about 200 million nerve fibres, divided equally between those going from the right hemisphere to the left one and those going from the left hemisphere to the right one. Thus, when all goes well, the two hemispheres are in a constantly balanced connection, and information can flow back and forth for processing. The corpus callosum can be regarded as a third specific processing system.

Its thickness correlates with the IQ measured in intelligence tests, which means that efficient inter-hemisphere communication and task division play an important role in problem solving. Interestingly, this correlation only applies to adult brains, while no such relationship has been found in the case of children. The development of the corpus callosum, similarly to that of the cortex, is uneven and highly dynamic. This might be responsible for the inconsistencies in the studies, but the results may also be affected by the well-known fact that IQ tests yield very unreliable results until the teenage years. (Thereafter, they are simply unreliable.) These two causes, if they hold true, are enough already to obscure any potential relationships.

The two hemispheres – the specific processing systems – develop at a different pace, and the growth of the left and the right hemisphere differs by age. In small children, it is the right hemisphere which will first develop strongly. The left hemisphere will start growing sharply at the age of 2–5 years, probably alongside speech development. From the age of about 8 years, the right hemisphere will again try to pick up the pace, but will not reach the same level as the left hemisphere. This pattern conforms well to a culturally expected development and might even be more or less appropriate until school age – although it would already be important in younger children to better link the two kinds of information processing, in order to ensure more neuronal traffic through the corpus callosum. "Use it or lose it" applies already in childhood, as this is the time when neural connections are sorted into those that are important and will get stronger and those that are inessential and are to be discarded. For this reason, there should be a more conscious interlinking of linguistic education and development to kinetic and visual experience, and this method should also be continued at school age.

School education is built on the functions of the left hemisphere, which in the digital age doesn't help to adjust to the culture. What children need in the third culture is to practise spatial, imaginative, and holistic functions and to link them to verbality, so that they have the opportunity to practise choosing the optimal information processing with their nervous system.

Dual-system thinking – fast and slow thinking

The cortex, which is responsible for rational thinking, is often suppressed due to a "fight or flight" stress response coming from the areas of the reptilian and ancient mammal brains and due to emotional influences which affect and override thinking. In other words, irrationality is neurologically hardwired into even the most intelligent creatures. But the subcortical structures are not the only ones responsible for irrational reactions. The source of mistakes is frequently precisely those cortical thinking methods which are otherwise of immense help in adaptation.

Cerebral energy needs to be expended sparingly, because – as we know – a large-sized brain and its operation is a luxury. This is why evolution generated a lot of functions that can save humans the effort of thinking. Most of these functions are useful: for example, we don't have to waste a lot of computation to be able to see a three-dimensional image, to estimate sizes, to recognise faces, or to identify emotions. We get these ready-made products from evolution.

Not thinking can save a lot of time and energy, but not thinking can also be dangerous. This is why evolution gave humans the handy option of being able to choose whether they invest into thinking in a given situation or instead save the time and energy.

Daniel Kahneman, psychologist, and Nobel laureate in economics, captures these two choices in his book as two cognitive systems: a dominant, fast mechanism called "System 1," which is always on; and a slower, more thorough mechanism called "System 2," which we can turn on at any time, but whose usage consumes a significant amount of mental energy.

> System 1 is automatic and fast, works with little or no effort, and most of the time without conscious control. It's emotional, stereotyping, and unconscious.

System 2 is slow and pays attention to sophisticated mental activities, including complex calculations. It is logical, computational, and conscious. It
requires conscious effort.

There is a clear evolutionary advantage to a dual system which on the one hand
makes quick reactions with ready-made solutions and conservation of mental
capacity possible, and on the other hand leaves open the option of in-depth reflection. Of the two kinds of thinking, **System 1** doesn't even seem like thinking
since it is unconscious and instantaneous. It may be more accurate to call it a cognitive function. Capabilities of this is system include, for example, the following:

- Focussing on the source of a sudden noise
- Estimating distances and sizes
- Quality judgements
- Identifying emotions expressed on the face
- Perceiving hostility in a voice
- Expressing disgust through facial expressions
- Simple calculations not requiring computation, such as 10 + 3
- Skills, such as walking, driving in a familiar location, reading
- Understanding simple sentences
- Making quick decisions

This package includes automatic reactions and mental functions that have
become automatic and which require so little mental capacity that it is possible
to perform more of them at the same time. **System 2**, in contrast, requires attention and conscious mental work, which we experience as thinking:

- Pay attention to the voice of a specific person in a crowded and noisy place
- Find a specific stimulus in the environment, for example, a white cat
- Recall a melody
- Walk in an unusual manner
- Drive a car in heavy traffic
- Give someone a telephone number
- Calculate the result of 43 x 27
- Fill out a form
- Check logical arguments
- Compare the advantages and disadvantages of two things

In contrast to the first list, we here used words that imply activity, because active
participation is necessary for this type of functioning. These are tasks which the
brain is only capable of handling at most one at a time. There is still some mental
capacity left over in such a case, though, so System 1 can take on problems while
the brain is doing the slow thinking. For example, we are able to drive a car
while looking for a white cat, and we understand when someone tells us to stop.

While System 1 meddles in everything, System 2 only starts up if there is an intent to do so: otherwise, it remains inactive. There is no sharp divide between two systems; in fact, things that used to be System 2 functions can turn into System 1 functions. The development of skills follows this path. For example, jugglers learning to throw a three-ball cascade will need to devote all their attention to it and consciously control their movements; but after a year of intensive practice, they would even be able to deliver a lecture on the neurological developmental effect of cascade throwing while keeping the balls in the air.

In addition, prior knowledge acquired through System 1 is often processed by System 2 if it is so instructed by the owner of the brain. (The reason for this convoluted wording is that we run into questions of the mind and consciousness at this point, and of who is talking inside our head anyway. Or perhaps not even inside of it?) Tasks of the System 2 type are thus filled with elements from System 1. For example, if someone is trying to compute 43 x 27, they will immediately perceive it to be a multiplication task and will probably feel they will need a pen and paper. They have a few vague intuitive ideas about the range of possible results, too. They could quickly reply that 31 or 700,000 are not the result of this product, but 821 is a viable suspect, and a quick answer would not be possible in this case.

When someone does undertake to painstakingly calculate this product using slow thinking, they will first need to take the method of multiplication they learned at school and then implement it step by step. They need to hold multiple details in memory, pay attention to the sequence of steps in order not to skip over any of them, and make sure that the numbers are in the proper place. Writing the numbers down is an automatic process, though, and some of the lines may not be as neat as others – which just goes to show that System 1 functions never leave us alone. Let us have no exaggerated illusions about how conscious our mental functions are, because only about 1 percent of our behaviour is methodical and deliberate, while the rest can be managed at the level of System 1. The only reason that the amount of System 2 thinking seems high to us is that this is the one we are aware of.

The use of fast thinking is not up to our making of a choice: it just happens. We cannot not recognise a tiger once it's taken a place in our memory – what is more, even our emotions associated with it will also surface at once along with it. But we can decide if we want to engage in the painstaking, slow type of thinking and, for instance, count the number of stripes on the back of the tiger.

Evolution has provided an excellent System 1 to most animals, and most of the time it suffices. Animals living in the wild rarely face highly complex problems, but they do need to make quick decisions most of the time, like having to react to certain smells or sudden movement. Even humans rarely need to analyse a situation and work out an answer: immediate reactions are far more typical, and these are automatically generated by the cortex. However, System 2 – opting for thinking – may be one of the most important keys to human existence.

Conscious mental coping requires mental energies, but the opportunity for methodical thinking can be a huge evolutionary advantage in the long term.

Dual system thinking is not a recent scientific discovery. We can already come across it in medieval philosophy under different guises. For example, Zohar, the mystic commentary on the Torah, brings up the distinction between *Chokhmah* – wisdom – and *Binah* – intelligence. The former is associated with the right-brain hemisphere and synthesising mental processes. The latter is linked to the left hemisphere and analytical thinking.

Jonathan Evans, a professor of cognitive psychology who himself developed a dual cognitive system, compiled a list of similar theories in 2008.

We are not simply talking about a left-right hemisphere difference in processing but about more complex systems of thinking involving neural structures and networks beyond the two-hemisphere division. van den Berg and colleagues studied the neurological background of the two types of thinking in 2020 and found that the difference lay not in the regions of activation but in the connectivity between regions. Engaging with tasks requiring more System 1-like processing elicited stronger connectivity primarily within the temporal lobe and between the occipital and parietal area, while tasks entailing a chiefly System 2-type thinking involved stronger connectivity between the frontal, temporal, and parietal areas, and between the posterior parietal cortex and the cerebellum. The temporal and parietal regions belong to networks contributing to memory and attention, respectively, which are relevant for both types of processing.

Tasks requiring predominantly System 2-type processing triggered considerably stronger connections in regions of the brain identified as key nodes in cerebral networks of executive functioning. The frontal lobe is an example. The researchers note that the cerebellum, which for a long time used to be primarily linked to motor control, had also proven to be involved in cognitive functioning, including executive functions like cognitive control – in other words, it supports executive functions as an important network node.

Thinking, especially of the voluntary, methodical System 2 type, is intricately linked to executive functions, which are necessary to persevere in the cognitive process, maintain the effort, and control the process – which is why they have come to the spotlight in the research on intelligence. In our framework, they are an influential satellite system, which will be studied in a separate section.

The existence of the numerous dual thinking theories shows that the cognitive functioning of the human brain is unequivocally dual, but also that this dual system can be approached in diverse ways, each of which can be valid. The proverbial "elephant" which the different theories perceive from different sides is in fact the result of a long developmental process which led to an efficient cognitive security system.

In a nutshell, we have a cognitive system which operates automatically at the level of the most primitive reactions and eases the burden on the brain through fast stimulus–reaction solutions, and we have a system which speeds up adaptation through methodical, in-depth information processing and analysis by learning about and understanding its environment and solving problems that have not yet been encoded in the fast system. The trick is again to use the appropriate processing system in the appropriate situation. Where possible, it is best to conserve energy and gain security through speed, but the effort should be devoted to in-depth processing where it's worthwhile to do so.

Another advantage of investing in System 2 thinking is that methodical cognition can, with time, enrich the fast system – that is, the newly acquired knowledge can be incorporated as an automaticity, which, enhancing adaptation to the environment, will mean new, ready-made knowledge requiring less mental energy. This process was one of the reasons human cognitive functioning has been able to depart from genetic-level information transfer and switch to cultural evolution. Slow thinking could speed up development because it generates knowledge necessary for adaptation.

Human thinking can be fast or precise, but the latter is extremely tiring. Humanity is taking the steps to augment itself with machines to be able – and, if possible, to be easily able – to make decisions quickly and accurately. This may prove possible, but it's best to pay close attention because, as we know, if you want to make really big errors, use a machine. This is because machines carry out whatever task humans set before them, and if the humans err even a little, the machine will be able to exponentially compound the error thanks to its efficient computation.

Fast and slow machine thinking

Understandably, humans wanted to transfer System 2-type functioning to machines first. This is why, for instance, calculators were among the first cognitive assistive tools. At this point, we are apparently contradicting our earlier statement that a key to human existence is the opportunity to switch to slow, analytical thinking. And indeed, that statement needs to be refined. Animals are also able to think through problem situations. Dogs, for instance, can look extremely cute when they start thinking hard. When they perceive something strange and uncommon, they will tilt their head and try very hard to understand what's going on. Apparently, they don't have a ready-made answer to what they perceive, so they start thinking it through using System 2. And this is only one of the diverse kinds of problem-solving methods animals employ. It is therefore not the use of System 2 itself which is the dividing line, but the efficiency and flexibility in its use, and – as mentioned already – the dissemination and storage in multiple brains of the information acquired via System 2, which has led to the cultural evolution.

Machines rapidly came to take first place in the dissemination and storage of information, but the appearance of AI means that a qualitatively new agent has entered the cognitive arena. The question arises as to what kind of role AI plays in terms of the two types of cognitive functioning.

In humans, System 2-type cognitive functions belong to higher-level intelligence, but in computer science, System 2 functions can be considered as the less-developed forms of programming. They comprise algorithms in which a series of predetermined steps is applied to the data to achieve the desired results. Given a specific situation, selecting the appropriate procedure and parameters will yield the answer.

Machines have an immense advantage over humans when performing System 2 functions because they don't tire, their attention does not get distracted, their working memory is excellent and upgradable, and they don't forget or omit either any data or any of the steps of the procedure. However, this is not the entire story about System 2 because it is necessary to specify the steps to perform – in other words, the algorithm itself. It's important to always choose an algorithm appropriate to the given situation. At present, we still need human agents to govern the System 2 functions for machines because a machine is reliably efficient only in clear-cut situations. In traditional programming, an important factor in computational performance is the programmer's ability to understand the details, causal relations etc. of the process when writing an algorithm.

Machine learning, an important component of AI, employs algorithms generating algorithms to replace those that would require tiresome work to prepare by a human brain. In machine learning, a machine "learns" the key elements of the patterns from a training dataset. The result is a "model" which can be applied to new data, and the "analysis" of the new data will take place quickly and automatically based on the knowledge built from the training data. Using machine learning, an AI will itself identify the best parameters without humans having to understand the causal mechanisms behind the problem. We are already relying on AI systems in everyday life whose operation we don't truly understand, but which we know from experience to be generally reliable. There are thus strong similarities between machine learning and the human System 1.

In learning a System 1-type decision, an important advantage of AI is that it is able to retain and analyse a lot more information than the human brain, and it is able to do so more reliably and accurately. What is more, machines are not affected by the emotional-motivational factors that influence human thinking. We should hasten to add, though, that these special biases can also constitute an advantage in processing, because they can modify the decision in diverse minor ways, which could prove useful. Possibly. Or they could be a drawback due to the bias they introduce.

Human thinking is influenced by several subconscious factors, and in some situations humans will form a judgement even before knowing what the issue is about exactly. An example is when a novel thing evokes liking or distaste even before we know anything about it. A part of these mechanisms is subsumed under the concept of heuristics, which has come to enjoy great popularity in the last years. Heuristics are quick, involuntary, evolutionarily wired decision processes, which are indeed quick and efficient, but – on the downside – not very reliable.

In superficial information processing, the simple decisions are made based on easily available and salient information. These simple pieces of information are persuasive heuristics, which bring about a prior attitude. An example of this is that the opinion of a professional or a more qualified individual is more reliable than that of a layman, or that the longer a message, the more reliable it seems, even if it is incomplete or illogical. Fast processing does not care about analysis and logic: it simply accepts the outcome of the attitude.

These heuristics have evolved and survived in human thinking, because despite the mistakes, they generally lead to acceptable results, and their speed makes them more advantageous than other cognitive strategies. So much so that System 1 functioning has even come to be employed in autonomous robots. Old-style robots, which try to analyse the world by calculating the total costs and benefits of all the potential actions, are slow and cumbersome. Newer robots – like humans – will behave in a dumb way in certain situations, but they are quick and efficient on familiar ground. In many respects, they are primitive imitations of the human brain.

Heuristics – attuning to the quick and more or less reliable solutions – has proved useful in the case of AI. This includes, for example, accepting a more or less correct solution, or using a "greedy algorithm," which always chooses the step that is the best one at that particular moment, irrespective of later consequences. Heuristic methods of search include the use of search trees in a way that instead of generating all possible solution branches, they select the branches that yield results with a greater probability than others. The human brain also uses heuristics like these.

The use of heuristics is especially efficient when coupled with a little wisdom and prudence, because otherwise even the most intelligent person can be led astray by their fast thinking. Kahneman and Tversky investigated heuristics and systematic mistakes in their research. One of the heuristics they identified was the anchoring bias, which anchors estimates to a number used as a point of reference. For example, if someone wants to buy a table, and they are shown some tables in the price range of around 300 EUR, they will more easily buy a table that costs 150 EUR than if they had been shown tables costing about 30 EUR. The availability heuristic – another heuristic they identified – means that people consider something more important if they recall examples about it or if they have heard about it. This is why people think shark attacks are more dangerous and frequent than they actually are. The presentation, or wording, is also far from irrelevant. For example, more people oppose inheritance tax if the term *death tax* is used than when it's called an *estate tax*.

System 1 is a very useful "invention" because there are a number of situations which are highly complex and/or in which case the dataset is too big for the human brain – to the point where even the most efficient mind is incapable of analysing it, and even machines could only do so at the cost of a lot of time. System 1 is also a good choice if key information is missing and it would be impossible to come to an efficient solution by thinking things through – or in the case of machines, via traditional programming. In these situations, applying machine learning techniques to come up with a decision model based on pattern recognition is a viable alternative. In the case of humans, we call this intuition.

Most human decisions are based on System 1-type functions, and AI is also employing it in increasingly more situations – and it can even surpass human fast thinking. Its results could be distorted by the training dataset, of course. The nature and composition of the data through which an intelligence learns about the world is extremely important – be this a human or a machine intelligence.

In the next chapter, we will continue to study the topic of satellite intelligences by exploring the functions which may or may not be classified as a part of intelligence, but which most certainly heavily influence thinking.

Enrichment

If asked nicely or otherwise a machine will carry out any task we set before them. If we ask them to do the wrong thing – we err a little – the machine is capable of generously compounding the error, even refining the error due to its incredibly tireless computing ability.

Identify seven key errors that humans have generated that you would seek machines to avoid replicating and developing. What remedial action would you propose a machine could undertake to limit, remove, and restructure human thinking to resolve the presence and effects of the errors you identify?

Are sins (pride, greed, lust, envy, gluttony, wrath, and sloth) key errors we could seek to eliminate from our lives through instructing machines on how to act? If so, what protocols would have to be put in place to guide machine activity?

Link pathways

What links the "greedy algorithm," heuristic thinking, and driving a car?

References

van den Berg, B., de Bruin, A., Marsman, J. C., Lorist, M. M., Schmidt, H. G., Aleman, A., Snoek, J. W. 2020. Thinking fast or slow? Functional magnetic resonance imaging reveals stronger connectivity when experienced neurologists diagnose ambiguous cases. *Brain Communications* 2 (1): fcaa023. doi:10.1093/braincomms/fcaa023.

Evans, J. 2008. Dual-processing accounts of reasoning, judgment, and social cognition. *Annual Review of Psychology* 59: 255–278.

Kahneman, D. 2011. *Thinking, Fast and Slow*. New York: Farrar, Straus and Giroux.

MacLean, Paul D. 1990. *The Triune Brain in Evolution. Role in Paleocerebral Functions*. New York: Plenum.

Metcalfe, B. 2013. Metcalfe's law after 40 years of ethernet. *Computer* 46 (12): 26–31. doi:10.1109/MC.2013.374.

Muthukrishna, M., Doebeli M., Chudek, M., Henrich, J. 2018. The cultural brain hypothesis: How culture drives brain expansion, sociality, and life history. *PLOS Computational Biology* 14 (11): e1006504. doi:10.1371/journal.pcbi.1006504.

Sternberg, R. J. 2018. Why real-world problems go unresolved and what we can do about it: Inferences from a limited-resource model of successful intelligence. *Journal of Intelligence* 6 (3): 44. doi:10.3390/jintelligence6030044.

Zollikofer, C. P., De León, M. S. 2013. Pandora's growing box: Inferring the evolution and development of hominin brains from endocasts. *Evolutionary Anthropology* 22 (1): 20–33. doi:10.1002/evan.21333.

Suggested further reading

Brockman, J. 2015. What to think about machines that think: Today's leading thinkers on the age of machine intelligence. New York, NY: Harper Perennial.

Burgess, A. 2018. *AI in action. The Executive Guide to Artificial Intelligence.* Cham: Palgrave Macmillan. doi:10.1007/978-3-319-63820-1_5.

Eliot R. Smith, Diane M. Mackie, Heather M. Claypool. 2015. *Social Psychology*, 4th edition. New York: Psychology Press.

Geary, D. C. 2004. *Origin of Mind. Evolution of Brain, Cognition, and General Intelligence.* Washington, DC: American Psychological Association.

Kaufman, S. B. 2011. Intelligence and the cognitive unconscious. In R. J. Sternberg, S. B. Kaufman (Eds.), *Cambridge Handbooks in Psychology. The Cambridge Handbook of Intelligence* (pp. 442–467). Cambridge: Cambridge University Press.

Mesoudi, A., Whiten, A., Laland, K. 2006. Towards a unified science of cultural evolution. *Behavioral and Brain Sciences* 29 (4): 329–347. doi:10.1017/S0140525X06009083.

Sun, T., Hevner, R. F. 2014. Growth and folding of the mammalian cerebral cortex: From molecules to malformations. *Nature Reviews. Neuroscience* 15 (4): 217–232. doi:10.1038/nrn3707.

Maguire, E. A., Gadian, D. G., Johnsrude, I. S., Good, C. D., Ashburner, J., Frackowiak, R. S. J., Frith, C. D. 2000. Navigation-related structural change in the hippocampi of taxi drivers. *Proceedings of the National Academy of Sciences* 97 (8): 4398–4403.

Pope, M. 2003. Placing boxgrove in its prehistoric landscape. *Archaeology International* 7: 13–16. doi:10.5334/ai.0705.

Savi, A. O., Marsman, M., van der Maas, H. L. J., Maris, G. K. J. 2019. The wiring of intelligence. *Perspectives on Psychological Science* 14 (6): 1034–1061. doi:10.1177/1745691619866447.

Sousa, A. M., Meyer, K. A., Santpere, G., Gulden, F. O., Sestan, N. 2017. Evolution of the human nervous system function, structure, and development. *Cell* 170: 226–247.

Tanaka-Arakawa, M. M., Matsui, M., Tanaka, C., Uematsu, A., Uda, S., Miura, K., Sakai, T., Noguchi, K. 2015. Developmental changes in the corpus callosum from infancy to early adulthood: a structural magnetic resonance imaging study. *PloS One* 10 (3): e0118760. doi:10.1371/journal.pone.0118760.

Westerhausen, R., Friesen, C. M., Rohani, D. A., Krogsrud, S. K., Tamnes, C. K., Skranes, J. S., Håberg, A. K., Fjell, A. M., Walhovd, K. B. 2018. The corpus callosum as anatomical marker of intelligence? A critical examination in a large-scale developmental study. *Brain Structure & Function* 223 (1): 285–296. doi:10.1007/s00429-017-1493-0.

3

FLUID INTELLIGENCE, OTHER SATELLITES, AND CONSCIOUSNESS

Our mental performance is influenced by our emotions, our instincts, and our impulses. At present, these are not issues that artificial intelligence must face, but even when it comes to AI, creativity and executive functions can be relevant factors for the quality of the resulting intellectual product. When it comes to human intelligence, these are factors that have to function properly in order to achieve good results in IQ tests. Each component of intelligence is based on some form and proportion of conscious and unconscious neurological processes. The extent and way in which an intelligent agent can influence its own cognitive processes is an important question in the development of both HI and AI.

Pattern recognition and fluid intelligence

Recognizing patterns is a key element of human perception and intelligence. Our survival used to depend and still depends on our brain being able to assemble coherent wholes from possibly even very small pieces. It must have been a huge advantage for some ancestor of ours when they were able to recognise a sabre-toothed tiger from yellow patches in a green thicket. It may be just a trick of light, and the yellow patches might not be after us – but if they are, then the danger is life-threatening, and it's better that we flee. And, vice versa, if we have to find a prey that is in hiding, then pattern recognition – being able to eliminate interfering elements and construct a consistent whole – again constitutes an evolutionary advantage.

Detecting the essential makes predictions possible. Once we see the pattern, we are in the position to imagine what the future will be like based on it (for example: will it attack or not?). From then on, there's no stopping anymore. The human brain keeps constructing patterns, whether we want it to or not. While logic and analysis are things we can do consciously, patterns just fall into place.

DOI: 10.4324/9780429356346-4

Still, this ability is crucial for intelligence, which might seem a contradiction, given that intelligence is linked to thinking. This is true sometimes, but as we have seen, a rather large proportion of our decisions are unconscious, like when patterns simply fall into place or when a solution simply takes shape in our head.

There are a lot of similarities between the way a computer scientist and a psychologist would describe pattern recognition. This is of course hardly surprising, seeing that psychology built heavily on technological sciences in the 20th century and so did subsequently the creators of AI on the way the human brain functions.

Thinking in terms of machine learning algorithms, pattern recognition is the classification of data based on acquired knowledge and/or statistical information extracted from the patterns. Psychologists have approached the same process in humans from a number of different directions. According to template- or prototype-matching approaches, for example, we store some kind of templates or prototypes of objects in our memory, and this is what serves as the basis for perception. In another approach, we compare the features of the perceived pattern with the features stored in our memory, and this is how we identify objects and shapes. Nature probably didn't leave things to chance, and the brain probably utilises all of these and other processes in parallel and in a mutually reinforcing way when it collects information about the outside world.

The human brain is perhaps best prepared for recognising patterns − better than for any other cognitive function. Our brains are, for example, inferior and slow in logical processing, in remembering facts or performing calculations. In processes like these, machines have long since surpassed us. But we are extremely efficient in pattern recognition. Machines are able to process a lot of information very rapidly and can therefore use extremely large databases for pattern recognition. The human brain, however, is able to distil the essence even from relatively little data. At the same time, evidently, it is true of the human brain, as well, that the more information it has at its disposal, the easier the recognition of patterns will be. If there is only little information available, it is easy to make huge mistakes. For example, we would see a tiger even where there is none. It's no coincidence that ghosts abound in foggy Great Britain and tend to prefer twilight. When there is a scarcity of clear and unambiguous information, imagination takes over, and anything may turn up in the patterns generated by the brain that is compatible with the few visual details at hand: a headless rider, a hellhound, or virtually anything else.

This also applies to AI − to err is not exclusively human. In fact, as we know, if you want to err big, use machines. To illustrate: researchers experimented with image recognition using the deep neural network ResNet-50, and it made a lot of baffling mistakes like misidentifying a squirrel as a sea lion. Such mistakes are not peculiar to ResNet-50, of course: anyone and anything attempting pattern identification can run into them.

Machine intelligence sees a dog where there is an ostrich? This phenomenon is clearly highly characteristic of human thinking, so we don't have much cause to look down on the machine for it. *Homo sapiens* is the product of millions of years, while the evolution of AI can as yet only be measured in decades. It would be terrific were our own brains able to filter out all noise in perception, because we would then no longer need to get scared of tigers and ghosts that are not there. Within the bounds of the current biological and technological solutions (human and artificial systems), however, there is as yet zero chance of such a perfect solution, because the possibility for mistake is coded in the design. Machines may still have a chance for change in this respect in the future, but human brains are what they are. In particular, there is an involuntary process in the brain that rapidly generates patterns, which a slower system that takes actual information and earlier experience into consideration attempts to keep in check and steer towards reality as much as possible. This dual system is responsible for producing percepts, be they visual, auditory, or tactile. The system also interprets information. The human brain invents the world – that is, it moulds it into patterns. What a person sees and thinks and what they understand depends on the patterns they form. And the truly adaptive path to this does not lead through thinking. Still, recognizing patterns lies at the core of intelligence. More precisely, our ability to generate patterns forms the basis for fluid intelligence.

When discussing intelligence, we have already touched on fluid intelligence, a concept by Raymond Cattell, which – in contrast to crystallised intelligence – makes an agent capable not of applying something learned previously, but of discovering novel connections. We call it pattern recognition, but it is essentially built on pattern generation, which is then subject to selection by a much slower system that can take all sorts of complex information into account. The cognitive processes collectively called "executive functions" are what likely play an important role in this selection process, which is why we will probably need to address that area.

In short, fluid intelligence consists only in part of pattern generation, because it is only in conjunction with the processes exercising control and critical selection that we can call it intelligence. The elements of the satellite system have a mutual influence on each other, and they contribute, as a function of earlier experience and the situation at hand, to different degrees to the assessment of the particular context – that is, the generated pattern.

In brief, patterns are generated, rather than recognised, by the brain. We can talk about recognition once we are certain that the pattern generated in the brain mirrors the actual situation precisely. This is something we can rarely be certain about. If we had endless information and a great deal of time for the analysis, we would arrive at the appropriate whole for certain. Typically, however, the available amount of both time and information is insufficient. This is especially true of an emergency or when the individual experiences a sense of emergency. In such cases, the rapid, but superficial, pattern-generation process can come to the fore, as it offers a greater chance of survival. In contrast, when we have the time to contemplate the world's affairs at our leisure, we have the opportunity to create crisp and clear concepts. A concept, as we have remarked earlier on, is itself a kind of pattern, a subjective grasp on a particular phenomenon. Theories, including theories of intelligence, are subjective. Scientific thinking is the process during which we form a pattern on the basis of a large amount of experience and studies. New experience and studies may supplant them, but scientific findings constitute relevant knowledge in a particular time period and context.

In the previous paragraph, we have referenced several satellites that influence intelligence and which can be grasped alongside the pattern generator. These include emotional and motivated thinking, instincts and impulses, the intersubjective reality, intuition, and creative thinking.

These satellites exert their effect in interaction with the given situation. At the same time, the extent and way in which satellites influence thinking is an individual neurological characteristic. In some individuals, it is emotions; in some others, it is motivations that affect the process – and, by extension, the result – more. If executive functions exercise less control over pattern generation, an idiosyncratic way of thinking may manifest itself.

Michelle Dawson and her colleagues showed in their study published in 2011 that individuals with high-functioning autism spectrum disorder achieved higher scores than others in Raven's Matrices, which measure fluid intelligence, in comparison to their scores on the widely used Wechsler scales assessing intelligence. Individuals with classical autism showed a similar pattern, and they had even been shown to give the correct answers in Raven's Matrices faster than non-autistics. At the same time, studies indicate that autistic individuals tend to make more mistakes in tests requiring executive functions. Autism is characterised by an instability in the executive functions, and so we can hypothesise that pattern generation can "get out of hand" to the extent that the executive functions allow it to.

On the approach of cognitive scientist Andrea Kuszewski, cognitive performance can be captured along the dimensions of cognitive control and levels of divergent thinking. She demonstrates the link between outstanding talent, creativity, and different mental disorders in her coordinate system.

The formula may seem oversimplified, but it shows how mutually interacting neurological processes bring about apparently highly different neurological functioning and performance connected at the level of deeper factors.

The surreality of schizophrenic and paranoid individuals is rooted in a loss of cognitive control. Their brains will accept images and connections which common sense would tell us cannot be real. In a way, they are constantly seeing ghosts. In milder forms, however, this can lead to noticing things many people would not, because their internal control system will not give full reins to the pattern generator. As the joke goes, "Paranoia is when you have some idea about what is really going on." There's a grain of truth in every joke.

Uncertainty, insufficient information, or – conversely – an unprocessable amount of information are all favourable to the less-controlled and fast-pattern generation. Those who are anxious or afraid switch to survival mode, and those in whom anxiety and fear have led to psychological disorders are more prone to function in survival mode. Uncontrolled pattern generation means that conspiracy theories and fake news find a good breeding ground in these cases. Highly creative minds are more susceptible to misleading news and, in absence of sufficient cognitive control, can become victims thereof.

In the 21st century, the amount of available information is incredible, and so fluid intelligence is gaining considerable importance, since it is the ability to interpret, "make sense," and create knowledge. Its key component is pattern recognition, which, however, only leads to usable knowledge when paired with appropriate control.

Emotions, motivations, and instincts unavoidably influence the human brain when it comes to pattern generation. AI is so far immune in this respect. Interest, faith, trust, will – these do not at present play a role in machine problem solving. The performance of AI is independent of emotions, although the kinds of information it is loaded with are highly relevant, because it can only form its patterns on the basis of what it learns from.

Awareness – that is, knowing the factors influencing fluid intelligence and bringing them under conscious control to the extent possible – can mean a lot in increasing HI efficiency. There's nothing new to this, of course: it has also been the focus of a number of ancient mental exercises, as well as, for example, the mindfulness techniques of our age.

From here on, pattern recognition, which is so influential on our thinking, will stay with us as we go along, and we will be addressing areas that influence it.

Emotional decisions – we are human beings

Even individuals who achieve good results in intelligence tests will often exhibit extreme stupidity. Rational behaviour is strongly influenced by important satellites connected to intelligence. One of these is emotion. Emotions affect the decisions of even the most intelligent and rational people. There is no purely rational decision if a human brain is making it. Emotions contribute to our thinking. Reason and emotions are so intertwined that many people will even bring up rational arguments to support emotional decisions. Why have I chosen this career? Why are they my friends? Why have I chosen someone as my partner in life? There are always rational reasons behind emotions, too.

Emotions manifest the subjective relationship of humans to reality. They depend on experience, thinking, intelligence, neural and hormonal control, and several other external and internal factors, which will often lead already in early childhood to the formation of cognitive schemata along which the individual interprets the world.

Reason would constitute the objective approach to the world for the human mind, but the schemata ingrained at an early age influence reason, too, and as a result, its objectivity is limited. There is thus no simple formula and no clear boundary between emotions and reason – which is also supported by neuropsychology. Emotional processes can influence cognitive processes, while cognitive processes can control or alter emotions. Both kinds of interaction can be brought about by changing the (either emotional or cognitive) variables of the mental state. Emotions and thoughts move in sync and can give rise to a new mental state. For example, losing a job can create anxiety. Thinking the situation through will evoke images and emotions: for example, the image of an unpleasant boss whom we won't have to see again. This thought will bring good feelings with it, and the individual will enter a new mental state.

Our thinking is heavily influenced by our mental state. Using the work of researchers (Salzman, Fusi, 2010) at Columbia University, we can succinctly put it, a mental state is a disposition toward some action, encompassing all aspects of the internal state of an individual that can contribute to its behaviour and reactions. This can include, among others, thoughts, emotions, convictions, intentions, memories, and perceptions of the individual at a particular moment in time. A mental state is a function of both internal variables and environmental stimuli, and it predisposes the individual to react in a specific way. The actions to which mental states can predispose us range from the cognitive (like decision-making) and behavioural (like fighting or fleeing) to the physiological (like increased blood pressure).

The concept of a mental state is strongly intertwined with, but different from, the physiological, neurological state of the individual's brain. There is of course a correspondence between mental states and the physical states of the neural brain circuits that can be described with variables like transfer speed. Such neural-physiological variables are what constitute a momentary state of the individual's brain.

The variables of mental states, in contrast, range from parameters pertaining to emotional processes like the degree of pleasantness or unpleasantness of a stimulus (called valence) or the level of stimulation (arousal) to parameters that can be attributed to cognitive processes, like perception, memory, and planning. Whether these variables are conscious or unconscious is irrelevant with respect to the mental state, because both kinds can predispose the individual to an action.

The amygdala, which we have discussed in the previous chapter, and which is associated with emotion control, has been shown to be involved in executive functions through special connections with the prefrontal cortex; and, vice versa, the prefrontal cortex also receives instructions from emotion control. The prefrontal cortex is the frontal part of the frontal lobe in the brain. The complex encoding and intricate connections of the amygdala, the prefrontal cortex, and the associated cerebral structures lead to the emergence of mental states and are responsible for interactions between cognition and emotions.

Of the executive functions associated with areas of the prefrontal cortex, working memory and voluntary ("endogenous") attention play a key role in the connection between cognitive and emotional functioning. What the brain pays attention to and what information it retains at a particular moment will determine how it evaluates the situation and, thereby, what kind of emotion is triggered. What the brain pays attention to and what it retains is not entirely up to chance, though: the amygdala feeds it "prompts" based on earlier experiences and their emotional character. This results in a closed loop that can become self-reinforcing. If certain types of reaction occur frequently, then the corresponding mental states will likewise be frequent and will be characteristic of the personality.

It is understandable in this light that neuropsychologists consider emotional reactivity, personality development, and awareness as the most important roles that the frontal lobe plays. This reveals to us the factors beyond the objective variables of a situation that determine the extent to which cognition is characterised by emotion and reason:

- Emotional reactivity
- Personality
- Awareness

If an individual's nervous system is more disposed towards emotional reactions, then, obviously, they will be less able to be rational. At the same time, how extensively this is built into their personality is no unimportant question. There may be those who are predisposed to emotional reactions, but their personalities may be essentially more of the reflective kind: such individuals will take a deep breath and return to their usual way of functioning, which is potentially less guided by emotions.

Even if someone is prone to emotional reactions and their personality is likewise so oriented, rationality is still not off the table, because there is still awareness to reckon with. There is always the possibility to rethink a situation and bring more awareness, and thereby rationality, into mental processes.

Emotions, however, do not just mean trouble. In fact, they are essential for efficient cognition and have several advantages when it comes to decision making:

Reactivity

An emotion-controlled decision is extremely fast compared to a rational decision. It is reactive and, for the most part, unconscious or subconscious. There are situations in which speed is more important than reflection because failure to make an instantaneous decision is the worst option. However, this only happens in emergencies. If there is no immediate danger, but time presses and the environment wants to provoke a quick decision, it is best to yield only in situations of minimal consequence – see the issues of System 1 of the dual-system theory of thinking.

Respecting human values

There are basic emotions that are always good to have influencing our decisions. We are not talking about anger or fear here, because these do not always "give good counsel," but about respect for life, for instance. A rational decision should be influenced by a respect for human values, or else humans could turn into monsters – selfish survival machines.

Defining human values is not trivial, though, because they depend on the particular culture and society: that is, humans come by them by being raised in a certain way. However, there is a basic striving toward harmony that characterises humans in general. For example, infants as young as 6 months old show empathy if someone is hurt, but only if the victim doesn't fake the pain experienced. Nearly all humans strive for love, peace, freedom, justice, non-violence – just as proclaimed by yogis and hippies.

Humans are social beings and, as such, a consideration for others is encoded in them at an emotional level, as well. It is of course possible to eradicate this with education, but it's not advisable if we want to think about the future of *Homo sapiens*.

Expert intuition

Emotions offer a chance for encoding and compressing experiences, making possible a swift choice of response. Experts intuit solutions without thinking their decisions through at that moment. Everyone is an expert of their own life. Emotions are signals from our subconscious; they provide us with information by distilling earlier experiences, and they offer a prepared response triggered by the specific situation, making our everyday lives easier. However, these decisions can also be maladaptive, because the responses prepared by the emotional-cognitive apparatus based on earlier experiences may not be appropriate in each new situation. The goal of cognitive therapies is, in fact, to create alternative attitudes and emotions from alternative thoughts in opposition to maladaptive practices.

Equivalent choices and involvement

Emotions may be needed in rational decisions when making the final choices, especially if we have to choose between near-similar options. Consciously bringing emotions into thinking is useful in any case because that way we can bring unconscious knowledge to the surface. Employing emotions in the final stages of decisions has especially profound significance when there are personal stakes in the results of the decision. Facing the results of a mathematical puzzle is an entirely different matter than deciding on what kind of car we should buy. Even when it comes to the latter problem, proceeding along a rational consideration of pros and cons is useful, but what we ultimately need to consider is whether we would like to sit in it: whether we like it at all. Although if you ask mathematicians, the solution to a puzzle is likewise only good inasmuch as it is beautiful, too.

New directions

Emotions can lead us in new directions that are different from the usual, logical avenues. It is worth taking diverse considerations into account in thinking and adding a speck of craziness – that is, emotions – to the path that logical analysis considers the most optimal one. This way, we retain logic and analysis while enriching them with new ideas.

People who appear to be highly intelligent on the basis of IQ tests are often unable to make a successful career or develop sufficiently: their performance does not reflect their test results. Intelligence cannot be reduced to rational, logical, analytical thinking, or else it would be out of touch with reality. This is the reason simple IQ tests are not really authoritative in terms of predictions, and the reason it is important for AI to become capable of involving emotions, as well. Indeed, the considerations listed here are all strong arguments that a purely rational machine cannot be an efficient companion to humanity. At most, it can be a tool, which, paired with a human emotional contribution, can help us in solving intellectual problems.

In sum, we can accept that we often function in an irrational way, and this is not always a problem. The ability and readiness for rational decisions cannot be taken for granted. Everyone lives within their own world view, the centre of which they occupy, and the role of individual emotions, stress, and instincts must be taken seriously.

As for the negative aspects of emotional decisions, the list would be so long that it wouldn't be worth enumerating here. It's one of the reasons the impressive and scientific-sounding field of "neuromarketing" thrives so easily nowadays. The main targets of manipulation are the unconscious processes, including, in particular, emotions. When someone appeals to emotions, it's always best to exercise caution.

Neuromarketing, however, does not appeal to emotions; it affects them. Psychology, and, by today, neuropsychology have succeeded in pinpointing how to best manipulate people without them noticing it.

Social existence unavoidably means mutually affecting each other, but the manner and intensity of this has changed considerably. Powerful professional systems of manipulation have been at work for several decades, guiding the masses along specific interests. The media and online social platforms do not play small; they have an immense influence on society. As long as it was only our family, friends, colleagues, neighbours, and numerous market vendors who strove to persuade us this way or that, we could still maintain some level of control over a situation. Today, however, our cognitive processes are influenced by infinite and unknown forces.

Humans in the 21st century are no longer part of only relatively small communities, but we live in an extended, open communication environment. The bigger and more open this space, the more awareness is needed for us to remain ourselves. It is not even easy to decide who exactly this "self" is.

An important difference between human and machine abilities is that emotions and intellect form an organic whole in human behaviour control, while this question is not even relevant for machines. Human information processing is not a purely cognitive algorithm, but a bio-psycho-sociologically determined process in which forces are at play that have been shaped since ancient times. Also at work in the background, in addition to emotions, are instincts, which our brains have retained and keep using, and which in turn keep influencing us from the inside – unconsciously and intensively.

The power of instincts and impulses – we are also animals

Those who managed to work their way through the brain physiological crash course in the preceding chapter will know that the sponge in our head weighing a little over 1kg that we call a brain houses both the indifferent ancient jellyfish, the aggressive reptile, the little shrew quaking with fear, and our ape-like ancestor beating on its chest. There's a large crowd and a scuffle when we must react to a situation. Each inhabitant of our little zoo wants to make themselves heard at each moment and to bombard us with a multitude of impulses.

The most important handhold for us humans is conscious self-control, meaning the ability to control the zoo inside us. *Homo sapiens* has actually tamed itself in the last 20,000 years.

David Geary (2004), a professor of psychology at the University of Missouri, and his colleagues have studied the changes in the skull size of our ancestors 1.9 million and 10,000 years ago. They found that – as we have noted already at one point – the brain grew smaller with the emergence of complex societies, because humans no longer needed to be so smart in order to survive. Humans didn't become dumber, though, but developed abilities that differ from earlier ones.

A smaller brain suffices. The important thing is for control, which is necessary for co-existence and conscious problem solving to work well. As such, it comes as no surprise that the frontal lobe, the location of the controls and the area of awareness, has developed strongly in the last 10,000 years. Interestingly, the same process can be observed in domesticated animals, too. For example, huskies have smaller brains than wolves, but they are more clever, can behave in a more refined way, and understand human gestures of communication.

Another important example concerns the closest surviving relatives of humans: the primate chimpanzees and bonobos. While chimpanzee brains are bigger than those of bonobos, they are less intelligent and less flexible than bonobos. Chimpanzees are aggressive, want power, and try to control and rule others, while bonobos wield violence to prevent others from ruling over them. Humans are both chimpanzees and bonobos by nature, and the question is how to release more bonobos and less chimpanzees in ourselves. Fortunately, it is within our grasp to help bonobos triumph since we have conscious control at our disposal. Our behaviour is governed by mutually independent factors: reflexes (Thanks, flatworm!), instincts (Our gratitude, reptile!), emotions (a gift from the shrew), and cognition (The primates are here, too!).

Nobel prize-winning ethologist Konrad Lorenz claimed that instinctive behaviour patterns differ fundamentally from all other animal behaviour patterns, "be they simple conditioned reflexes, complex conditioned behaviour or the highest feats of intelligence based on insight" (Lorenz, 1970, p. 116).

According to him, there are factors at work in the ontogeny of instinctive behaviour patterns that are similar to those of the ontogenetic development of organs – more similar, in fact, than to the factors at work in the development of intelligent behaviour.

In other words, the characteristics of instinctive behaviour are like those of an organ. Instincts carry precise and rigid behaviour patterns. Intelligent behaviour is not genetically coded; it is flexible, and its results are uncertain. Environmental stimuli play a role in both the triggering of instincts and in intelligent behaviour since both of these can be a response to these stimuli. However, instincts cannot be altered by the environment: they only have a triggering effect, meaning that the exact same thing will happen in each new situation. Intelligent behaviour, in contrast, is influenced by prior experience, and the response to a later triggering stimulus may be different.

Machines will never have a problem with their ancestors (although "software archaeologists" might contend that, at the very least, old legacy code pervades a lot of systems) or instincts that persist and intervene in emotions and, there-through, cognition. That is, machines do not have to consciously choose cognition. At the same time, they cannot turn into real intelligence without having awareness. Machine learning without true understanding is only competence, or simply reactivity, but not learning. As long as machines are not conscious, sentient beings, learning is ensured by a pre-defined helper function rather than insight. Machines don't learn something in order to avoid some danger next time, to acquire something that is important for them or perhaps out of curiosity, but because their algorithm dictates that they do so. Just like genetically encoded instincts.

Machines are able to react, that is, function as some form of reflex. Perhaps the closest thing to instincts is ANI (artificial narrow intelligence). What is certain is that irrespective of how many signal-response paths are encoded in a machine, simply a multitude of such "instincts" will not turn into machine intelligence – it will simply become a machine that is able to carry out a lot of tasks, which has no awareness of its own knowledge. An entirely different solution would be for an AI and a being with consciousness to form a joint unit. In that case the conscious being augmented with machine knowledge – the humachine – could have the potential to become a superintelligence. The question remains open, though, what such a being, enhanced with a slew of special competences, would do, if it is not even able to rein back its genetically given instincts at all times.

Motivation for thinking and motivated thinking

If we're talking about instincts, then the most exciting topic is motivation. It has several layers, going as far back as the ancient jellyfish and starting from "eat and exist," that is, the deepest motivation of self-preservation behaviour. The well-known Maslow pyramid of needs can be populated with the zoo in our brain (see Figure 3.1). At the reptilian level, the focus is on striving toward security – the

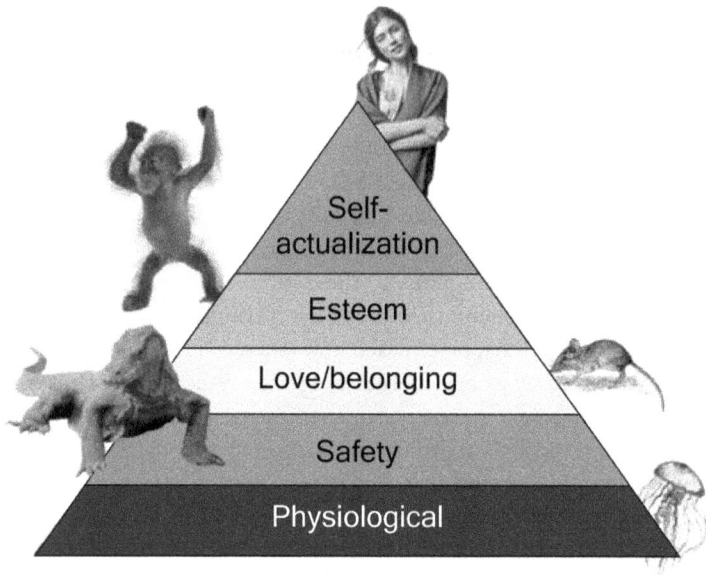

FIGURE 3.1 Maslow's motivational levels with the inner animals

fight or flight motives. Our shrew is a sensitive soul and is motivated by love and social emotions, but also by fear. Our primate motives include achievement motivation, as well as the wish for recognition, power, and freedom.

A human motivation is to accomplish everything we can, to grow, and to reach the sky even. This human motivation is what is currently giving birth to AI. At the point where *Homo sapiens* reached the boundaries of its abilities, it started looking for tools, then subsequently started to make tools, and finally started producing them at an industrial level. Today, there are tools making the tools, and humanity is no longer extending only its physical abilities but its cognitive abilities, as well.

As we have observed, machines are free from several factors resulting from human biology that influence thinking. This applies to motivation, too. A machine is not motivated, but programmed, for achievements. It's true that so-called reinforcement learning is incredibly successful in AI and has been extremely successful in competitive games (like chess and Go). This is not because AI is competitive or wants to win, but because it works along a specific algorithm. Reinforcement learning in AI is practical for humans because the programmers don't need to label a vast amount of training data: they just need to specify a system – for example, a neural network – to look for a certain "reward," such as a victory in a game. The neural network then learns by replaying the game over and over and optimises for any step that can bring it to the final feedback, the one which signals its victory. This is by and large the method by which a dog can learn different feats in return for a treat. But, in fact, anyone can be conditioned to carry out even some nonsensical series of actions if it brings rewards. Let's compare this to superstitions, which work on a similar basis. Assume that I step on a particular stone on my way to school so that there is no test that day. If this works out a couple of times, then we have a connection, even though there is definitely no real causal relationship to be identified here.

The question is why humans don't get rid of their superstitions if they have turned out several times not to hold true. In other words: there was a test at school, even though I stepped on the stone! This is actually also a part of training, called "alternating reinforcement." It is used in animal training when the behaviour has already formed and the goal is to make it operate independently. At this point, the behaviour will be rewarded increasingly more rarely, and as such will be internalised, because there is no external cause for it anymore. Machines are not so easy to trick; they are far more goal-oriented than to retain a bunch of unreinforced links. Of course, they can be hacked in other ways. But human intelligence can likewise be tricked in a number of ways.

We are often not even aware of where a particular behaviour comes from and what motivates us. None of our "internal zoo" inhabitants particularly want to step on a stone to avoid something: it's not a need. However, adapting to the outside world is. Environmental effects play a large role in the development of motives, because they are beneficial for adaptation if the internal drive motivates an individual toward a behaviour appropriate for the external circumstances.

Motivation is the totality of internal factors driving the individual towards some behaviour. Its unit is the drive, the internal impulse, which develops from internal needs to motivate the individual towards satisfying that need. There are primary drives, which are the most fundamental needs, such as hunger, thirst, a desire for security, or the sexual instinct (the desires of the reptilian brain). Then there are so-called secondary drives, which are forces built on top of primary drives – that is, they serve the satisfaction of those needs indirectly. At the reptilian level, for example, money can indirectly serve the need for security or the satisfaction of sexual instincts, possibly both at the same time. It can also be a tool of self-actualisation, too, though. Motives can thus mix or be compounded and cannot be cleanly separated from each other in practice – only when we submit our internal drives to a deeper analysis.

Motivation influences thinking, learning, intelligence, and behaviour in several ways. The first crucial question is whether the individual is motivated for intellectual coping. A second question is what the individual is motivated to think through or learn. But the most complex issue is how motivations alter thinking, and in what directions they steer learning and behaviour.

When solving a situation, we can choose the cognitive path, but we can just as well take the Alexandrian way of cutting the Gordian Knot. It's unequivocally the environment, society, and culture, but most especially family, from whom individuals obtain the impulses that predispose them to use cognitive resources. It is of key significance how much someone believes the use of intelligence is expected and what they think of themselves and of what they should use: that is, whether they detect cognitive abilities in themselves that can make them successful. The ways that children choose to cope is far from irrelevant when it comes to the future.

A lot of adults are of the belief that it's best to praise children and call them intelligent and clever and that, as a result, children will in turn consider themselves clever. This is for sure much better than calling children stupid, but it's not the best solution. Carol Dweck (2006), a researcher at Stanford University, urges a change in approach. She has shown that praise can be a hindrance and can cause individuals to become unmotivated, and can even engender anxiety and a compulsive desire to live up to expectations. This is because the exact target of a praise is of extreme relevance. According to the development-oriented approach, the most important function of a praise is to reward effort, so that the learner focuses on the process itself, rather than the end result. This is similar to intrinsic motivation, when the individual performs some work for the sake of the activity itself or when they learn in order to grow and develop. In other words, praising the endeavour, diligence, and effort brings more positive results than praising intelligence and ability.

What someone is willing to think through and what they want to learn is likewise down to their internal drives. This is merely a special case of the foregoing, but it's worth adding that interest – the directed form of motivation – should receive far more attention. Once the individual starts engaging in an activity in some area, then the soul is set in motion, and it is easier to move forward. The word *interest* has, perhaps not coincidentally, a meaning similar to *profit*. Interest goes beyond motivation, as it has a stronger emotional content, and as such energises an individual more strongly and more deeply.

Motivated thinking also has significant emotional content, but it's on an entirely different plane than in the case of interest. When it comes to motivated thinking, the "profit" doesn't appear on the surface, even though it is extremely strong: the goal is the safeguarding of the self.

In motivated thinking, an individual will come up with arguments as a form of self-justification that corroborate what they want to believe. This leads to false beliefs and an insistence in them to an extent that not even contradicting proof will convince them. The desired cognitive result functions as a sort of filter, which shuts out other viewpoints and potentially even scientific proofs. This is how cognitive dissonance works. If some new piece of information or experience contradicts the prior beliefs of the individual, it is dissonant. Dissonance leads to internal stress, which in turn leads to a feeling of anxiety. It is harder to re-evaluate one's own convictions than to question new information: and this is how motivated thinking starts.

When an individual is motivated to maintain their original beliefs, it can create paths in their neural network which deepen their convictions along similar neural networks in which logical thinking happens. As a result, a strongly emotionally loaded idea will face contradictory pieces of information again and again, which need to be repelled again and again through further distortion.

This is also called affective contagion, but instead of "infecting" other people, the individual will infect their own thinking with their arguments and conclusions. The result can be a truly sick system of thoughts.

Not even the most intelligent people are immune to this contagion, because its source is motivation, not intelligence. A high intelligence level could even assist the spread of this "infection," since a more efficient cognitive system is more efficient at distortions, too. For example, an excellent professional or researcher can become entirely blind to a mistake they have made and can defend the mistaken method with success and over a long period of time. This is all the more easy if we recall that the world is put together from small pieces, and if the pattern generator has been hijacked by emotions and motivations; then we can assemble anything. Our world is made up of individual subjective realities, and if there are a sufficient number of people who accept one of these subjective realities, then it could even turn into a worldview. Any kind of worldview.

Subjective and intersubjectivity reality, and the world of beliefs and memes – we are sociable animals

Humans must manage to see themselves as rational beings amid all their emotions, instincts, and motivations, which is no small feat but sometimes successful. We are often faced with the fact that reality is not entirely unambiguous, and so rationality must build on rather uncertain foundations.

Subjective reality is the product of our brains, which function as excellent pattern generators. As we have observed, the human brain invents the world – that is, moulds it into shapes – although there is a starter pack of a few ready-made wholes genetically encoded in our neural networks. To illustrate: new-born infants already discern human faces from the visual environment, even though they are not yet capable of much in the area of visual processing. We could thus conclude that we put together and process nearly everything from experience. Perception itself is not equivalent to simply taking things in, but it is an active processing of the stimuli. We have our inborn basic tool kit at our disposal for this, but beyond that, the brain must depend on individual experience – that is, it is compelled to rely on subjective perception.

In his book entitled *What Is It Like to Be a Bat?*, American psychologist Thomas Nagel argues that bats, for instance, perceive the environment in a wholly different way than humans, and it is thus impossible to talk about what it is like to be a bat. Their tool kit of ready-made materials in the brain is different from that of humans, as is their perception, as well. Each organism has a unique viewpoint, which no other organism is able to experience – and each organism creates their own reality from their individual viewpoint.

Obviously, the more similar the bio-psycho-sociological characteristics of two organisms, and the more similar the experiences they have had, the more similar their subjective realities will be. The difficulty – and let us add, excitement – of social coexistence is rooted in the fact that everyone puts together the world differently, and as such, social interactions entail the meeting of mutually independent worlds. If the communication between the parties is frequent enough, then common patterns can be formed, which can serve as a basis for joint thinking. The expression "intersubjectivity" refers by and large to what happens during the interaction of multiple minds.

At the centre of intersubjectivity we find shared experience, shared attention, and shared concepts. Primary intersubjectivity is based on sensory-motor abilities, which make it possible for an individual to grasp the meaning of others' movements, gestures, facial expressions, eye direction, and intentional actions during social interactions. This is the first connection between an infant and their carer. These are the abilities that are required in order for humans to enter into shared attention situations. Small children learn from observing activities and picking up on movements, and this efficient way of learning continues to assist humans throughout their lives.

The first historical intersubjective interaction must have involved one of our ancestors showing something to another and managing to get them to pay attention to it. Shared attention makes the co-ordination of movements and actions in the shared world possible, and with that we already have the basis for secondary intersubjectivity. From then on, our ancestors could use gestures to express what they wanted: for example, that they should go somewhere together, or that their peer should give or take something somewhere or perhaps, conversely, that they should accept something. Whether animals are capable of intersubjectivity is under debate. They can certainly be taught shared signs. They are even capable of mentalization, that is, putting themselves in the shoes, or more precisely the mental state, of another being. For example, a subordinate chimpanzee will target bananas that its dominant peer cannot see. Similar mentalization has also been observed in dogs.

Social interaction stepped up a level when another ingenious ancestor of ours, who commanded some basic linguistic knowledge in addition to social skills, no longer only pointed and gestured, but linked the elements of the world to sounds – that is, abstracted away from the concrete object and substituted it with an auditory stimulus. This ancestor somehow convinced the others to accept that saying "stick" referred to the longish piece of wood lying on the ground. In a way, humans "hacked" intersubjectivity – an efficient tool of social behaviour – with language, and there was no stopping from then on. People started giving names to their own subjective patterns and adopted these from each other in social situations.

The seemingly clear distinction between subjectivity and objectivity hinders a fuller psychological understanding of these concepts. It is therefore perhaps better to describe the different aspects of the phenomenon using the terms *individual versus collective* and *private versus public*. The four patterns we get with the permutation of these four categories can be covered by the terms *intrasubjective*, *intersubjective*, *interobjective*, and *interobjective*. We can thus think in terms of public-personal, private-social, etc. domains.

American philosopher Ken Wilber (2001) argues that reality is made up of four domains (or "quadrants"), each of which has its own standard of truth:

1   Interior-individual: the subjective world, the individual subjective perspective
2   Interior-collective: the intersubjective world, the cultural perspective
3   Exterior-individual: the objective state of affairs
4   Exterior-collective: the interobjective perspective, the "functional fit," the way entities fit together in a system

When a group of people accept an element of reality generated by some subjective reality and incorporate it into social interactions, it then becomes intersubjective reality. These range from signalling gestures through our concepts to scientific theories. These are all patterns accepted by sufficiently many individuals, but they can still be subject to change or be rejected, and new theories and concepts introduced in their place.

According to Hungarian evolutionary biologist Eörs Szathmáry, hypotheses supported by proof tend to win over alternative suppositions and to oust the latter akin to the way better adapted genotypes oust the ones less suited to the particular environment during evolution. In the evolution of human culture, the intersubjective reality that is most suitable in terms of adaptation in that particular time will be the one to spread.

For example, the concept of intelligence is typically identified on the basis of definitions born of the "Western" culture. Human intelligence has different meanings depending on the culture. In many Eastern cultures, intelligence is primarily related to the social roles and responsibilities of the individuals. The Chinese approach to intelligence captures it as the ability to sympathise with and understand others, although this is of course far from the only way it's defined in China. Intelligence is likewise approached from a social-emotional aspect in several African communities. Sometimes the main criterion is social responsibility instead of social roles. For example, in the Chi-Chewa language, which is spoken by about 10 million people in Central Africa, intelligence means not just cleverness, but also the ability to take responsibility. And as we have seen, there are several different interpretations even within the Western culture. Crucially, culture influences individual thinking, and so the culture or subculture of an individual will influence the individual's notion of intelligence. In other words, the process through which subjective content becomes intersubjective is not a one-way path, but a system of mutually influencing back-and-forth processes.

In the 21st century, the expansion of social media accelerated and spread the construction of intersubjective reality. Individual subjective realities can be rapidly disseminated, and as soon as they reach a sufficient number of people and take hold, they immediately become intersubjective.

Culture, analogously to biological processes, changes constantly. Some of its elements are preserved; others change or disappear. Memes are units carrying cultural information, akin to the DNA in biological evolution. Memes are information patterns taking a hold in the individual's brain, which will get passed on. Superstitions, ideas, apt expressions, or images can all become memes if they are somehow advantageous from the perspective of the individual. The advantages of social memes go beyond the individual level, and they become culturally defining.

Owing to limited capacities, not all memes survive in the brain. The ones that stick are typically those which are able to connect to the existing individual cognitive structures. The same applies at the social level. It's not the suitability of a meme in itself that matters, but whether it fits the specific environment. And this is where things get interesting. To paraphrase a pertinent observation widely (though incorrectly) attributed to Darwin, it is not the best that survive, but those who can adapt best.

As long as humanity had no scientific facts at its disposal, humans chiefly used imagination to comprehend the world and the way it functions, and they believed in explanations of unfathomable phenomena without any scientific proof. Prior to the scientific revolution, humanity had no high-level knowledge of nature and technology, and people would learn about the patterns in nature at a level that can be directly experienced. The difference between the situation before the scientific revolution and today is that in the pre-scientific revolution eras, the anointed would keep the relatively limited amount of knowledge to themselves and use it to control the communities. Scientists, the anointed priests of science, in contrast, have been uncovering increasingly more powerful forces and making these available. Then again, science is delving increasingly deeper and is going more and more into details, which is no longer easily understandable or accessible to the vast majority of the people. Science has reached such depths that in most areas, everyday people simply have to believe in it, because they are unable to verify the truth content of a supposedly scientific fact.

A large gap has opened up between science and the knowledge of the majority of humanity. While the opportunities and tools born from the evolution of science and technology are widely in use today, the users are far from aware of how exactly these work. The development of science and technology has thus returned humanity to belief. In absence of knowledge, intersubjective reality can be far removed from scientific reality – so much so that the gap can become insurmountable, forcing people to choose one or the other in equivocal situations. Common sense and imagination can be combined, though: that is what we call creativity, which doesn't just grow by itself but is a highly energy-intensive luxury service provided by our brain.

What comes easily and automatically are intuition and imagination. As Yuval Harari wrote in his book *Homo Deus*, the source of *Homo sapiens'* success lies not in its intelligence, but its imagination. Intersubjective functioning only requires that a sufficient number of people are able to conceptualise the product of imagination proffered by someone, and it is henceforth easy to think and act in concert.

Human knowledge is based on imagination, while machine imagination is based on knowledge. As Hungarian professor of mathematics László Lovász once put it, the essence of human mental activity is not the execution of algorithms but the creation of algorithms.

We can only actualise things we can imagine – that is, the only limit for the human mind is imposed by imagination. Imagination builds upon objective subjective realities, and is thus not as free as we would think, since it must use the available realities as building blocks. It will arrange knowledge into new algorithms and thereby create a new reality. As a result, depictions of the future are a rearrangement of the given present into an alternative algorithm. Art, as the imagination of humanity itself, can thus discover the future and its inventions sooner than science. It draws on intersubjective and interobjective realities in creation. Science is then like the contractor simply implementing it all.

Imagination hardly requires any control – indeed, it is best to let it soar free. However, creating even a subjective reality entails some control, because it involves a choice from among the possible realities. And at this point, the so-called executive functions become definitive. The closer a reality is to what we can call objective, the more the brain needs the networks that are capable of planning and control.

Executive functions – staying in the process

When discussing intelligence, researchers always put the conscious processes into the foreground. Accordingly, the so-called executive functions are gaining increasingly greater respect in the eyes of intelligence researchers. These are necessary, but far from sufficient, components of the process. The relation between IQ results and the executive functions manifests itself on the performance side. That is, as the terminology itself suggests, these functions are not direct components of intelligent functioning but belong to its satellites. Without execution, intelligence – whatever it may be – couldn't even come near its full potential.

Already as early as 50,000 years ago, *Homo sapiens* possessed an intelligence similar to today's humans and the characteristics described earlier. The reason we can say this with certainty is that there is evidence of symbolic thinking from 50,000 years ago, which is the basis of language, among other things.

Executive functions, in contrast, became a defining cerebral network at a relatively late stage in the development of *Homo sapiens*. The frontal lobe area of the brain – the primary location of executive functions – only increased in size in the past 10,000 years. That brain development took this direction is to a great part attributable to the dramatic culture change that happened when humanity swapped the nomadic, hunter-gatherer lifestyle for a settled, agricultural one. Agriculture and husbandry have changed history and the human brain.

As for which cognitive functions exactly belong to executive functions, not even psychologists are certain. These are essentially the processes that make it possible for someone to get from A to B without deviating from their goal, and to be able to change, if necessary.

Executive functions have three main groups:

1 Control functions: inhibition, resisting temptation, retaining attention, shutting out distracting stimuli
2 Working memory: keeping information in mind (making it possible to link one thing with another or to use information to solve a problem and thereby sustain the mental process)
3 Cognitive flexibility: changing the perspective of or approach to the problem, flexibly adapting to new needs and rules – in other words, mentally choosing directions

Executive functions thus assist the individual's control of their behaviour and perform tasks like planning, decision making, problem solving, self-checking, and acting with long-term goals in mind. They are groups of top-down mental processes that are needed when we must concentrate and pay attention, when relying on automatic actions and instincts is not the appropriate choice. Executive functions are cognitive processes at which humans are significantly better than other animals. Only machines are our betters in process control.

The use of executive functions requires effort. It's easier to continue doing something than to change; easier to give in to temptation than to resist; and it's easier to act automatically than to reflect on what the next step should be. The frontal lobe in the brain thus houses the keys to internally controlled activity and the organization of thoughts.

Machines are built, among other reasons, to serve as an extension of our executive functions. They are reliable monitoring and control systems, which, if necessary, are capable of replanning the procedure, and thus they appeared quite soon in automatization. "If-then-else." Again, we see a sort of reverse process inasmuch as when it comes to humans, executive functions have only become truly efficient over the last 10,000 years. On the contrary, machines have become suitable for precision functioning and for activities based on flexible algorithms in an early phase of their evolution. Programming machines is easier for humans than controlling their own actions. Executive functions play a large role in conscious behaviour, but if that were all that is necessary for consciousness, then DeepBlue, for example, would be aware that it was the first machine in the world to defeat a human chess champion in a match. AI is, however, incapable of reflecting on itself, even though it is in possession of the knowledge and all its details.

Being conscious of consciousness

Consciousness as a subjective experience means by and large that an agent perceives and is aware of its own thinking and existence. It is currently still beyond doubt that even the most intelligent machine is unaware of thinking and solving problems. Whether it will ever be possible to create an AI with consciousness is a big question.

At the level of phenomena, perceived consciousness follows natural rules and is determined by psychophysical laws. We don't know anything beyond this, and science is unable to supply us with reliable answers to questions like: what is consciousness; where is it located; and does it exist at all beyond us knowing about it, feeling it, experiencing it? People give names to a lot of things that don't otherwise exist.

The term *consciousness* is often used as a synonym of *mind*, but just as frequently it is only assumed to be an aspect of it. Consciousness means knowing about the internal and external experiences, about understanding, feelings, and percepts – that is, it means not simply possessing these, but possessing knowledge about that possession, as well. Why this is all necessary is quite inexplicable. At least from an evolutionary point of view, the luxury of being conscious of a part of our actions, and especially of our existence, doesn't seem to make much sense. From an evolutionary point of view, we would be quite well-off without the "big black pebble:" intelligence and its satellites would take care of existence and the computations required for it. In this case, of course, we wouldn't know about everything, including our existence and its purpose. The purpose of our existence is not really clear, anyway, so we are not much further ahead or farther back with our consciousness.

By having a consciousness, we can debate what it is and where it is, because our starting point is that it exists. The majority of researchers accept consciousness as a given, and they attempt to understand its relationship with the objective world as described by science.

Many think that consciousness belongs to some external entity – that is, that there is a soul and there is a separate body, in which the brain is a sort of information processing centre, but in our physical-physiological existence we are not much more than a drone that is externally controlled by our soul, just as we do a drone. We can state with quite a bit of certainty that drones have no philosophical views about this, but what is equally certain is that we do. The question is whether this is simply a question of intelligence. If machines were smart enough, then could they also have a consciousness? Or is consciousness an entity entirely independent of intelligence, so not even the most intelligent machine ever created could possess consciousness?

On another approach, our consciousness is nothing more than the functioning of the neuronal network in our brain. This simplifies the situation in that in this case it is unequivocally, although as yet only theoretically, possible to create an artificial neural network that makes a machine not only intelligent but turns it into an agent with consciousness.

However, there are again two diverging theories at this point. One of them is the Global Neuronal Workspace (GNW), a theory of neuroscientists Stanislas Dehaene and Jean-Pierre Changeux (2011). In this theory, when someone is conscious of something, then many different parts of their brain can access that information. If, however, the action is not conscious, then the information is only localised in the affected sensory motor system.

According to the GNW, consciousness is a mode of information processing in which special programs connect to a small, shared storage space. The data located there become accessible to several assistive processes, including working memory, language, the planning module, etc. Consciousness manifests itself when the incoming information that was stored in such a space exists globally into multiple cognitive systems, which process this data for speech, storage, or the execution of an action.

The network of neurons broadcasting the messages is presumably located in the frontal and parietal lobes. When these data are broadcast along the network and become globally accessible, the information becomes conscious. Since the storage space has only limited size, only a limited amount of information can be consciously processed at one time.

The GNW allows for the possibility of computers of the future becoming conscious, because although today's machines haven't reached this level of cognitive refinement, it is only a matter of time before it will happen.

In opposition to this all, the Integrated Information Theory (IIT) asserts that we cannot infer the existence of consciousness from the physical systems as a starting point. The starting point for Italian neuroscientist and psychiatrist Giulio Tononi (2008) in his theory was experience itself. Every piece of experience has certain essential features, and every complex and mutually connected mechanism whose structure encodes a set of causal relations possesses these features, and thereby some level of consciousness, as well. On the inside, this manifests as some kind of feeling, but if the mechanism lacks integration and complexity, then no awareness is achieved. According to the IIT, consciousness is an internal causal force, which is linked to complex mechanisms like the human brain. Consciousness cannot be computed: it must be built into the structure of the system. This would mean that machines will never have consciousness.

In sum, we can at least be certain that machines may or may not be capable of possessing consciousness – but we still know nothing certain about the nature of consciousness.

In the foregoing, we have concluded that our brain houses a menagerie of jellyfish, a couple of reptiles, shrews, and the sabre-toothed tiger, as well as a variety of primates. All of this is kept in order by executive functions, an innovation of our brain uncannily similar to automatic process control in the field of production, which has gained strength in the past 20,000 years. These ensure that we are capable of acting consciously, as well.

In light of this, at which level exactly consciousness appears, and if animals possess it, is a very good question. It is quite clear that at least some of them possess will and intentions: anyone who has a dog and/or a cat will experience it each day, so at least when it comes to mammals, we can be certain of the answer. For those without such experience or who don't consider this approach scientific enough, there is the fact that the brain structure of mammals bears a high level of similarity to that of humans. The efficiency of information transfer in the cerebral neural network is the same in all mammals, including humans. True, the relative size of the neocortex compared to the rest of the brain tends to be significantly greater in humans than other living beings. Well, dolphins give us a run for our money, and there is even a species with a higher neocortex ratio than humans.

The ability of animals to learn from others, invent new behaviour, and use tools plays a key role in the evolution of the brain. And these are areas in which humans are not just quantitatively, but perhaps also qualitatively, different. At the same time, there is no qualitative difference to be found in the hardware between mammals and humans. The cerebral networks of intentional actions are also very similar; the pre-supplementary motor areas and the prefrontal and parietal cortex areas generate information for the next actions and trigger the characteristic experiences of consciousness of the intention to act, and subsequently that of planning and controlling the actions.

When it comes to machines, we certainly cannot talk about intentions: intentions are to be found in the programmer and in the user of the machine, since the machine itself does not "want" to execute what it does. The series of decisions is subsequently within the grasp of machines, too, though. They are able to "decide" whether they need to act, and if so, what action is to be executed and when – all without intentions or will.

Machines and animals, including humans, process data and information and can be extremely different in how they go about it. Let us take the pyramid of data-information-knowledge-understanding-wisdom from the first chapter and pair it with different modes of thinking. The level of "wisdom" entails that the neural network achieves a complex synthesis from concrete data by abstracting away from them, thereby arriving at a higher-level insight not bound to concrete objects. Consciousness could be an event occurring at an incredibly high level of abstraction and synthesis, if we think of the GNW approach, that is, when a sufficiently large proportion of the brain gets involved in the process as a network – not actively, but in an abstract way – and "the pieces fall into place." At this point, consciousness appears, and the agent becomes aware of their own existence and actions. This process is always active. The individual must reflect on the knowledge of their actions and existence. And this means that we are talking about some kind of ability.

The tricky point is, what brings the agent to the level of being able to abstract away from everything else and put together self-awareness, which apparently has no sense or utility. This is one of the reasons the IIT approach may have a valid point. The twosome of abstraction and synthesis requires a qualitative jump, which must be a characteristic of the agent. One candidate may be the internal drive for development for its own sake, which is purposeless and, as such, independent of everything. This may be what helps us over the magical boundary by extending knowledge to reach the level of "wisdom" – that is, knowledge about knowledge. From this point, there isn't much abstraction and synthesis needed for humans to create their own subjective reality that we call identity.

The point of hybrid systems is that each component delivers its performance in the field of abilities characteristic of it, and in areas where its performance is poorer, it gives way to other components in the spirit of the division of labour. Machines can do a lot that humans need for their further evolution, but for which they are unwilling to wait at least a couple of hundred thousand years to develop biologically. A humachine is a hybrid system to which humans contribute consciousness, identity, and the drive for progress and to which machines contribute everything that humans want to acquire for their development. The evident conclusion is that human agents need to become stronger in the areas they contribute to the joint system. This is the path to both development and self-defence.

The level of ability in other areas is irrelevant; for example, dolphins and dogs possess better cognitive abilities than humans in several areas. Consciousness is, however, a peak in an area resulting from the maturity of an agent. As yet, we can only be certain of its existence in humans despite the fact that advanced animals are also capable of abstraction, demonstrate intentions, and show signs of consciousness. The theory of Australian philosopher David Chalmers goes as far as stating that consciousness is in everything, being a fundamental, autonomous constituent of reality. As such, it is perhaps only a question of maturity what level of consciousness a thing – or perhaps already an agent that can be called a "who" – has reached. Even if it is not the machines, there can theoretically be agents who have a level of consciousness surpassing even that of humans. But just as a dog cannot understand human consciousness, humans are incapable of understanding entities beyond their own level of abstraction and synthesis.

Human intelligence is likewise a hybrid system whose components function in different ways and at different levels. But, coincidentally, or for some to-us-unknown reason, a neural network structure has come into existence that is driven by development for its own sake, and this has opened up huge mental possibilities.

Enrichment

The extension of knowledge – wisdom (knowledge about knowledge) breaks through magical boundaries. What can't we imagine?

A meme (short for *mimeme*) can be described as something such as a video, picture, or phrase – a unit of cultural information, concept, belief, or practice – that spreads from person to person in a similar way to the transmission of genes. Choose a method of transmission/dissemination for a meme of your own creation, and follow the meme's journey. Does it come back to you?

Link pathways

What links consciousness, mind, wisdom, and memes?

References

Chalmers, D. J. 2005. The matrix as metaphysics. In Christopher Grau (Ed.), *Philosophers Explore the Matrix*. Oxford: Oxford University Press.

Dawson, M., Gernsbacher, M. A., Mottron, L. 2011. The level and nature of autistic intelligence II: What about Asperger Syndrome? *PLOS One* 6 (9): 657–662. doi:10.1371/journal.pone.0025372.

Dehaene, S., Changeux, J. P. 2011. Experimental and theoretical approaches to conscious processing. *Neuron* 70 (2): 200–227.

Dweck, C. S. 2006. *Mindset. The New Psychology of Success*. New York: Random House.

Geary, D. C. 2004. *Origin of Mind. Evolution of Brain, Cognition, and General Intelligence*. Washington, DC: American Psychological Association.

Harari, Y. 2017. *Homo Deus: A Brief History of Tomorrow*. New York: Harper, an imprint of HarperCollins Publishers.

Kuszewski, A. 2009. *The Genetics of Creativity: A Serendipitous Assemblage of Madness*. Methodology Working Paper No. 58.

Lorenz, K. Z. 1970. *Studies in Animal and Human Behaviour* (Vol. 1). Translated from the German edition (Munich) by Robert Martin. Cambridge: Harvard University Press.

Maslow, A. H. 1943. A theory of human motivation. *Psychological Review* 50 (4): 370–396.

Nagel, T. 1974. What is it like to be a bat? *The Philosophical Review* 83 (4): 435–450. Cited in Chalmers, D. J. 1996. The conscious mind. In Christopher Grau (Ed.), *Search for a Fundamental Theory*. New York: Oxford University Press.

Salzman, C. D., Fusi, S. 2010. Emotion, cognition, and mental state representation in amygdala and prefrontal cortex. *Annual Review of Neuroscience* 33: 173–202. doi:10.1146/annurev.neuro.051508.135256.

Tononi, G. 2008. Consciousness as integrated information: A provisional manifesto. *The Biological Bulletin* 215 (3): 216–242. doi:10.2307/25470707.

Wilber, K. 2001. *A Brief History of Everything* (2nd ed.). Boston, MA: Shambhala.

Suggested further reading

Brockman, John. 2015. *What to Think About Machines That Think: Today's Leading Thinkers on the Age of Machine Intelligence*. New York, Harper Perennial.

Cocodia, E. A. 2014. Cultural perceptions of human intelligence. *Journal of Intelligence* 2: 180–196. doi:10.3390/jintelligence2040180.

Harré, R., Sammut, G. 2013. What lies between? In G. Sammut, P. Daanen, F. M. Moghaddam (Eds.), *Understanding the Self and Others: Explorations in Intersubjectivity and Interobjectivity*. New York: Routledge.

Koch, C. 2018. What is consciousness? *Scientific American* 318 (6): 60–64. doi:10.1038/scientificamerican0618-60.

Lindenfors, P. 2005. Neocortex evolution in primates: The "social brain" is for females. *Biology Letters* 1 (4): 407–410. doi:10.1098/rsbl.2005.0362.

Madgwick, P. 2017. From instinct to intelligence: Has AI taken a wrong turning? Exploring Artificial intelligence & What it means to be human. https://becominghuman.ai/from-instinct-to-intelligence-has-ai-taken-a-wrong-turning-e84582dc4600.

Mason, M. F., Banfield, J. F., Macrae, C. N. 2004. Thinking about actions: The neural substrates of person knowledge. *Cerebral Cortex* 14 (2): 209–214. doi:10.1093/cercor/bhg120.

Racine, T. P., Wereha, T. J., Leavens, D. A. 2012. Primates, motion, and emotion: To what extent nonhuman primates are intersubjective and why. In A. Foolen, U. Lüdtke, T. P. Racine, & J. Zlatev (Eds.), *Moving Ourselves, Moving Others: Motion and Emotion in Intersubjectivity, Consciousness and Language* (pp. 221–242). Amsterdam: Benjamins.

Roberts, J. 2016. Thinking machines: The search for artificial intelligence. *Distillations* 2 (2): 14–23.

Serpell, R. 2000. *Handbook of Intelligence* (pp. 549–578). Cambridge: Cambridge University Press.

4

THE CHANGING NATURE OF EMPLOYMENT AND FUTURE LEARNING BEHAVIOURS

FIGURE 4.1 Work (1852–1865), Ford Madox Brown

Source: Manchester Art Gallery/Bridgeman Images

The challenge we face as a global society seeking civic and economic stability within chaotic reinvention is what do we teach people to ensure they have the right skills, attitude, and resilient enthusiasm to evolve and energise their part in the new global and outer space economies? What basic knowledge will be relevant? What knowledge will carry young and older learners through the

DOI: 10.4324/9780429356346-5

storms of disruption to a place where work is redefined in a time that robots will increasingly create the wealth and governance to run a healthy society?

The truly remarkable thing about the pandemic catastrophe that is coronavirus (COVID-19) as we write is the fact that it has dramatically advanced our journey into inevitable global economic, socio-cultural, spiritual, and psychological changes that the modern period was going to bring. The world of employment and the learning models and ambitions of our world are now changed forever. While many people will desire a return to pre-pandemic normality, others see opportunities to exploit for good (and unfortunately sometimes malevolent reasons) a situation of global disruption. The nature, style, purpose, and content of working lives cannot return to any sense of historic normality. Complex changes in manufacturing, finance, and distribution methodologies using AI are too efficient and cost beneficial to "go back." The changing world of work requires that we look forward and learn from the past. Simultaneously we must also recognise that education and training have also undergone, in a remarkably short time, an astonishing period of intense change.

A close examination of the painting "Work" by Ford Madox Brown presents a world where everyone has a place and an economic status, if not paid employment creating wealth. Seen to the right in the picture are the workers in their mind – here represented by portraits of Thomas Carlyle, thinker and writer, and Frederick Maurice, writer and Anglican theologian. In the left of the painting, we can see a fashionable lady, an evangelist, and a ragged flower-seller who is selling Forget-Me-Nots. These two groups are the representational edges of a highly structured society in which work and status are carefully delineated.

Carlyle held the view that,

> "an endless significance lies in Work;" a man perfects himself by working. Foul jungles are cleared away, fair seedfields rise instead, and stately cities; and withal the man himself first ceases to be a jungle and foul unwholesome desert thereby. Consider how, even in the meanest sorts of Labour, the whole soul of a man is composed into a kind of real harmony, the instant he sets himself to work! Doubt, Desire, Sorrow, Remorse, Indignation, Despair itself, all these like helldogs lie beleaguering the soul of the poor dayworker, as of every man: but he bends himself with free valour against his task, and all these are stilled, all these shrink murmuring far off into their caves. The man is now a man. The blessed glow of Labour in him, is it not as purifying fire, wherein all poison is burnt up, and of sour smoke itself there is made bright blessed flame!
>
> *(Carlyle, 1843)*

While governments across the world struggle to maintain meaningful coherence of employment through financial mechanisms such as the United Kingdom's COVID-19 furlough scheme, irrevocable changes are being rehearsed whereby employment changes would and will continue to be driven by AI, economic forces, and political and social disruption. The world of work and employment is having the shock of the future thrust upon it as economies restructure their income and employment models. The surety of the 19th-century vision of work as expressed by Thomas Carlyle and Ford Madox Brown's painting is now a vision template and reflective resource in understanding that which is historic in recent employment models and a stepping stone to allowing us to reflect on the changing world of work and leisure.

> Every step in the rise of the modern world involved a situation of transition or crisis, where the taken for granted order became shaken, even turned upside down, requiring a new solution.
>
> *(Szakolczai, 2017)*

One critical review of the pandemic financial governmental responses clearly hints at these deep changes in employment patterns being unavoidable. People are having to consider what would have happened in relatively recent history if jobs had been protected from disappearing as working and buying practices changed. Think and reflect for a minute to consider the extraordinary changes and adaptations that have been made in just the last few decades to see how relentless change in employment patterns can be. Mitigating economic damage is not the same as managing the effects of a pandemic while also recognising the new conditions at work in the world. Immeasurable changes happened before the pandemic and will continue to happen during and post-pandemic. Employment and learning behaviours driven by AI will change everything regarding work and learning for what work will become in societies.

Ancient work

The first work-jobs required skills which needed to be applied and improved to be effective and to ensure the desired return for effort. It is important to note the difference between a job as a task which has a value in itself and a job that is rewarded either financially or through other acceptable payment.

Early occupations such as agriculture, hunting, and shelter-making required the development of tools. These tools had to be creatively modelled and then manufactured. Tool-making and carpentry emerged as a result of human intelligence developing and creating solutions to problems of survival. The reward was a community benefit rather than a financial-capital creation one. The reward was meeting a need of increasing both well-being and security. With a little imagination we can see that practically all early jobs continued to develop, and despite industrialisation and more recently the development of technology, these ancient work activities still exist throughout the world for the simple reason that they continue to meet the most basic human needs.

Creative teachers, farmers, builders, musicians, artists, miners, storytellers, carpenters, butchers, hunters, and soothsayers – or now in the 21st century futurists, fortune tellers, and an often-neglected category of rewarding employment, criminals – remain fundamental components of global economic activity. As the complexity of economic activity developed from humble beginnings, writers, accountants, architects, and medical practitioners appeared in job-focussed employment.

New jobs are constantly being developed and have been created since the ancient world of employment. Essentially however they remain aspects of the earliest requirements of a developing and stable community. Agriculture is a staple of employment, an area with serious issues of growth and demand increases being met. Demands in the future cannot be met until one applies AI technologies and thinking. The simple but important point is that while the activities of agriculture remain the same, the complexity of sustaining agricultural activity at a level required to sustain and meet global demands means increasing complexity of both management and methodologies of production and control.

Artificial intelligence holds, as with practically all human activities, the promise of driving for example an agricultural revolution at a time when the world requires increased food production using fewer resources efficiently and effectively.

The case in the United Kingdom reflects the state of many countries with regard to AI readiness.

Recent findings show that compared to global averages, the UK suffers from lower relative AI maturity and technology adoption. As a more pressing global and localised skills gap becomes more problematic, a failure to promote AI reskilling of the worldwide workforces will have serious consequences for all aspects of economic life. Old jobs are beginning to disappear, and we remain unprepared to support new areas of work and new ways of working. Functional governments across the world are now preparing for a time when robots will carry out low-skilled repetitive jobs. A recent European commission report suggested 43 percent of jobs in the UK could be filled by robots in the future.

There will be attempts to hold on to "old" jobs and familiar methods of maintaining employment models and reducing civil unrest. The world of jobs and employment is fundamentally changing to a socio-economic model whereby the majority of people do not work and rather like a football crowd they will be important as consumers of others work but will be a challenge for society to offer them meaningful lives. Those who will have careers and interesting, meaningful employment will be both AI-skilled and possess skills and abilities remaining beyond the ability of AI in the near and mid-future.

The invention of AI has and will change our ways of living, thinking, and how we regard what intelligence is and how we nurture it beyond recognition. Normally change of this magnitude would take many decades to evolve and be realised. Through COVID-19, many of the cruel events that would have taken decades to occur have literally happened overnight. In 2020, less than one year has witnessed the world of work and employment changing forever. Millions of people are being paid by government not to work in lockdown; this is a rehearsal economic strategy for the new lifetimes of working leisure in the near future. In less than a year, globally, millions of people are no longer employed, and the circumstances of their employment are going to be unstainable and will disappear forever. Changes in work location, office working restrictions, cost benefits of home office employment, shorter working weeks, and compacting hours are all becoming familiar aspects and models of the changing and emerging work-life-learning experience. A global economic model shattered beyond repair is being redesigned.

Anticipated change

Credible predictions indicate that more than 5 million Australian jobs will simply disappear in the next 15 years as a result of technology. That's 40 percent of the jobs that exist in Australia today. The situation in Australia will be largely typical of other economies. The unnerving fact is that this projection was made before the pandemic occurred.

As a matter of urgency, societies need to closely examine their understanding of:

- The nature of employment
- The nature of education in relation to changing employment or otherwise economic activities
- The effect of AI-driven change regarding old and new forms of employment, changing community structures, and education for a post-work-as-we-knew-it society

In other words, actual change needs to be prepared for and quickly. Economies will fail because they are behind with reskilling people to work with AI and supporting the relentless AI world waiting to be realised as we live in a time of restless and constant change.

Employment that has disappeared

- Dispatch motorcycle riders were employed during World War I and World War II to deliver urgent messages
- Herb strewers of the 17th century were employed to spread herbs and flowers throughout royal residences to assuage unwelcome odours
- Toad doctors worked in 19th century, treating sick people in England with what is best described as folk-magic medicine
- In the period known as the Industrial Revolution, people were paid to wake people up for work by knocking on their doors and windows with long sticks; knocker-ups were mostly found in Britain and Ireland, but as alarm clocks became more accessible, the job eventually became redundant

- In the early years of telephones, switchboard operators would have to connect callers to each other via a switchboard; the American Bureau of Labor Statistics estimated that some 80,000 people were switchboard operators still working in this role as late as 2017

Employment that will disappear

Price Waterhouse estimates that 44 percent of jobs will become fully automated in just two decades. Employment either as or serving the needs of sales staff, office staff, receptionists, secretaries, farm workers, cashiers, plasterers and tilers, dispatchers, financial advisers, accountants, holiday agents, drivers, farmers, postal workers, broadcasters, jewellers, fishermen, printers and publishers, telemarketers, manufacturing workers, sports officials, and referees, will all disappear as jobs in the near future. Some forms of jobs will reinvent themselves as the digital disruption advances, and specialist jewellers or carriage drivers and wig makers will find niche employment existences; however hundreds of thousands of jobs are going to disappear forever with huge economic repercussions.

Many jobs once regarded as secure will simply disappear through digital disruption, developing, and implementing AI and the social upheaval that will hallmark employment changes in the early 21st century.

Employment that will be retained

Artists and creatives, media technologists, teachers, nature conservation work, agronomists, sports and gaming therapists, healthcare professionals, doctors, nurses, psychotherapists, physiotherapists, epidemiologists, care workers, accountancy supervisors, managers, cyber security consultants, robotic engineers, software developers, skilled trades such as carpenters, bricklayers, plasterers, glass makers, and home designers/architects. While many of the jobs in this list will survive, they will increasingly disappear as AI and HI become more able at mimicking and enhancing existing human expertise. Other skilled areas of employment and income generation will cease to be heavyweight activities such as bricklayers and plasterers; these occupations will become increasingly niche-artisan activities on par with specialised wood carvers or glass blowers.

In all areas using technology, diagnostic engineers and technicians will be required to develop and maintain automatic machines. Other both retained and developing employment will call for data analysts, artisan hospitality and catering professionals, and engineers; legal professionals such as paralegals, barristers, solicitors, and judges; and policing/security services. With regard to law specialists and political decision-making, while humans will retain the policy oversight, corruption in elected offices and law enforcement agencies could in theory become a thing of the past through using AI robots. The robot is largely free of any inducements to act in a corrupt way; it cannot be compromised or rewarded by sex, money, preferment, or power. People have weaknesses.

No list will prove exhaustive, but this list demonstrates the huge change in employment opportunities that the next decade or so will create. Many of these jobs will disappear as AI will increasingly learn and develop sophistication and expertise to carry out even more human face-to-face creative roles in the world.

AI learns very quickly, and machines never get tired or bored or need to take a break; they don't expect a pension or pay raises. Increasingly, the way millions of people live their lives will change in ways that will constantly adjust employment opportunities and pathways for human development – some for the next decade and others for the foreseeable future.

The new learning AI world and new forms of employment

It would seem that no aspect of the growth of AI in the world of employment opportunities and needs as we know them will remain unaffected. For the purpose of looking at what may be described as "new learning" and our need to increase our species' imaginative and operational intelligence, we can focus on three disparate areas of economic activity: the military, agriculture, and criminal employment. It is an irony that a good education can support a successful career in criminal activity as easily as it could in any professional employment activity.

AI and the military market

The application and development of artificial intelligence in the military market has grown from USD 5.42 billion in 2016 to an estimated USD 8.70 billion in 2022.

A moment's consideration generates a picture of the new jobs and tasks that will result from AI applications in the military and its associated support functions. New developments in military capabilities border on the realisation of science fiction and the familiar roles and expectations of military functioning. There will be soldiers. There will also be insect-sized robots that can explore a disputed or dangerous area, swarms of small killer drones described as "biomimetic" or "nature-imitating," and weapons that are currently being developed. The soldier, sailor, or airman and their space-force colleagues will still need to eat and have clothes supplied, so while science fiction is realised, developments in supply and service (including clothing manufacturing) will remain a necessary area of work as well.

Battlefield military applications of AI – new manufacturing, design, control, and management jobs

- Artificial intelligence weapon control, autonomous weapons, unmanned fighting vehicles, unmanned ground vehicles, air defence systems, command and control systems, naval ships, submarines, unmanned maritime vehicles, fighter aircraft and helicopters, transport and cargo aircraft, ariel vehicles, space launch vehicles, cyber security, logistics, transportation, target recognition, battlefield healthcare, simulations and training, planning, threat monitoring, situational awareness, information processing, military organizations, antipersonnel weapons detection and neutralisation weapons, computational science, autonomous navigation control systems, swarming technologies, personnel management, artificial neural networks, artificial intelligence software, collision avoidance systems, contingency operations, killing machines, self-repairing machines, decision support systems, facial recognition, big data analytics, cybersecurity solutions, autonomous drones, lasers and military satellites, software modeller, ethics and protocol generators, pattern recognition machines

In addition to military platforms concerning physical and intelligence data analysis, other professional requirements are being developed:

- Philosophical and ethical governance will need to be agreed upon; as the development of military capability proceeds, the necessary legal and ethical protocols of AI-enhanced military actions will require realisation and international agreement
- Cyber-AI ambiguity of action will also require a function of military action to adjudicate, control, and prevent inappropriate actions resulting from the application of AI miscalculation and misdirection as and while AI machines learn from experience
- AI-to-human communication, the possibility that an AI system can create its own unique language that humans are unable to comprehend, could be an issue; linguists and translators of AI communications will be required

AI robots and machines are perfect for military use. The wide-scale military adoption and application of AI is happening now, flying planes and drones significantly in cyber war and gathering intelligence. The changing nature of the military will mean that combat roles will become a matter of fighting machines which are replaceable and self-repairing. The expensive asset to protect will be distant to any theatre of ward and therefore easier to physically protect. Asymmetric warfare and the personnel to work with AI are and will increasingly be very able and highly intelligent – constantly learning, highly skilled and trained intelligence cyber-operative controllers who will come at a significant cost in training and recruitment. AI protects both other AI machines and AI technologies within the same protection aims as it will protect HI workers to keep human casualties to a minimum. As an example, a fighter aircraft will soon be operating as drones do now, without a human pilot but with AI flying the combat plane. America's Defence Advanced Research Projects Agency (DARPA), a department of the USA Pentagon, has considered the future of air-to-air combat and the role of AI. It is investigating AI as the frontline disposable asset, rather than a human deployment with the human element providing the strategic command. It is only a matter of time before we see AI machines actually deployed on the battlefield and used as infantry or in more specific areas like bomb detection and disposal, operating in toxic or radio-active situations.

Agriculture

Agriculture is a vital part of the global economy and employs a huge number of people performing unskilled work. In the USA, agriculture and its related industries provide 11 percent of U.S. employment. In 2018, 22.0 million full- and part-time jobs were related to the agricultural and food sectors – 11.0 percent of total U.S. employment: a USD 5 trillion industry.

Agriculture also plays a vital role in the UK economy, providing 61 percent of the raw materials for the wider UK agri-food industry which is worth around £108 billion to the national economy and provides over 3.7 million jobs. At the time of writing, the agri-food sector as a whole generates around £18 billion of gross export earnings for the UK each year. As the world population continues to grow and productive land becomes scarcer, people have needed to get creative and become more efficient about how we farm, using less land to produce more crops and increasing the productivity and yield of those farmed acres.

The agricultural industry is turning to AI technologies to:

- Help improve yields and increase the optimum conditions to produce healthier crops
- Control diseases and pests
- Monitor soil and growing conditions
- Organise data for farmers for maximum efficiency
- Analyse weather conditions, temperature, water usage, and soil conditions
- Create seasonal forecasting models to improve agricultural accuracy and increase productivity
- Transfer workloads and repetitive tasks to improve the use of human resources
- Improve and manage logistic tasks throughout the entire food supply chain
- Reduce accidents and areas of work that may be the causes of health issues and detect diseases
- Accurately identify and eliminate weeds
- Reduce costs for farms by having a 24-hour seasonal application while also reducing labour costs

Other AI applications are real-time and increasingly accurate weather forecasting data. Seasonal forecasting is useful for efficient management of resources both agrarian and livestock farming.

The professional criminal

The four key dimensions of a criminal career identified by Blumstein 1986 are participation, frequency, seriousness, and length, and are all linked to research

Detecting illegality	Theft by employees Transportation of illegal goods Insider financial trading Detecting and preventing fraud and money laundering Blocking illicit content like child pornography on social media

FIGURE 4.2 Detecting illegality

AI applications to prevent illegality	Predict and prevent crimes Financial transactions flagging Automatically recognise anomalies in data sets Uncover and remove terrorist recruitment videos and message detecting and interpret patterns Prevention and awareness of terrorist activities Automatically recognise known faces and make estimates about the age and gender of individuals in the photographs. Preventing and reducing human trafficking Developing evidence recognising tools that uses artificial intelligence to identify objects in police photographs – and search for links with other crimes Analyse photographs, and CCTV footage Software is currently being developed which will automatically sifts through potential

FIGURE 4.3 AI applications to prevent illegality

on individual offending behaviour and societal-level crime trends. Conflict and discussion amongst researchers exists about how these four concepts are understood and defined. What can be observed with a degree of certainty is whatever the crime or frequency of criminal activity data, deduction and intuition can be embraced to examine both the journey and pattern of individual criminality. AI can at the moment be used to interrogate big data to seek out patterns of criminal behaviour: AI can calculate and see patterns to expose criminality and criminals, while intuition will for a while remain the human intelligence skill which AI cannot replicate or improve/learn from. AI can be and is already being utilised and developed to deal with a wide range of criminal activity.

Ironic that a good education can all be in service of a criminal career. Learning to write – frauds and corrupt contracts. Learning mathematics and arithmetic – corrupt accounting, gambling fraud, illegal share-trading. Learning interpersonal skills – impersonation, financial grooming, theft. Learning to be computer literate – leading to new areas of criminality, and so on. Simply put, every piece of knowledge can have an ambiguous future whereby what is meant to be used for good is in fact used for corrupt and illegal purposes.

The different guises and activities of career criminals are well known, as is the employment that criminals engender by civic society wishing to control, eliminate, or at the least mitigate their activities and success. Police officers with specialist and general skills, forensic experts, prison management and service professionals, insurance agents, judges, paralegals, barristers, law makers, loss-prevention officers, psychologists, financial crime analysts, security officers, and many other jobs and professions are all part of the employed and volunteer activity existing because of criminal activity.

Additional AI areas of application to prevent and detect illegality

The use of AI by law enforcement agencies will have to demonstrate not only that there are tangible benefits from adopting such systems, but also that the uses are legally and ethically transparent.

Policing and law enforcement are like many institutions now, entering and adjusting to an unknown but hopeful future. AI tools will both speed up existing tried and tested practices while also creating new methods of crime detection and desirable crime prevention. Human law makers and enforcement agents will have to learn to manage and supervise at highly skilled levels of competence. Their education will be an ever-changing experience of constant learning and skill upkeep.

Having looked at three contrasting major areas of economic life, we can begin to speculate as to what future learning behaviours will be required to maximise the effective use of AI working with and enhancing HI in a changing employment environment.

Core learning needs

"I would be against trying to cram knowledge into the heads of children, even if we could agree on what knowledge to cram, and could be sure that it would not go out of date, even if we could be sure that, once crammed in, it would stay in. Even then, I would trust the child to direct his own learning. For it seems to me a fact that, in our struggle to make sense out of life, the things we most need to learn are the things we most want to learn. To put this another way, curiosity is hardly ever idle. What we want to know, we want to know for a reason. The reason is that

> there is a hole, a gap, an empty space in our understanding of things, our mental model of the world. We feel that gap like a hole in a tooth and we want to fill it up. It makes us ask How? When? Why?"
>
> *(Holt, 1977)*

We can easily recognise the basic knowledge and skills we have historically sought to develop and inculcate into learners through mass state education: language use, reading comprehension, writing, and mathematics. We also have sought to teach learners about science, government civics, economics, the humanities and arts, foreign languages, history, and geography. Additionally, we would also need to recognise that physical education, however limited, is still seen as an important element of any curriculum. What we must now ask ourselves is why we should or need to continue with this type of familiar curriculum in a rapidly changing world. We also need to consider the socialising effect of formal school attendance and the role of protector-surrogate parent that many schools represent for a large group of children.

From our examination of the three areas of human activity and employment `– the military, agriculture, and criminal employments – we can identify amongst many others a number of core skills and general education required for transitional and future employment success.

Applied skills for 21st-century AI-HI living and working

- Critical thinking: distinguishing lies from facts
- Creativity
- Collaboration
- Oral communication
- Written communication
- Information literacy
- Media literacy
- Technology literacy
- Flexibility
- Ethical sophistication and knowledge
- Efficacy and self-direction/motivation
- Leadership and the management of diversity
- Teamwork and collaboration
- Initiative: confidence and maturity of responsible actions
- Productivity
- Social interpersonal skills including gender expectations
- Physical and mental health including well-being

Learning to renew and learning to engage in a broader HI-AI community – old employment circumstance disappearing and new employment opportunities coming into existence – will be painful for many communities of work and working practices. There will be attempts to create bridges of working practice to ameliorate the worst outcomes of mass unemployment and recognition of the fact that considerably fewer jobs exist, as we presently understand the concept of employment is changing. With an overhaul of the employment concept will be a necessary and inevitable overhaul of the education system. AI will become a highly skilled and nuanced teacher-trainer. AI machines will learn the patterns of learners and intimately respond to the individual's mind to achieve planned learning goals.

Things will change

AI technology directed by HI is changing, and will continue to change, the world we live in. Some changes will be radical and unnerving, difficult to adjust to; other changes will appear to be gentler, as the familiar ways of doing things adjust to change. Some giants of our infrastructure will however demand serious change, for example, education. Education will never disappear. It will just be reinvented for the 21st century. The important player in the changing face of education will be who is defined and seen as being the "learner." The learner of the future will now be young people. Young people will increasingly be self-directing as to what and how they will learn. They can expect to share learning company with teachers, parents and carers, and the rest of their community. We will find ourselves learning new skills to address economic needs and new skills to manage the changing nature of the way we will need to use the time we will increasingly have to not work; but we will still have an income produced by AI-working/wealth-generating activity.

The place of learning will evolve beyond the classroom, as learning and skill theory can take place anywhere there is an internet connection. The practical skills will need to be taught, demonstrated, and mentored within venues where the school science room becomes the community learning laboratory, and the physical education area is a 24-hour function devoted to physical and mental well-being and skill development activity, rather than (as in many schools) an area that is cleared away for meals to be served midday. Similarly, the music room becomes the community recording studio. Classrooms and many school buildings will need to change their use to meet broader needs of communities as the factory model of education withers away, as it will have no relevant place in an AI-HI world. There will be no central learning venue and no reliance on teachers to teach everything. Distinctions between academic and skill learning for the sole purpose of earning a living and contributing to the functioning of an economy will cease. Learning will become leisure learning for many, and highly skilled learning will be provided for those with particular aptitudes and ambitions. These changes will happen, and the number of people in employment will fall rapidly as we move from the early impact of AI and HI learning from each other to enriching our human ability to creatively increase our learning intelligences and letting them blossom.

eLearning and connectivity will mean learning can be an opportunity available over 24 hours and happen anywhere. A fixed timetable mimicking the working day will be a historic function. Learning will become a self-pacing opportunity whereby when help is required, it will be increasingly available to the learner in a learner-centred diagnosed form. AI will work to enhance HI through the interrogation of large data sets indicating what will work to enhance an individual learner's success.

Learners will find their own speed without the restraints of mass teaching; in particular, the gifted, able student will be able to learn at a speed appropriate to their needs.

Learning that we now regard as both essential and basic to our individual and collective needs will disappear. For some, writing will remain an interesting activity; for others, perhaps the mass of people, writing will be an unnecessary skill as a machine can take the spoken word and convert the words into grammatically correct text for communication to others. Increasingly arithmetic and mathematics will simply not be necessary for many people to learn. Ask why? A machine can deal with all the number activities normally experienced in daily life. Manual functions such as data collection and interpretation (including statistical analysis as part of mathematical literacy) will become irrelevant in the near future.

Following what a learner wants to learn will define the help they need and the learning resources they need, with the teacher evolving into the creative mentor and guide. Learners will learn in ways appropriate to their preferences, and learning will use different devices appropriate to individual needs and skills. Personalised learning will recognise gender identities and exceptions. Every learner deserves the same opportunities in life, and unless we stop treating boys and girls differently this will never be possible.

As careers are adapting to the future freelance economy, students of today will adapt to project-based learning, and working can be taught as basics that every student can use in their further academic careers.

Like many jobs and professions, the role of the teacher will change as they become a part of the learning leisure society. They will, however, be and will remain an essential and vital societal resource.

We believe schools in their present form are a lost cause in society that is essentially educating for the 19th century when children now are thinking in the 21st century. It is not science fiction to envisage that some people alive today may in the future become what we would currently describe as a machine or cyborg. This will be true of many societies, even those with basic resources for teaching basic maths, science, and languages.

As connectivity accelerates, we will see unprecedented learning and creativity taking place. The issue for schools will be to reinvent their use to society, both as:

- Intellectual, socialising centres
- Buildings – the physical stock of school and colleges

Schools will fail increasingly, as they cannot in an age of connectivity keep up with being a sole source of educational development for young minds. They are no longer the well of wisdom. It follows that the socialising functions of schooling are also under a radical deconstruction as different political, religious, and secular beliefs are empowered by technology to have their say about the how and what of educating the young. The complexity of schools is that their function is plural rather than singular, in that childcare functions are confused with education basics needed for a functioning society as understood by policy makers.

Like Marx's view about capitalist production, schools, ultimately, may even bring about conditions in which they like capitalism can be done away with. To ignore the huge changes that AI and HI working together can present to us will reveal a desperate ideological repression of change that will be an increasingly severe exploitation of proletarians.

Asking the question "What do you want to be when you grow up?" is going to be increasingly more difficult to answer in a high-change, HI-AI global economy, as is the question of how and what we as a society should be teaching. Answering both questions is only going to get harder as many future forms of employment we would recognise as a "job" have not been invented yet. The number of existing "safe" professions will be eroded as AI becomes more able and abilities mature. In other words, an algorithm can manage a complex conversation with a human being (and of course another AI machine) without having higher skills of empathy and creativity which will be developed as AI becomes an increasingly able teacher-learner. We will need to reconsider the training of teachers, parents, all learners, and employers as to their new roles in an AI-HI society and a new world of vanishing jobs and raining educational needs, training, and adjustments for changing jobs and the new jobs we do not yet know will be available. The *World Economic Forum* has forecast that 133 million jobs globally could be created with the help of technological advances over the next decade, compared with 75 million that could be displaced. All the new jobs will require new teaching and training methods, new curriculums, and new learning environmental models. The need to develop new social and individual learning models (skills for today and future generations), the end of the classroom, and a flattening of provision through social media and self-directed learning is happening around us now. What part will you play in this new world of 360 learning? "Your future self is completely dependent on you" (Oettingen, Sevincer, 2018).

Enrichment

1 Artificial General Intelligence (AGI)

Imagine machines that could successfully perform any intellectual task a human being could carry out. What would life be like for human beings freed from making a living, without a need to earn money or fill their time with work rather than pleasure activities?

As AI develops into Artificial General Intelligence, whereby HI is superseded, what new intelligences do you expect human beings to develop as thinking is enhanced by AGI?

2 Forensic AI

A century ago, fingerprint evidence was becoming admissible in courts around the world – but it didn't happen overnight. The first UK criminal trial in which fingerprint evidence convicted a person took place in 1902.

Look back to "now" from 100 years in the future and ask/discuss what AI-driven evidence will be available to solve crimes and whose job will it be to collate/present/evaluate evidence when making a judgement about guilt or otherwise of people involved in criminal acts.

3 Work

Ask yourself and/or your students to study Figure 4.4.

- How many jobs and professions can be seen?
- Can different socio-economic groups be determined?
- What jobs can be seen that still exist, and what jobs can be seen that no longer exist?

FIGURE 4.4   Work (1852–1865), Ford Madox Brown

Source: Manchester Art Gallery/Bridgeman Images. https://en.wikipedia.org/wiki/Work_(painting)

- Why have some jobs remained in place for hundreds of years?
- What jobs will still be with us in 100 years, and what new jobs will come into existence?

With all questions and answers in mind create:

- An updated version of this picture. It would be interesting to create an updated painting.
- A picture reflecting the changes you or your group will consider to be in place in 50 years' time. What will be new? What will remain unchanged, and what will be absent or in decline? Will you use oil paint or a design software to produce your work of art?

Link pathways

What links Thomas Carlyle, Tim Berners-Lee, Henry Faulds, and Edwin Sutherland?

References

Brown, Ford Maddox: WORK, 1852–1865. https://en.wikipedia.org/wiki/Work_ (painting).

https://elearningindustry.com/9-things-shape-future-of-education-learning-20-years.

Carlyle, Thomas. 1843. *Past and Present*. Newton Stewart, Dumfries & Galloway, UK: Ancient Books. ISBN: 978-1-544-98446-9.

Holt, J. 1977. *How Children Learn*. Victoria, Australia: Pelican. ISBN: 0-1402-1133-0.

Oettingen, G., Sevincer, A. T. 2018. Fantasy about the future as friend and foe. In G. Oettingen, A. T. Sevincer, P. Gollwitzer (Eds.), *The Psychology of Thinking About the Future* (pp. 127–149). New York: The Guilford Press.

Szakolczai, A. 2017. Permanent (trickster) liminality: The reasons of the heart and of the mind. *Theory & Psychology* 27 (2): 231–248. doi:10.1177/095935431769409.

Recommended further reading

ABC Robotic revolution. 2015. *Is Your Job Going to Disappear?* www.abc.net.au/7.30/is-your-job-going-to-disappear-in-the-digital/6724638.

Air Combat. 2010. www.economist.com/science-and-technology/2020/11/15/fighter-aircraft-will-soon-get-ai-pilots?utm_campaign=the-economist-today&utm_medium=newsletter&utm_source=salesforce-marketing-cloud&utm_term=2020-11-16&utm_content=article-link-5&etear=nl_today_5.

Art, science or applied science (pedagogy). 2018. https://lepole.education/en/pedagogical-culture/27-history-of-pedagogy.html?start=1.

Could a robot due your job? 2017. www.abc.net.au/news/2017-08-08/could-a-robot-do-your-job-artificial-intelligence/8782174.

COVID-19 cybercrime. 2020. www.theguardian.com/technology/2020/nov/03/covid-related-cybercrime-drives-attacks-on-uk-to-record-number.

Crime in England and Wales: Year ending. 2020. June. www.ons.gov.uk/people-populationandcommunity/crimeandjustice/bulletins/crimeinenglandandwales/yearendingjune2020.

Criminal careers. 2020. www.encyclopedia.com/law/legal-and-political-magazines/criminal-careers.

Criminal gangs target NHS. 2019. www.theguardian.com/technology/2019/aug/07/robot-heal-thyself-scientists-develop-self-repairing-machines.

Deep Leaning. 2016. https://synapse.koreamed.org/upload/SynapseData/PDFData/1088HIR/hir-22-351.pdf.

Goodwin, Paul. 2020. *Statistics*. www.theguardian.com/commentisfree/2020/oct/31/think-statistically-truth-falsehood.

Home schooling beyond lockdown. 2020. www.theguardian.com/education/2020/sep/19/seeing-my-sons-development-was-incredible-the-parents-sticking-with-home-schooling-beyond-lockdown#comment-143868680.

History of Education. 2020. https://en.wikipedia.org/wiki/History_of_education

Learning in Ancient times. 2020. https://lepole.education/en/pedagogical-culture/22-history-of-education.html?start=1.

Major crimes in the United Kingdom. 2020. https://en.wikipedia.org/wiki/List_of_major_crimes_in_the_United_Kingdom.

Michael, F. 2020. *Shaughnessy Education Views*. www.educationviews.org/an-interview-with-john-senior-the-runaway-nose/.

Microsoft AI Skills in the UK Report. 2020. https://info.microsoft.com/DE-DIGTRNS-CNTNT-FY21-07Jul-24-AISkillsintheUKreport-AID-3013784-SRGCM3647_01Registration-ForminBody.html#:~:text=While%20digital%20transformation%20has%20been,urgent%20shift%20to%20remote%20working.&text=35%25%20of%20UK%20business%20leaders,in%20the%20next%20two%20years.

Military Application of Artificial Intelligence. 2020. www.marketsandmarkets.com/Market-Reports/artificial-intelligence-military-market-41793495.html?gclid=EAIaIQobChMI6cSei4SK7QIVl-N3Ch0JXAgVEAAYASAAEgLjKvD_BwE and https://apps.dtic.mil/sti/citations/AD1097313.

Multiple discovery. 2020. https://en.wikipedia.org/wiki/Multiple_discovery#:~:text=The%20concept%20of%20multiple%20discovery,by%20multiple%20scientists%20and%20inventors.

OECD Report 21st Century Skills. 2008. www.oecd.org/site/educeri21st/40756908.pdf.

Pasquate, Frank. 2020. *New Laws of Robotics: Defending Human Expertise in the Age of AI*, 344 pages. Cambridge, MA: Harvard University Press. ISBN: 978-0-674-97522.

Parents warned of fines for absences. 2020. www.theguardian.com/education/2020/aug/24/coronavirus-parents-in-england-could-be-fined-if-they-keep-children-off-school-says-minister.

Procter, Kate, Elgot, Jessica. 2020. Schools in England will have to provide remote learning if closed again. *The Guardian*, August, p. 244.

Rapid robot rollout. 2019. www.theguardian.com/technology/2019/jun/26/rapid-robot-rollout-risks-uk-workers-being-left-behind-reports-say.

Reinforcementlearning.https://deepmind.com/blog/article/deep-reinforcement-learning.

Sullivan, Christopher J., Piquero, Alex R. 2016. The criminal career concept: Past, present, and future. *Journal of Research in Crime and Delinquency*. https://journals.sagepub.com/doi/abs/10.1177/0022427815627313.

Rycroft-Smith, Lucy, Andre, Graham. 2020. *The Equal Classroom: Life Changing Thinking about Gender*, 304 pages. Abingdon, UK: Routledge. ISBN: 978-1-138-49102-1.

Walch, Kathleen. 2019. How AI is transforming agriculture. *Cognitive World AI*. www.forbes.com/sites/cognitiveworld/2019/07/05/how-ai-is-transforming-agriculture/?sh=226ccb5c4ad1.

5

INCLUDED, EXCLUDED, EXTRAORDINARY, EFFICACIOUS

Transitional and open curriculums

On 19 November 2020, the *Guardian* (a UK newspaper) reported that: "More than 870,000 children are not attending school" and "1 in 10 pupils are missing school over COVID-19." For several years now, New Zealand has recorded a steady and significant rise in children missing from schools by choice. While the COVID-19 pandemic may have been an influence on the accelerating number of children missing from schools, it is not the main driver of absenteeism. It is more an accelerant feature of the changing needs of learners. Absenteeism is a global issue and reflects the times we are living through. According to data from the UNESCO Institute for Statistics (UIS), about 258 million young learners were out of school for the school year ending in 2018. The total includes 59 million children of primary school age, 62 million children of lower secondary school age, and 138 million children of upper secondary school age. Globally, schools have been working on an unsustainable 19th-century model, whereas young people are freer now than ever to desire a 21st-century model of education as they lay the foundations for the 22nd century. The rise of the self-learning community is the withering away of mass education. The classroom is becoming a museum.

Absenteeism is a human community, a creative phenomenon intricately linked to the development of human and machine neural networks.

> Human creativity is more a matter of deviance, while machine creativity is more a matter of intelligence. The challenge is the co-operation of the human and machine neural networks on the highest levels of creativity. Co-operation could be achieved by the acceptance of diversity in the different ways people think and learn; it will be possible to act jointly with the machine's neural networks and to be able to become the creative being.
>
> *(Gyarmathy, Senior, 2018)*

DOI: 10.4324/9780429356346-6

Two questions being asked and answered by young and older learners are: 1) Which learning opportunities prove to be most successful for indicating a meaningful future? and 2) Where is the best environment to enjoy successful learning? An additional question might be: How do I develop my individual human intelligence (HI) growth with artificial intelligence (AI) and other humans? Different roads can be taken to increase both individual and collective intelligence.

Russ Juskalian, in his paper examining Germany's Ausbildung vocational programme, brings some interesting observations we can apply to the then, now, and future debate regarding education.

Addressing the complexities of higher unemployment, he writes:

> But unemployment goes up and lifetime earnings fall when workers get into their mid-40s. At that age, the outdated skills of someone with vocational training can make it harder to stay in the labor force. University graduates – who learned more generalized knowledge, analytical thinking, problem solving and organisation, the skills that experts predict will grow increasingly valuable in an AI-driven economy – adapt better.

Education priorities are always intricately linked to the economic and technological developments in all nations. Juskalian writes further:

> During a period of slow change, "training people to do one job, because they can expect to do the job for the rest of their life, is a useful thing." Krueger, an economist mentioned in Juskalian's paper is quoted as saying that in a rapidly evolving technological economy training workers to solve problems as opposed to fixating on one job might be a better alternative.
> *(Juskalian, 2018)*

Here we can see how closely in education the overwhelming function of the relationship between employment and education remains. What happens, however, when the need to consider employment activity for the many is transformed by technology to being a need to see the relationship reformed to become a relationship between education and meaningful leisure? As accepted work pathways disappear, how do we educate people for both individual and collective change management and increasing leisure? What will give meaning to workers who do not have work to define themselves by and who do not need to earn a living as the increased use of applied AI maintains and increases wealth?

The traditional curriculum (including assessment, testing, and accountability) serves a world in which a young person learns skills at 16 which are sufficient to sustain them as a basis for a lifetime of employment in a job that affords minimal change and therefore minimal training/development. This model has changed almost beyond recognition with training modifications extending retirement age further into the future from (for example) 60 years old to 70 years old as a retirement age. AI transforms a growing number of industries and commercial activities, which may tortuously extend employability without affording a fundamental change in the traditional curriculum.

The open curriculum, however, (including assessment, testing, and accountability) plus new ways for increasingly accurate feedback diagnostics is growing and redefining what it means to be a learner and how that learning will be applied.

We need spend any time on the traditional view of education; we are all familiar with the writing, reading, and arithmetic curriculum. We do need to spend some time reflecting on what type of learner is emerging, what type of learning situation is growing around us, and what this means for the transitional curriculum.

Will we find ways to develop and conjoin with new trends in education and AI's involvement? We should briefly consider how some open curriculums view their learners (included, excluded, extraordinary, efficacious, and invisible) and how they may develop the intelligence potential by the use of AI machines and robots.

The range of learners both in and out of our schools is widely accepted to be:

- Auditory and musical learners
- Visual and spatial learners
- Verbal learners
- Logical and mathematical learners
- Physical and kinaesthetic learners
- Social and interpersonal learners
- Solitary and intrapersonal learners

However, if we accept the idea that learners can move from one preferred learning style, creating a portfolio of learning styles appropriate to the learners' needs, we can encourage learning in a changed situation while also encouraging plasticity of thinking in a social context.

Applying Vygotsky's theory of learning – which asserts that learning is a social process in which the support of parents, caregivers, peers, and society play a fundamental responsive and flexible formative, underpinning influence – we should perhaps look at the possible social learner identities that we can identify, rather than solely reducing a learner to possessing a fixed mindset.

It is interesting to think of learners now, in the 21st-century transitional curriculum as:

- Included learners
- Excluded learners
- Extraordinary learners
- Efficacious learners
- Invisible learners
- Machine learning

Included learners

This learner is less a category of learner and more a complex or otherwise amalgam of all the normally accepted types of learner familiar to most teachers and
educationalists. The included learner is the learner who is biddable within state
and formulaic educational settings, receiving wisdom and obligingly regurgitat-
ing what they are presented with. In this setting we can think of learners not
learning how to be independent learners and certainly not having the skill set
for an emerging, still-being-realised world. Within a unrestructured traditional
curriculum, this type of learner is at a disadvantage as they are not being educated for now and tomorrow; they are being educated for the 19th century. What
is of interest here is not how the learning takes place as much as the fact that
learning does not take place for all learners when the teacher is generally prefer-
ring to teach in the way they best learn. In a class of 30–60 one size does not fit
all, and it is not surprising when some children fail to flower or prosper both at
exam time and in a complex future where constant change requires flexibility
and skills to manage change.

Excluded learners

The excluded learner is an interesting category. By choice or design or situation,
the excluded learner is excluded from mainstream education. Often the experience for the excluded learner is one whereby they are educationally exhorted to
reach a standard at which they can participate in included learning situations.
Pause for a minute to reflect on why an excluded learner may find themselves
excluded from the mainstream. Of course, one reason would be the need for
extremely specialised teaching for young learners who face particular learning
challenges and need specialist environments to learn in, highly trained teachers
to enable and encourage learning, and upon occasion supportive counselling and
mental health support. However, their educational prosperity will always be very
largely dependent on technology and individualised wrap-around teaching.

Extraordinary learners

The extraordinary learner is just that: exceptionally gifted, very able, and creative. Often more able and intelligent than their teachers, lecturers, and upon
occasion their professors. Often neglected, usually citing the excluded learner's
needs for additional help, the extraordinary learner cannot always manage on
their own. We as educators know the reality is that all learners need different
pathways to learn, and the extraordinary learner is largely establishing new and
exciting pathways based on the little we give them in schools.

> Later when I asked (Lisa's) mother how often Lisa (pre-kindergarten) asked
> what a word was. She thought for a bit, and said, Not very often. Maybe

once or twice a week, at most Then as an afterthought, It's interesting, though; when she asks a word, she never forgets it. Interesting, but not surprising; the things we learn because, for our own reasons, we really need to know them, we don't forget. But if she only asked other people for words once, or even a few times a week, this would only account for at most perhaps two hundred of the fifteen hundred or more words that she knew. Where had she learnt the others? Clearly, she had figured them out for herself.

(Holt, 1970)

Efficacious learners

The efficacious learner is successful in achieving a desired ambition or intended result. They are effective, tenacious learners. These learners need little encouragement to apply and excite their mind and thinking. Combine the extraordinary learner and the efficacious learner profile, and whatever challenges they find – physical, mental, geographical, or economic – they will overcome them and be successful in terms that have value for them despite a restricted formal curriculum setting. These learners value rewards that may well not be economic.

Invisible learners

By definition, the invisible learner cannot easily be addressed; they can only be surmised. As of September 2020, the reported data for 2018/2019 shows that 75,918 children were recorded missing by UK police forces. However, there were 218,707 incidents of missing children in 2018/2019, as some children go missing multiple times in the same year.

At the very worst we have missing children who are being criminally trafficked and in fear and to all our shame exploited.

> One Albanian teenager, now 19 but who was trafficked into the UK aged 15, said he was struggling to survive with no support and just £45 a week to live on.
>
> He said: "Friends of mine have disappeared – they live underground. The people who get you to work know you are illegal, and they tell you after you have worked for the day to go or they will call the Home Office and get you sent back to Albania. The only other option is to sell drugs. I don't want that life."

There will also be invisible learners who are not engaged in criminality. They and their parents/carers will have withdrawn from society and be offering an invisible curriculum. The question of the nature and ambitions of the invisible curriculum are fascinating to think about. What would you include in their curriculum as "essential"?

Machine learners

Machine learning is a genuinely exciting concept, as is the existence of the "self-repairing machine."

Machine learning is the study of computer algorithms that improve automatically through experience. It is seen as a subset of AI. Machine learning involves computers discovering how they can perform tasks without being explicitly programmed to do so. In cases where vast numbers of potential answers exist, one approach is to label some of the correct answers as valid. This can then be used as training data for the computer to improve the algorithm(s) it uses to determine correct answers for simple tasks assigned to computers. It is possible to program algorithms telling the machine how to execute all steps required to solve the problem at hand; on the computer's part, no learning is needed. For more advanced tasks, it can be challenging for a human to manually create the needed algorithms. In practice, it can turn out to be more effective to help the machine develop its own algorithm, rather than having human programmers specify every needed step.

The discipline of machine learning employs various approaches to teach computers to accomplish tasks where no fully satisfactory algorithm is available.

Machine learning approaches are divided into three broad categories, depending on the nature of the "signal" or "feedback" available to the learning system:

- Supervised learning: the computer is presented with example inputs and their desired outputs, given by a "teacher," and the goal is to learn a general rule that maps inputs to outputs.
- Unsupervised learning: no labels are given to the learning algorithm, leaving it on its own to find structure in its input; unsupervised learning can be a goal in itself (discovering hidden patterns in data) or a means towards an end (feature learning)
- Reinforcement learning: a computer program interacts with a dynamic environment in which it must perform a certain goal (such as driving a vehicle or playing a game against an opponent); as it navigates its problem space, the program is provided feedback that's analogous to rewards, which it tries to maximise

Other approaches have been developed which don't fit neatly into this three-fold categorisation, and sometimes more than one is used by the same machine learning system.

As of 2020, deep learning has become the dominant approach for much ongoing work in the field of machine learning. Other significant developments are:

Unsupervised learning

Unsupervised learning is an approach to AI where algorithms learn from data without human guidance. The future development in AI will not be supervised by human interventions. Unsupervised learning more closely mirrors the way that humans learn about the world: through open-ended exploration and inference, where what is understood is predicated upon what is inferred. The system learns about some parts of the world based on other parts of the world, rather as a new-born baby learns. Achieving unsupervised learning is the development challenge ambition in machine learning and AI.

Federated learning

Federated learning may one day play a central role in the development of any AI application that involves sensitive data: from financial services to autonomous vehicles, from government-use cases to consumer products of all kinds. Paired with other privacy-preserving techniques like differential privacy and homomorphic encryption, federated learning may provide the key to unlocking AI's vast potential while mitigating the ethical considerations regarding individual data privacy.

Transformers

The key technology breakthrough underlying this revolution in language AI is the transformer. Transformers' great innovation is to make language processing parallelised: all the tokens in a given body of text are analysed at the same time rather than in sequence. In order to support this parallelization, transformers rely heavily on an AI mechanism known as attention. Attention enables a model to consider the relationships between words regardless of how far apart they are and to determine which words and phrases in a passage are most important to "pay attention to."

> If a curriculum is not adaptive, it becomes rigid. There is no such thing as a perfect curriculum that does not need updating, because the world continues to change and the goals of an optimal curriculum changes with it. Depending on the subject, the change can happen at different rates. For example, relevant programming language changes every two years, but ancient philosophy remains much more constant. This does not mean that the curriculum should fall victim to fads, but rather that there should be built-in mechanisms for keeping the curriculum up to date with modern findings and new breakthroughs.
>
> *(Fadel, Bialik, Trilling, 2015)*

The "modern findings and new breakthroughs" Fadel writes about are in fact the individual human members of a learning society working as a collective, interconnected influencer group and AI in the learning machine mode. Both groups are relentless learners who in fact share a great deal as they explore and expand human-machine intelligence. Both groups, as they conjoin in a variety of ways, will set the learning agenda which will increase intelligence.

While schools continue working to a traditional model of education, our new learners will be working to what can be described as an orthodox alternative mix of education beliefs and methodologies creating a transitional curriculum. Let's look at some examples of the how and what of significant alternative models of social/democratic "schoolings" where it is the learner who has a significant influence in what they learn, when, how, and where they learn it.

Outlier alternatives to state directed models of education can offer a guide to how the open curriculum working with AI and HI will be formed.

Summerhill School

Summerhill School is an independent boarding school in Suffolk, UK. It was founded in 1921 by A S Neill, who believed that a school should be made to fit the child, rather than the other way around. Members of the community are free to do as they please, so long as their actions do not cause any harm to others, according to Neill's principle "Freedom, not Licence." This extends to the freedom for pupils to choose which lessons, if any, they attend. Summerhill is noted for its philosophy that children learn best with freedom from coercion. At Summerhill, all lessons are optional, and pupils are free to choose what to do with their time. Neill founded Summerhill with the belief that "the function of a child is to live his own life – not the life that his anxious parents think he should live, not a life according to the purpose of an educator who thinks he knows best."

Célestin Freinet

Freinet was born in Provence, France. He was an extraordinary man. His early life was to say the least challenging and would form his approach to teaching methods. After his war service (he was severely injured), he became a village school-teacher where he began to explore ideas and methods of teaching. With his own printing press, he printed free texts and newspapers for his students. His was a generous contribution to the development of a compassionate approach towards the education of children (Célestin Freinet).

> "It is a new range of academic values that we would like to work here to establish, with no bias other than our preoccupation for the search for truth, in the light of experience and common sense. On the basis of these principles, which we shall regard as invariable and therefore unassailable and sure, we would like to achieve a kind of pedagogical code."

- Pedagogy of work: pupils were encouraged to learn by making products or providing services
- Enquiry-based learning: group-based trial and error work

- Co-operative learning: pupils co-operate in the production process
- Centres of interest: the children's interests and natural curiosity are starting points for a learning process
- The natural method: authentic learning by using real experiences of children
- Democracy: children learn to take responsibility for their own work and for the whole community by using democratic self-government

The Pedagogical Code has several coloured lights to help educators judge their psychological and pedagogical situation as teachers: The constants cited below are only a small selection underpinning the pedagogical work of Celestin Freinet.

> The child is of the same nature as us adults.
> A child's academic behaviour is a function of his constitution, health, and physiological state.
> No one likes to be forced to do a certain job, even if this work does not displease him or her particularly. It is being forced that is paralyzing.
> The normal path of [knowledge] acquisition is not observation, explanation and demonstration, the essential process of the School, but experimental trial and error, a natural and universal process.
> Punishments are always a mistake. They are humiliating for all and never achieve the desired goal. They are at best a last resort.
> There is also a constant that justifies all our trial and error and authenticates our action: it is the optimistic hope in life.

- Green light: for practices conforming to these constants, in which educators can engage without apprehension because they are assured of a comforting success
- Red light: for practices not conforming to these constants and which must therefore be proscribed as soon as possible
- Orange and blinking light: for practices that in certain circumstances may be beneficial but which are likely to be dangerous and towards which one must advance only cautiously in the hope of soon moving past them

Key elements of the pedagogical work of Célestin Freinet:

1. The child is of the same nature as adults
2. A child's academic behaviour is a function of his or her constitution, health, and physiological state
3. No one – neither the child nor the adult – likes to be commanded by authority
4. No one likes to move mindlessly, to act like a robot, that is to do acts or to bend to thoughts that are prescribed in mechanisms in which he does not participate

5 We [the teachers] need to motivate the work
6 The normal path of [knowledge] acquisition is not observation, explanation, and demonstration, the essential process of the school, but experimental trial and error, a natural and universal process
7 Intelligence is not, as scholasticism teaches, a specific faculty functioning as a closed circuit, independent of the other vital elements of the individual
8 The school only cultivates an abstract form of intelligence, which operates outside living reality, by means of words and ideas implanted by memorization
9 The child does not like the work of a herd to which the individual has to fold like a robot; he loves individual work or teamwork in a co-operative community
10 The new life of the school presupposes school co-operation, that is, the management by its users, including the educator, of life and schoolwork
11 The democracy of tomorrow is being prepared by democracy at the school; an authoritarian regime at the school cannot be formative of democratic citizens
12 One can only educate in dignity; respecting children, who must respect their teachers, is one of the first conditions for the redemption of the school
13 There is also a constant that justifies all our trial and error and authenticates our action: it is the optimistic hope in life

Montessori education

Maria Montessori was an Italian physician and educator best known for the approach to education that is known by her name: the Montessori method. While Montessori schools are most common for younger children, Montessori middle schools and high schools exist as well. Montessori focuses on educating the whole child, including physical, spiritual, social, mental, and emotional education. This means that you might find a Montessori 3-year-old carefully walking on a line while carrying a glass of water, learning to control his or her body and movements. You might find a child meditating or doing yoga while you see another practicing subtraction nearby. Each of these components is considered equally important. Maria Montessori lived during a time of world wars and global upheaval. She placed great emphasis on peace education.

Her method contains five basic principles, which are shown in the following subsections.

Respect for the child

Respect for the child is the major principle underlying the entire Montessori method. Montessori believed children should be respected. Respect is shown for children by not interrupting their concentration. Respect is also shown by giving students the freedom to make choices, to do things for themselves, and to learn for themselves. Teachers model respect for all students as well as peaceful conflict resolution and must learn to observe without judgement.

The absorbent mind

Montessori education is based on the principle that, simply by living, children are constantly learning from the world around them. Through their senses, children constantly absorb information from their world. They then make sense of it because they are thinking beings.

Sensitive periods

Montessori pedagogy believes there are certain periods during which children are more ready to learn certain skills. These are known as sensitive periods, and they last only as long as is necessary for the child to acquire the skills. The order in which sensitive periods occur (i.e., a sensitive period for writing) as well as the timing of the period varies for each child.

Through observation

Montessori teachers must identify sensitive periods in their students and provide the resources for children to flourish during this time. All authentic Montessori schools have long, uninterrupted work periods (generally 2–3 hours depending on age). Rather than having 30 minutes for math and then 30 minutes for language, children have a long morning and afternoon work period in one classroom that includes all of the subjects. This long time period allows children to engage with the materials deeply and reach intense concentration.

The prepared environment

The Montessori method suggests that children learn best in an environment that has been prepared to enable them to do things for themselves. Always child-centred, the learning environment should promote freedom for children to explore materials of their choice.

Teachers should prepare the learning environment by making materials and experiences available to children in an orderly and independent way. Children in Montessori schools learn by working with specially designed materials. Rather than memorizing data, they begin by counting and adding concrete materials. They use little objects and a set of wooden letters known as the *movable alphabet* to learn to read and write. Maria Montessori observed that children need to move and learn through experiences, rather than through sitting and listening to a teacher.

Auto education

Auto education, or self-education, is the concept that children are capable of educating themselves. This is one of the most important beliefs in the Montessori method. Montessori teachers provide the environment, the inspiration, the guidance, and the encouragement for children to educate themselves. Montessori classrooms include mixed ages and mixed skill-levels, generally divided into three-year groups. Peer learning is encouraged as the little ones learn from observing their older friends, and the older children solidify their knowledge and gain valuable leadership skills through giving lessons to the younger children. If a Montessori class has 25 different students, each of those 25 will be at a different academic level that is observed and tracked by the teacher. Rather than giving group lessons, Montessori teachers give one-on-one lessons to each student depending on his or her specific level and needs.

In addition to math, language, and science, Montessori schools include two other academic areas: practical life and sensorial.

Practical life consists of exercises to help children learn everyday life skills. For young children, this includes carefully pouring water, tying their shoes, and scrubbing a table. For older children, this may include things like budgeting and starting a small business.

Sensorial is the education of the senses, and it is most prevalent in classrooms for young children. Montessori believed that children learn through their senses, and there are materials specifically designed to help them refine their senses.

Reggio Emilia

The Reggio Emilia philosophy is based upon a learner-centred set of principles that exclaim the view that each child is seen as beautiful, powerful, competent, creative, curious, and full of potential and ambitious desires. The child is viewed as being an active learner, a constructor of knowledge. Rather than being seen as the target of instruction, children are seen as having the active role of an apprentice.

- The young learner must have control over the direction of their learning and learn through their sensory faculties through listening, observing, and moving
- The young learner has a relationship with the world they are exploring, both relationships with other people and with material objects

- The young learner should have their curiosity developed through expressing themselves
- Children have rights and should be given opportunities to develop their potential

Much of the instruction at Reggio Emilia schools takes place in the form of projects where they have opportunities to explore, observe, hypothesise, question, and discuss to clarify their understanding. Children are also viewed as social beings, and a focus is made on the child in relation to other children, the family, the teachers, and the community rather than on each child in isolation. They are taught that respect for everyone else is important because everyone is a "subjective agency" while existing as part of a group.

Reggio Emilia's approach does challenge some conceptions of teacher competence and developmentally appropriate practice. A major teaching strategy is purposely to allow mistakes to happen or to begin a project with no clear sense of where it might end. Another characteristic that is counter to the beliefs of many Western educators is the importance of the child's ability to negotiate in the peer group.

One of the most challenging aspects of the Reggio Emilia approach is the solicitation of multiple points of view regarding children's needs, interests, and abilities, and the concurrent faith in parents, teachers, and children to contribute in meaningful ways to the determination of school experiences. Teachers trust themselves to respond appropriately to children's ideas and interests, they trust children to be interested in things worth knowing about, and they trust parents to be informed and productive members of a co-operative educational team. The result is an atmosphere of community and collaboration that is developmentally appropriate for adults and children alike. Parents are a vital component to the Reggio Emilia philosophy; they are viewed as partners, collaborators, and advocates for their children.

Personalised learning experiences

The future of education will see the teacher and new forms of educational provision remaining at the core of our human development. AI in many forms will of course improve supporting differentiation, assessment models, and subtler nuanced forms of promoting personalised learning experiences. Teaching and learning mentors will be central to the development of educational competence and success for learners in the future. The future however is going to be turbulent; both learner and teacher will need to be willing and able to cope with rapid change and new forms of extreme connectivity.

Learners will need to acclimate to a learning environment of a hyperconnected world requiring tolerance for other cultures and an ability to act and behave in a creative solution-seeking manner.

TABLE 5.1 Connected people

Topics and themes	Knowledge areas (Traditional and modern)	Learning outcomes
Social skills Emotional intelligence	Psychology Sociology Anthropology Political science World history Civics and global citizenship Comparative religions World music and theatre	Understanding the thoughts, feelings, perspectives, and motivation of others Collaboration and teamwork both virtually and viscerally across numerous cultural differences
Global literacy	Cultural studies (geography, global history, ethnography, music) Media/Journalism Foreign languages and linguistics International business and economics	Global perspectives: understanding global events, cultural practices, and behaviours in a variety of cultures
Systems thinking	Maths (complex systems) Integrated disciplines (i.e., robotics, biosystems, business) Environmental and ecological studies Future studies	Interconnectedness Causality Ecological forecasting

Source: CCR

We are, with relation to AI and HI, experiencing the learning situation of a to-be-born and born child. No guidebook or curriculum exists to assist a new-born human being as to how to use their eyes, ears, senses, and tactile information in developing and growing a mind. As a new-born baby enters the world, so we will enter a new world of AI and HI growth. Many words have and will be written about the dangers of conjoining with AI, expressing fears about "killer robots," machines "stealing jobs," and the end of human life. For schools, the reality will be the creation of safer learning environments with on-line learning, reducing the need for children to perform in judgemental situations – learning comes first. The machine and the human teachers will be able to introduce learning and respond very particularly to the needs of the learner.

A reasonable observation after a few moments' reflection is that these worst-case scenarios speak of humanity's fears about the present rather than an informed understanding of possible futures. Many people fear change, but change is a hallmark of our present global experience, and to succeed we need to develop our infant understanding of the implications of AI for humanity and for the development of our intelligences. Just as you and I had to work out how to see and hear and think, we advanced beyond the basics to a more sophisticated view of the human experience because of teachers, mentors, and mindful communicators.

Learning shifts are increasingly redefining what it means to be intelligent. The future focus of learning will be on developing both a mastery of technology and, importantly, the expansion of the human learner's ability to be creative, curious, and conscientiously tenacious. The learner's key task will be one of synthesising a complex world in which "learning" is applied as breathing is to keep us alive and functioning.

The changing nature of learning, as briefly represented in Tables 5.1 and 5.2 is the huge task we must collectively undertake as to how we learn to learn with AI as the better part of our intelligent existence.

Increasingly we will move towards listening to and acting upon the needs of learners. What do they need to learn? What do they want to learn? When and where do they want learning to take place? On a distant horizon when AI and HI methodologies and protocols reach a level of excellent competence, the division between "learning," "work," and "leisure" will cease to exist. Learners increasingly will have more opportunities to learn at different times in different places. eLearning tools will facilitate opportunities for remote, self-directed learning. The concept of the classrooms will change, as the theatre of learning becomes more varied and fluid. Congregating learners will still be an essential part of many aspects of learning, but this will not be a standard provision, as AI and HI can grow in many different ways.

Students will learn with study tools and styles that adapt to the capabilities of a student. This means above-average students will be challenged with harder tasks and questions when a certain level is achieved. Students who experience difficulties with a subject will get the opportunity to practice more until they reach the required level. Students will be positively reinforced during their individual learning processes. This can result in positive learning experiences and will diminish the number of students losing confidence about their academic abilities. Learners will become more and more involved in forming contemporary relevant curricula and learning journeys. A responsive curriculum will emerge that is relevant and rewarding whether the learning and teaching concerns how to maximise the football fan experience or an advanced professional understanding of how to construct a cold-fusion power generator or prosthetic brain.

The seeds of a new curriculum

A summary

We can learn from our brief glimpse of pioneering educators who saw the need to educate a learner to learn in a social way that benefits the individual and the community of which that individual is a part.

TABLE 5.2 Learning summary

Intelligence is not, as scholasticism teaches, a specific faculty functioning as a closed circuit, independent of the other vital elements of the individual.	Learners are also viewed as social beings, and a focus is made on the learner in relation to other learners, the family, the teachers, and the community rather than on each learner in isolation.	Respect is shown for learners by not interrupting their concentration. Respect is also shown by giving learners the freedom to make choices, to do things for themselves, and to learn for themselves.
As careers are adapting to the future, freelance, technologically driven economy, learners will find themselves adapting to project-based learning and working.	As the factual knowledge of a learner can be measured during their learning process, the application of their knowledge is best tested when they work on projects in the field.	A school should be made to fit the learner.
Lessons are optional, and learners are free to choose what to do with their time.	Ethical philosophical moral education will need to be central to the 21st/22nd-century core curriculum.	There is also a constant that justifies all our trial and error and authenticates our action: it is the optimistic hope in life.
Learners will be able to create their learning process with the skills and tools they feel are the best fit at a particular time for their particular learning focus.	The normal path of [knowledge] acquisition is not observation, explanation, and demonstration (the essential process of the school), but experimental trial and error, a natural and universal process.	The young learner must have control over the direction of their learning and learn through their sensory faculties by listening, observing, and moving.
Montessori teachers provide the environment, the inspiration, the guidance, and the encouragement for learners to educate themselves.	Teachers trust themselves to respond appropriately to learners' ideas and interests, they trust learners to be interested in things worth knowing about, and they trust parents to be informed and productive members of a co-operative educational team.	The human interpretation of data will become a much more important part of the future curricula.
The young learner should have their curiosity developed through expressing themselves.	Though mathematics is considered one of three literacies, without a doubt the manual part	

(Continued)

TABLE 5.2 (Continued)

	of this literacy will become irrelevant in the near future. Computers will soon take care of every statistical analysis, describe and analyse data, and predict future trends. Applying the theoretical knowledge to numbers and using human reasoning to infer logic and trends from these data will become a fundamental new aspect of this literacy.	Montessori education is based on the principle that, simply by living, learners are constantly learning from the world around them. Through their senses, learners constantly absorb information from their world. They then make sense of it because they are thinking beings.
Learners will learn with different devices and software based on their own preference.	Because technology can facilitate more efficiency in certain domains, curricula will make room for skills that solely require human knowledge and face-to-face interaction.	Project-based learning in high school is when organizational, collaborative, and time-management skills can be taught as basics that every learner can use in their living careers.

As Rosemary Luckin observed, "No one promised that learning would be easy. But it will take us to new places." We are living through a time of enormous and fundamental global change.

At the heart of the changes churning our world is the question of how we learn to be more intelligent as we enjoin with the most significant learning tool we have ever created, where mind and machine move to a new paradigm of being.

> Advances in prosthetic genetic and pharmacological supports and human enhancement are redefining human capabilities while blurring the lines between disabilities and super-abilities. At the same time, increasing innovation in virtual reality may lead to changes in self-perception and sense of agency in the world.
>
> (Fadel, Bialik, Trilling, 2015)

The whole picture, influence, and character of the changes we are living through needs to be separated out as strands of knowledge and ignorance entwine, weave, or knot and then are remade as we prepare for advances in both intelligence and what Schleicher describes as "amplified humans." We need to develop an amplified open curriculum if we want to grow our intelligence as a relevant partner and not as a sub-set of artificial intelligence.

TABLE 5.3 Smart machines topics and themes

Topics and themes	Knowledge areas (Traditional and modern)	Learning outcomes
Digital literacy	Computer science Programming Engineering Robotics Synthetic biology Maker/DIY skills (i.e., 3D printing, laser cutting)	Computational thinking (logic, recursiveness) Data collection and analysis
Design thinking	Customer surveying Design and prototyping Project management Entrepreneurship	Critical and creative thinking Conscientiousness in carrying out all aspects of complicated projects
Synthesis and integration	Writing (literature, journalism, technical writing) Research	Ability to define projects, develop plans, carry out complicated processes, evaluate results, and present findings with precision and clarity
Ethical mindset	Philosophy (Ethics)	Ethical behaviour Self-reflection

Source: CCR

Enrichment

The invisible curriculum

As an exercise, consider the "invisible curriculum." What do you think this will contain? Two main areas of learning will be taking place: criminal training and development, and alternative community values. Choose one of (or both) these curriculums, and map out what you think it would encompass. Then, when you have finished your mapping exercise, consider the actual value of such an education to the society we are living in. What could we learn about learners' needs for the 21st/22nd centuries?

You may also wish to reflect on what you may have unintentionally learned today or, even more interesting, what you unintentionally taught someone today.

Link pathways

What links a "prepared learning environment;" the 21st century; and advances in prosthetic, genetic, and pharmacological supports and human enhancement?

References

CCR: Table 5.1. *Connected People*. 2012. Source CCR.

CCR: Table 5.3. *Smart Machines Topics and Themes*. 2012. Source CCR.

Fadel, Charles, Bialik, Maya, Trilling, Bernie. 2015. *Four-Dimensional Education* (p. 177). Boston, MA: Centre for Curriculum Redesign. ISBN-13: 978-1-518-64256-2.

Célestin Freinet. https://en.wikipedia.org/wiki/C%C3%A9lestin_Freinet.

Gyarmathy, Eva, Senior, John. 2018. *The SAGE Handbook of Gifted and Talented Education*. Thousand Oaks, CA: Sage Publications. ISBN: 0-1402-1133-0.

Holt. John. 1970. *How Children Learn* (p. 173). Australia: Pelican Books. ISBN: 0-1402-1133-0.

Juskalian, Russ. 2018. *Rebuilding Germany's Centuries-Old Vocational Program*. Cambridge, MA: MIT Technology Review. https://www.technologyreview.com/

Suggested further reading

Andreas. 2015. *Four-Dimensional Education* (p. 177). Boston, MA: The Centre for Curriculum Redesign. ISBN: 978-1-518-64256-2.

Berliner, Wendy, Judd, Judith. 2020. *How to Succeed at School*, 183 pages. Abingdon, UK: Routledge. ISBN: 978-0-367-18645-6.

Carlyle, Thomas. 2019. *Past and Present* (p. 114). Newton Stewart, Dumfries & Galloway, UK: Anodos Books. ISBN: 9781544984469. (Originally published 1843).

Hasse, Catherine. 2020. *Posthumanist Learning* (p. 349). Abingdon, UK: Routledge. ISBN: 978-1-138-12517-9.

Clark Amanda. 2019. *What Are Some Alternative Forms of Education?* www.classcraft.com/blog/features/alternative-forms-of-education/.

Clemer Christina. 2020. *What Is Montessori? 10 Key Principles All Parents Should Know*. A school meant to appeal to children's nature, rather than fight it. www.mother.ly/child/what-is-montessori-10-basic-principles-you-need-to-know.

Emilia, Reggio. 2020. https://en.wikipedia.org/wiki/Reggio_Emilia_approach.

Frydenberg, Erica, Deans, Janice, Liang, Rachel. 2020. *Promoting Well-Being in the Pre-School Years* (p. 177). Abingdon, UK: Routledge. ISNB: 978-0-367-02862-6.

Henny, Christiaan. 2018. https://elearningindustry.com/9-things-shape-future-of-education-learning-20-years.

Luckin, Rosemary (Ed.). 2018. *Enhancing Learning and Teaching with Technology: What the Research Says* (p. 334). London: UCL Institute of Education Press, University College. ISBN: 978-1-78277-226-2.

Macfarlane, Bruce. 2017. *Freedom to Learn* (p. 139). Abingdon, UK: Routledge. ISBN: 978-0-415-72916-1.

Machine Learning. 2020. https://en.wikipedia.org/wiki/Machine_learning.

Myburgh, Susan, Tammaro, Anna Maria. 2013. *Pedagogies and Teaching Methods in Exploring Education for Digital Librarians*. www.sciencedirect.com/topics/psychology/vygotskys-theory.

OECD. 2020. *Trends Shaping Education Spotlight 21*. www.oecd.org/coronavirus.

Out of school children: UIS. 2019. http://uis.unesco.org/en/topic/out-school-children-and-youth.

Rasmussen. 2019. *Different Types of Learners: What College Students Should Know*. www.rasmussen.edu/student-experience/college-life/most-common-types-of-learners/.

Summerhill. 2020. https://en.wikipedia.org/wiki/Summerhill_School#Notable_former_pupils.

Toews, Rob. 2020. The next generation of artificial intelligence. *Forbes On-line Magazine*.

Townsend, Mark. 2020. *Number of Missing Vulnerable Children Soars as Safeguarding Is Cut During Pandemic*. www.theguardian.com/society/2020/jun/06/alarming-rise-in-cases-of-missing-children-following-safeguarding-cuts.

UIS. 2020. http://uis.unesco.org/en/about-us.

Unintentional Learning. 2020. www.edutopia.org/blog/3-types-unintentional-learning-to-make-intentional-ben-johnson.

Tibke, Jon. 2019. *Why the Brain Matters* (p. 216). Thousand Oaks, CA: Corwin. ISBN: 978-1-4739-9290-0.

Suggested viewing

School for Scoundrels. (1960). https://en.wikipedia.org/wiki/School_for_Scoundrels_(1960_film).

6

ACCEPTING CHANGE

A brief history of the future

We are sentient, dynamic beings capable of change: but we can be trapped not only in the learned sense of what we are not, but also in a powerful negative mirror image of ourselves that we perceive emanating from others. Yet, we can be released through enabling interactions with those special mentors who offer constant and strong scaffolding that we are, indeed, of great worth and significance as individuals with potential.

(Wallace, 2008)

There are reportedly 93 million selfies uploaded to Instagram every day.
(BBC, 2019)

In the future, everyone will be world-famous for 15 minutes.
(Warhol, 1968)

The psychology of seeing and inventing the future

The future is a strange concept. All of us, every individual has a past as real as can be evidenced. Thoughts, memories, and memory enhancers – pictures, recordings, letters, emails, and other artifacts – point to the past having happened. However, no one sees the same past as another even when they may have attended an event or experience such as a wedding or special anniversary or political protest. There are as many pasts as there are people alive, who in turn have internalised other memories as a part of what an individual can recall. But the future has no consolidating view either, and like the ephemeral past the evidence points to what might be based on what is our understanding of how the past evidences itself. Now, however, our memories are going to become very distant and dark as a globally linked pandemic change of the most fundamental kind is upon us. COVID-19 and AI are new experiences which require us to

DOI: 10.4324/9780429356346-7

adjust our view of the future. What they may bring and how we make it as we would wish remains to be imagined.

How do we invent the future?

The future, like the past, is not a frozen film. Both are continually moving targets for subjective interpretation – that is, the future is perceived relative to where we stand in the present.

Whether or not we care about the future largely depends on how we view ourselves in a possible future – which, in turn, leads us to focus on what it means to a person that they exist over time or cease to exist. How you see the future depends on how you see yourself as connected with others or not.

The viewpoint of a future self as another self suggests that the future self will have different needs and life requirements. To effectively manage change, however, within a changing world would suggest a belief in the continuous self being one that changes and develops both as an individual and in a community of selves constantly seeking redefinition and improvement. With this view, providing for and positively working for a successful future is central to what it is to be a self – in a community that changes and holds true to clear ethical and moral beliefs about how the world present and future should treat the self.

With a sense of the self travelling to a future as the other side of a temporal divide (e.g., a birthday, significant externally validated event such as graduation or a collective experience affecting the whole human community such as New Year's Day), the self is motivated to make changes more likely to achieve a better future self. To hold this viewpoint requires a series of creative acts in which possible futures are explored or imagined. Seeing the future self as continuous in being a community self expands the sense of community responsibility, which is not just a matter, for example, of having health insurance for some when it should be for all. Being connected to the future requires courage, as does the acceptance of constant change being acceptable in the everyday lives of selves locating and rooting themselves in their existence.

To a degree it is axiomatic that the future is what we make of it or at least what we imagine we will make it. Certainly, our actions have consequences.

Let us imagine the future:

- In the story of our journey, how did we and how do we manage change?
- How will learning about the future of evolutionary change management, as a must have a set of skills such as literacy and numeracy become regarded as an essential pedagogic activity?
- Will robots be able to perceive the world as meaningful in the way humans do, or will it be the conjoining of human intelligence with machine intelligence that provides for an evolutionary event with regard to developing intelligence?

The future is the time after the present. I started this sentence in the past. I imagine you the reader in the future. As you read this, I am in the past writing; you are in the present, reading. It is held to be the case that the future (in what form is the question) is inevitable due to the recognition of time and the laws of physics. Predictability and probability are key components in any discussion or reflection upon anticipating and predicting actual futures.

The impact of AI on the past/present and our sense of what it means to be intelligent is of such enormity that it offers the educator and learner a difficult challenge in simply quantifying possibilities as well as in preparing for the enormous change management we all will be and are involved with.

We have explored, in this book, both the technological changes AI is bringing and will increasingly bring to our sense of what it means to be intelligent and how we can increase our intelligence with AI and a revision of how we learn. The management of change is a creative act.

We will have to unlock our conscious and unconscious stories to embrace conjoining our intelligence with machines. A process of acceptance is the only language and range of stories through which we can begin to understand how we can be a machine/human. It will take time, and very few people will be able or want to adopt the changing future – first will be the unseen, unusually fluid minds; then the young (below 20 years old) who think what is happening is normal and have the brain plasticity to swim in an exciting river of change. As humans age, their ability to avoid "hardwired" thoughts is reduced as is their ability to manage and embrace change. For this reason, it is important to link early years education once again with later years thinking plasticity. This consideration is a pre-description with regard to AI. We tell the story of the AI robot acting in ways that are not in our interest while forgetting that we invented AI and will join our creation in being greater than our parts. Strangely simple is the binary choice we tell ourselves, the basic story of our future as yet unrealised. The story goes simply thus: AI and robots, bad – AI and robots, good. More precisely, however, the story of interest is whether human intelligence blended and responsive to the universe with artificial intelligence will be good or bad. It will, in fact, be what we make it.

However, realistically we must accept as an orthodoxy a learning platform and environment alien to older human beings. The language of the future is a language few will understand as they have learned a language for the world they grew up in and not the world developing around them. This is a truism as demonstrated by the largely unknowable language and sub-languages developing around AI in all of its different manifestations.

Being creative in thinking and evaluating meaning

Very little is truly known or understood as to how the physical brain and body operate as the primary or secondary contributor to creative acts.

Creativity is a fundamental activity of human information processing (Boden, 1999). It is generally agreed to include two defining characteristics: "The ability to produce work that is both novel (i.e., original, unexpected) and appropriate (i.e., useful, adaptive concerning task constraints)" (Sternberg, Lubart, 1999).

Work on data collection, neuron links, connectivity, manufacturing and development of connected devices, and brain plasticity all are mirrored by the growth of the self-learning machine's creative application to the "now" of our world. The impact of AI is everywhere, and we must learn to recognise the limits (at the time of writing) of what an intelligent machine can and will be able to learn. One view of how intelligence will develop is simple: "The future of schools lies in networks rather than hierarchies, in lateral rather than vertical organisations" (Elmor, 2011). Most of the work gets done in networks, not hierarchies. The education system will essentially functionally be replaced by a series of networks. Networks cannot be managed the same way that hierarchies are managed. Social networking is a different highly complex way of organising.

Learning is refining our understanding of what we know – expanding our knowledge. True creativity is a matter of epiphany, a view from another side of our reflection, seeing ourselves and what we understand and what we are in ignorance of.

A cat knows how to be a cat. It has invested its whole life in being a complete cat. With the cat tool-box, the cat is limited as to how it can negotiate or redefine itself to manage change. It is not only an old dog that can't learn new tricks. And here is the key issue at a time of great change: how do we support learners – the reluctant, reserved, challenged, and that most challenging learner (from an educator's perspective), of all, the insatiable learning enthusiast?

A 'core' creative change curriculum

From the future, looking back, we will see that all success in engaging learning awareness will be related to the development of individual and community creative acts, thoughts, and adaptive communications that both promote and accelerate connectivity. As (Dietrich, 2004) observes:

> Research on insightful problem solving, creative cognition, and expertise acquisition, as well as historic case studies of individuals with exceptional creative accomplishments have replaced the view that the creative act is a mysterious or even mystical event (Simonton, 2000). Creativity is grounded in ordinary mental processes (Boden, 1999; Ward, 1999; Weisberg, 1993), making creative cognition an integral part of cognitive science and thus neuroscience. Indeed, the view has been expressed that "any theory on creativity must be consistent and integrated with contemporary understanding of brain function.
>
> *(Pfenninger (Editor), Shubik (Editor) 2001)*

This is an important point, and it gently reminds us that while we discuss creativity as an important aspect of our understanding of what it is to be a human being, any idea of what creativity actually is will change as we change in creating a new relationship between ourselves, AI machines, and the new language of connectivity that will evolve between all involved in creating the future. Creativity is about plasticity of thinking, and as we journey to a closer relationship with machines we will need to deal with a future echo which will need to focus on grief and mourning and loss in order to conceive of renewing what it will mean to be human. The classroom and the curriculum will become an obsolete feature of the human experience; even the classroom of the mind will cease to be as we cease to be what we understand it is to be human.

Humans do not share a universal consciousness, just as they do not share universal perceptions. Meaning-making in the Vygotskyan sense may be a universal and special feature of all humans, but this is precisely because it is cultural and not universal.

This is different for machine learning. As rational agents, machines may run on the same global logic everywhere. Posthumanist learning concepts include a willingness to believe machines can learn. However (within the phenomenon of Posthumanist learning proposed in this book), it is not possible for machines to learn like humans. Posthumanist learners are not posthuman (Hasse, 2020).

Teaching and learning will become obsolete terms, and the concept of education will become redundant to our being. The future we need to prepare for is one where the story of intelligence is not a vicarious experience but a truly lived experience. Connectivity with the machine and the adjustments to our creative appreciation of the universe will mean that our intelligence will become all things, and the "internet of things" will become the "being of all things."

What stories will we tell ourselves about what we are and how we arrived to be beyond human?

Teaching learners to solve problems through being creative where there are no obvious solutions to obvious problems and/or teaching learners how to identify the actual problem that needs solving is our present approach to teaching learners to become creative. We allow, in a controlled way, learners to be curious in exploring problems. We require the learner to use problem-solving techniques and controlled adventures while they draw on existing knowledge which is necessarily limited by our ability to assimilate knowledge about the world they live in. Looking back from the future it will be clear that this approach is limited and archaic.

The story telling from the future will be about a rapid and accelerated change in machine-human development, a history story about loss of a traditional human identity and all the things we define ourselves by. The orthodox approach to teaching about change/creativity will fade away. The story of what it is to be human seen from the future looking back will be one of incredible excitement and anticipation as we realise the awesome potential for an intelligent existence going beyond what can be taught and learned to one whereby we are of the moment and all things become accessible through the embracing of machine and human – the ability to move and think about everything, at once and at the speed of light.

AI (as narrow AI) will give *Homo sapiens* time to think. Consideration of a minimal list of the main areas that currently occupy our minds and thinking lives of our communities indicate how much time and energy we will gain to think and learn when freed from repetitive and brain-dehydrating work demands.

One collective view in education is that creativity is about:

- Connecting: seeing relationships and combining in new ways
- Risking: having the self-confidence and freedom to fail and keep trying
- Envisaging: being original and imaginative about what might be
- Analysing: asking critical and challenging questions
- Thinking: taking time for reflection and soft thinking
- Interacting: sharing ideas and collaborating
- Varying: testing options and trying in different ways
- Elaborating: exploring and fiddling and doing the unnecessary with love

Creativity is seen not merely as a bolt on to the curriculum but as central to the whole process (Burgess, 2007).

Singularity (one story for us all): the creative being

Human life will be irreversibly transformed. Whether the biological body is perceived as a problem to be dealt with in achieving singularity by using engineering or as something that can lead to an enhancement of the human body, the singularist vision – the creation of learning machines – will gradually replace humans in the biological form we presently recognise. Intelligences will expand. Machines capable of learning and therefore capable of enhancing human thinking into a singular state of an expanded creative curiosity that asides age or the effects of growing old – forever humans having the plasticity of thinking demonstrated by a 20-year-old human mind with the gigantic power to ruthlessly manage data will mean an unknown and unimaginable intelligence beyond our lonely brain's ability to fully comprehend. We will need to embrace artificial intelligence and transform to a cyborg state to even begin our understanding of our intelligent status in any future universe. We don't yet have comparable communication ports in our biological brains to quickly download the interneural connection and neurotransmitter patterns that represent our learning. That is one of many profound limitations of the biological paradigm we now use for our thinking, a limitation we will overcome in the singularity (Kurzweil, 2005).

"'Attention,' a voice began to call, and it was as though an oboe had suddenly become articulate. 'Attention,' it repeated in the same high, nasal monotone. 'Attention'" (Huxley, 1962).

According to Darwinian theory, human imagination is an instrument of survival. In order better to learn about the world, and therefore be better equipped to cope with its pitfalls and dangers, *Homo sapiens* developed the ability to reconstruct outer reality in the mind and to conceive situations that it could confront before actually encountering them (Manguel, 2015).

To construct our sense of reality requires imagination and a relationship with our sensual reading of the world we inhabit. AI, ML, and DL are areas of powerful tools to think beyond the restrictions we face in solving problems, creating responsive time/energy saving machines, and generally supporting a developing sense of our expanding intelligence.

The conventional orthodoxy regarding the teaching of creativity aimed at enriching the learning experience and desired outcomes of schooling will cease to be relevant as singularity develops. The transitional learningscape will be one of rapid and intense change. Technology, as has been discussed, is advancing and maturing at an unprecedented rate, and while creativity will be an early key to both solving problems and addressing the identification of new, novel problems creativity be required to respond to how new technology impacts our lives, our thinking and particularly our increasing intelligence.

Motivation

"If you could bottle motivation and sell it in the supermarket, you'd be very rich. But you can't" ((Berliner, Judd, 2020).

Currently motivation is regarded as an important feature, with problem solving, of promoting creativity in learners. A great deal of time and effort and other resources are directed at boosting and locking into the learner's functioning learning personality. As what is taught to learners becomes of less interest or perceived relevance to the learner, the more desperate becomes the need to either coerce an imitation/pseudo-motivation amongst learners or a more draconian approach to engendering motivation in learners through a kind of enforcement motivation. These efforts will, of course, be seen as (at the very best) well-meaning and (at worst) a form of educational criminality whereby irrelevant curriculum content that does not reflect the urgent needs of learners is forcibly rejected by learners. Imagine forcing learners to use a quill pen and ink to record ideas while voice-activated technology can write your spoken word. Very quickly motivating learners to do something they rightly and increasingly reject will be seen as a ridiculous waste of everybody's time and resources. It is a simple problem to solve to ask learners what they want to learn. Find ways of making the learning and development of what learners want to learn, and they will not require gentle persuasion or sticks to be motivated. A learner who sees value in the learning does not need motivation.

Curiosity

We have invented artificial intelligence. As discussed elsewhere in this book, the AI we have realised is still in the clumsy state of establishing the ordering and management of a growing and massive amount of data. We as humans are curious with regard to every aspect of this busy form of emergent intelligence. Our active curiosity is a key part of the development maturity of AI and our own desire to continue our quest to understand the universe. We can reflect on the words of Dr. Johnson and Eliezer Yudkowski.

Curiosity is one of the most permanent and certain characteristics of a vigorous intellect. (Berliner, Judd, 2020).

AI does not hate you, nor does it love you, but you are made out of atoms which it can use for something else (Yudkowsky, 2008b).

Unintentional collective learning futures

Our education systems today by and large refuse to acknowledge the second half of our quests (failing in order to get better and to learn). Interested in little else than material efficiency and financial profit, our educational institutions no longer foster thinking for its own sake and the free exercise of the imagination. Schools and colleges have become training camps for skilled labour instead of forums for questioning and discussion, and colleges and universities are no longer nurseries for those inquirers whom Francis Bacon, in the 16th century, called "merchants of light." We teach ourselves to ask, "How much will it cost?" and "How long will it take?" instead of "Why?" (Manguel, 2015).

Like the autopoiesis and the cybernetic approach, Clark (2003) works from the notion of a "system" in which extended minds unfold themselves. *System*, like *category* and *discourse*, attempts to grasp the collective features of humans with a humanist eye on the collective as a "generalised" being. Clark, with his eye on the longer history, forgets the conceptual process behind any *we* – for example, the child, who at first sees the clock as a white circle with black dots before it is learned as a *watch* (Vygotsky, 1978).

The child is an ultra-social experienced learner who learns in her daily practice that when other humans pay attention to the white and black shapes there is something to learn. The learning is already enclosing the child in the collective from where they can make individual choices, such as neglecting going to school at 8:00 once the meaning of the wristwatch is learned. In the big picture, evoked by Clark, these small processes of collective learning go unnoticed – and the culture–culture divide in knowing through practices (what comes about as ignorance when people from different cultures meet each other) is ignored as well (Hasse, 2020). "Maybe intelligence is more about noticing than knowing?" (Netolicky, 2019).

The intentional future

And here we are in the future – how does it feel?

If from the future we can in our most extravagantly positive, creative, and wishful dreams look back to the now we are living in, we can wonder and accept (for the purposes of creating the imagined future that AI as a subset of Deep AI has helped us create) that our dreams can be golden. If, in this imagined future, not only have our lives become free of disease, starvation, violence, and unexpected natural disasters, what should we be doing now, at this moment? We should be enriching our minds, exercising our responsible intelligence in all its aspects as we prepare to eventually be at one with a technology that can and increasingly will work for us and improve our lives beyond recognition. This is not a utopian view or a science fiction fantasy. The world we are now in is taking a colossal step into new realities as a result of our creation of artificial intelligence. To play our part, we must attend to the positive and learn to manage and accept change. New politics and new economic beliefs will have to develop and become as historic as communication by semaphore signalling. We must learn to learn, learn to mentor, and share learning rather than remain involved in a hierarchy of learning. We must intend to achieve a new bright future in which killer robots and death-delivering cyber-swarms have no place in our reality other than as positive manifestations of our unique, creative intelligence.

There is a strong collective view that the emerging future will be exceedingly different from the past.

How would teachers teach if the exams were in 20 years' time? There is not an achievement gap, there is a relevance gap. Harvard Professor of Teaching and Learning David Perkins argues that most of what is taught beyond the basic literacies quickly gets forgotten, and a huge information base may not be the right priority for our times. Instead of fixating on educating for the known, we need a vision of educating for the unknown, for the kind of thinking and understanding that foster nimble adaptive insights in a complex world (Paterson, Caple, 2019).

The complexity of what AI is and is developing into is increasingly difficult to encompass and mentally embrace. For all our advances, we are still in transition, where tribal affiliations to the different and developing approaches to what is AI and how it is developing restricts our ability to respond to AI creatively. In all the excitement of making the future, it is easy to forget that *our* intelligence invented artificial intelligence. We now need to look back from the future and see how we journeyed from a confusing, work-orientated, unhealthy environment – moving from a disastrous, political, failing place to a place where we can feel protected and secure. A place of well-being, a future place whereby as a truly liberated intelligence both individually and collectively we move from our identity as *Homo sapiens,* the "wise man," the intelligent primate and we live the life of *Sapient partum intelligentia*, the "wise creative intelligence," being as one with general AI.

We will look back at our ignorance and be amazed at our journey to becoming human-bio-machines. After looking at a history story which anticipates and demonstrates our journey into a future present, one thing will remain and be clear to us: no matter how particularly singular we will be, our enhanced intelligence being what we are, that core driver that is the historic river of being a human now with the machine, we will (as a new being) still want to know more, to create, and to remain curious about future futures.

However, one important caveat as to the glorious potential and our projected, imagined future for human-machine learning and intelligence development is offered by Eliezer Yudkowsky: "By far the greatest danger of artificial intelligence is that people conclude too early that they understand it" (Yudkowsky, 2008a).

Enrichment

What motivation do you think we have for seeking to improve/enhance our intelligence? Why bother? What is in it for *Homo sapiens*? Why bother inventing or seeking a future in which we may be either increasingly intelligent or perhaps increasingly infantilised?

Defining what it is to be intelligent will not perhaps be on the top of great, historic, important events that changed the history of humanity. What, then, will be important – a flexible, generous understanding of change-management development and a spiritual understanding of the strengths and potential of the atypical, post-robotic, post-cyborgian being?

Now look back to "now" from a hundred years in the future. Imagine and assume the technology and your psychological state are such that you can safely travel in perception real time backwards. What do you think will surprise or shock you with your future sensibilities? Do you like what you find?

As an incidental experience to imagining looking back, look at yourself as you imagine yourself in the best possible future you can imagine for yourself. Are you human? Part machine? Part bio-mass? Are you engineered? Evolved artificially? Draw yourself as you imagine yourself to be (alive certainly, likewise as a healthy entity) a hundred years from now. Look at what you have created. How did this happen? What does your future picture tell you about the you in the early 21st century?

The challenge is to make what we "know" into a diaphanous, permeable event which allows what we know and believe to become like a cloud. As Nietzsche comments, "Convictions are more dangerous foes of truth than lies" (Nietzsche, 2008).

Is the future you travel back from a place where intelligence is increased, humans and machines are conjoined, and a golden age of peaceful creation exists? Or does our future present a time of uncertainty and danger?

Link pathways

What links Arthur C. Clarke, Ursula K. Le Guin, and Eliezer Yudkowsky?

References

BBC. 2019. https://www.instagram.com/bbcnews/?hl=en.
Berliner, Wendy, Judd, Judith. 2020. *How to Succeed at School: Separating Fact from Fiction What Every Parent Should Know* (p. 184). Abingdon, UK: Routledge. ISBN: 978-0-367-18645-6.

Boden, M. A. 1999. Is metabolism necessary? *The British Journal for the Philosophy of Science*. academic.oup.com.

Burgess, Tim. 2007. Lifting the lid on the creative curriculum. *Deputy Headteacher*, Holy Trinity Junior School, Surrey. https://dera.ioe.ac.uk/7340/1/download%3Fid%3D17 281%26filename%3Dlifting-the-lid-on-the-creative-curriculum-full-report.pdf.

Clark, A. 2003. *Natural-Born Cyborgs: Mind, Technologies, and the Future of Human Intelligence*. Oxford: Oxford University Press. ASIN: B00EKYPQPQ.

Dietrich, Arne. 2004. The cognitive neuroscience of creativity. *Psychonomic Bulletin & Review*, 11 (6): 1011–1026.

Elmor. Richard. 2011. Network leadership. https://search.informit.org/doi/10.3316/INFORMIT.639103672191722

Hasse, Catherine. 2020. *Posthumanist Learning: What Robots and Cyborgs Teach Us about Being Ultra-Social*. Abingdon, UK: Routledge. ISBN: 978-1-138-12517-9.

Huxley, Aldous. 1962. *Island* (p. 286). London, UK: Vintage Classic, Random House. ISBN: 978-0-099-47777-8.

Kurzweil, R. 2005. *The Singularity Is Near: When Humans Transcend Biology*. New York, NY: Viking. ISBN-10: 0715635611.

Manguel, A. 2015. *Curiosity*. New Haven, CT: Yale University Press. ASIN: B017PO8U78.

Nietzsche, Friedrich. 2008. *Man Alone with Himself* (p. 96). London, UK: Penguin. ISBN: 978-0-141-03668-7.

Netolicky, Deborah M. 2019. *Flip the System Australia: What Matters in Education*. Abingdon, UK: Routledge. ISBN:978-1-138-36786-9.

Paterson, C., Caple, K. 2019. Schools for the future: Networks and innovation. In *Flip the System Australia: What Matters in Education*. Abingdon, UK: Routledge .

Pfenninger, Karl H. (Editor), Shubik, V. R. (Editor). 2001. *The Origins of Creativity*. Oxford: Oxford University Press. ISBN: 0198507151.

Simonton, D. K. 2000. Creativity: Cognitive, personal, developmental, and social aspects. *American Psychologist*, 55 (1): 151–158. doi:10.1037/0003-066X.55.1.151.

Sternberg, R. J., Lubart, T. I. 1999. The concept of creativity: Prospects and paradigms. In R. J. Sternberg (Ed.), *Handbook of Creativity* (pp. 3–15). Cambridge: Cambridge University Press. ISBN-13: 978-0-521-57604-8.

Szakolczai, Arpad. 2017. *Permanent Liminality and Modernity: Analysing the Sacrificial Carnival through Novels* (p. 271). Abingdon, UK: Routledge. ISBN: 978-1-4724-7388-2.

Vygotsky, L. S. 1978. *Mind in Society*. Cambridge: Harvard University Press. ISBN: 0-674-5-76292, 978-0-674-57629-2.

Wallace, B. 2008. A vision of Paulo Freire's philosophy: Understanding his essential dynamism of learning and teaching. In M. Shaughnessy, E. Galligan, R. Hurtado de Vivas (Eds.), *Pioneers in Education: Essays in Honor of Paulo Freire* (p. 164). New York: Nova Science Publishers Inc. ISBN-10: 1600214797.

Ward, Stephen. 1999. Requirements for an effective project risk management process. *Research Article: Project Management Journal (SAGE)*. doi:10.1177/875697289903000306.

Warhol. 1968 15 minutes of fame. https://en.wikipedia.org/wiki/15_minutes_of_fame#:~:text=15%20minutes%20of%20fame%20is,Moderna%20Museet%20in%20Stockholm%2C%20Sweden.

Yudkowsky, Eliezer. 2008a. Artificial intelligence as a positive and negative factor in global risk. In Nick Bostrom, Milan M. Ćirković (Eds.), *Global Catastrophic Risks* (pp. 308–345). New York: Oxford University Press. ISBN: 978-0-199-60650-4. https://intelligence.org/files/AIPosNegFactor.pdf.

Yudkowsky, Eliezer. 2008b. *Friendly Artificial Intelligence*. https://en.wikipedia.org/wiki/Friendly_artificial_intelligence.

Weisberg, R. W. 1993. *Creativity: Genius and Other Myths* (2nd ed.). Oxford, UK: W. H. Freeman & Co Ltd. ISBN-10: 0716723670.

Suggested further reading

ABC. 2017. www.abc.net.au/news/2017-08-08/could-a-robot-do-your-job-artificial-intelligence/8782174.

Alison, Gopnik, Meltzoff, Andrew, Kuhl, Patricia. 1999. *Title: How Babies Think: The Science of Childhood* (p. 279). London: Weidenfeld & Nicholson. ISBN: 0-297-84227-7.

BBC. 2019. *What Will Art Look Like in 20 Years?* www.bbc.com/culture/article/20190 418-what-will-art-look-like-in-20-years.

Benjamin, Walter. 2008. *The Work of Art in the Age of Mechanical Reproduction* (p. 111). London, UK: Penguin Books. ISBN: 978-0-141-03619-9.

Brooks, Rodney. 2003. *Flesh and Machines: How Robots Will Change Us.* London, UK: Vintage. ISBN: 978-0-375-72527-2.

Carnie, Fiona. 2017. *Alternative Approaches to Education* (p. 256). Abingdon, UK: Routledge. ISBN: 978-1-1138-69206-0.

Clark, Arthur C. 1953. https://en.wikipedia.org/wiki/The_Nine_Billion_Names_of_God.

Dietrich, Arne. 2004. The cognitive neuroscience of creativity. *Psychonomic Bulletin & Review,* 11 (6): 1011–1026.

English, A. 2013. *Discontinuity in Learning* (p. 177). Cambridge: Cambridge University Press. ISBN: 978-1-107-02521-9.

Four Corners: Future Proof. Australia. ABC. 2014. www.psychologytoday.com/us/ blog/science-choice/201412/basics-identity.

George, Danielle. 2017. *Professor in Microwave Communication Engineering at the University of Manchester Guardian.* www.theguardian.com/science/2017/dec/24/early-man-micro plastics-the-year-in-science

Gyarmathy, Eva, Senior, John. 2019. *The SAGE Handbook of Gifted and Talented Education* (p. 545). Thousand Oaks, CA: Sage Publications. ISBN: 978-1-5264-3115-8.

Holt, John. 1970. *How Children Learn* (p. 173). Australia: Pelican. ISBN: 0-1402-1133-0.

Hölscher, L. (Ed.). 2007. *Das Jenseits: Facetten eines religiösen Begriffs in der Neuzeit* [*The Beyond: Facets of a Religious Concept of Modern Times*] (p. 267). Göttingen, Germany: Wallstein. ISBN: 978-3-8353-0201-3.

Luckin, Rosemary. 2018. *Machine Learning and Human Intelligence: The Future of Education for the 21st Century* (p. 157). London: UCL Institute of Education Press, University College. ISBN: 978-178277-251-4.

Lyotrad, J. F. 1984. *The Post-Modern Condition: A Report on Knowledge.* Minneapolis, MN: The University of Minnesota Press.

Macfarlane, Bruce. 2017. *Freedom to Learn* (p. 139). SRHE. Abingdon, UK: Routledge. ISBN: 978-0-415-72916-1.

Manguel, Alberto. 2015. *Curiosity* (p. 337). New Haven, CT: Yale University Press. ISBN: 978-0-300-21980-7.

Oettingen, Gabriele (Ed.). 2018. *The Psychology of Thinking About the Future* (p. 554). New York, NY: The Guilford Press. ISBN: 978-1-462-53441-8.

Srnicek, Nick, Williams, Alex. 2015. *Inventing the Future: Post Capitalism and a World Without Work* (p. 245). London, UK: Verso. ISBN-13: 978-1-78478-096-8 (PB).

Thomas, M. 2020. The future of artificial intelligence. *Built In.* https://builtin.com/ artificial-intelligence/artificial-intelligence-future.

TwinCitiesView. 2017. *How Do People Define Themselves and Others?* twincitiesview.com/ people-define-others/.

Viney, Wayne, Woody, William Douglas. 2017. *Neglected Perspectives on Science and Religion* (p. 260). Abingdon, UK: Routledge. ISBN: 978-1-315-21375-0.

Wardman, J. 2015. To act or not to act? Academic acceleration worked in the past, so what's the current hold-up in NZ? *APEX: The New Zealand Journal of Gifted Education*, 19 (1). www.giftedchildren.org.nz/apex.

Suggested further viewing

Arrival. 2017. *DVD Studio: eOne Entertainment*. Science Fiction. BARCODE: 50390360 79273.

Arrival: Sound-track. 2016. www.youtube.com/watch?v=HzNBrns1xPk&list=RDHz NBrns1xPk&start_radio=1&t=101.

7

THE MENTAL HEALTH
OF MACHINES

> We are feeling and thinking creatures and to the possible disadvantage of science,
> feeling may often appeal as a deeper source of truth.
>
> *(James, 1979)*

In developing and learning to be empathetic, special artificial intelligence (SAI) may well find that a mental health issue such as depression is an unwanted consequence of emotional development. Further, while learning to be creative and to be able to generate original questions, AI may well need to consider how to cope with and manage degrees of, for example, anxiety and obsessive-compulsive disorder (OCD). Given that psychologists cannot agree on the causes of mental health illnesses and diagnose them in a securely uniform manner, we cannot predict how the mental profile of SAI will be affected by increasing intellectual and emotional autonomy – all we can say for sure is that any emotional mix functioning as an aspect of intelligence may be susceptible to mental health issues of widely different potential for the appearance of disabling illness in SAI. The positive side in helping realise SAI into autonomous existence is that we will certainly learn more as to what it means to be human and intelligent.

> The greatest minds are capable of the greatest vices as well as of the greatest virtues and those who proceed very slowly may, provided they always follow the straight road, really advance much faster than by those who, though they run, forsake it.
>
> *(Haldane, Ross, 1911)*

We think of others, and within this thinking we have one overriding principle which is a basic truth: that, as human beings, we care. We care for one another; we care for our world and other people we have never met nor will ever meet.

DOI: 10.4324/9780429356346-8

We care about strangers in the now, and for people in the future who do not exist. The level and fullness of how we care, and when we may appear to fail to care, are matters for discussion and enquiry. A "failure of care" is the exception to our human condition. We care; it is what we do. We are never separated from the world we exist in; we are never truly isolated or insulated. As others care for us, we are a part of the life of others. We share thoughts and values that afford an understanding, incomplete as it may be, of how the world works and how we fit into the world community with different models of care (none being perfect or definitive, none offering a singularity of being). Dependant, totally dependent, at our birth and infancy, we develop in a basic environment of care for the vulnerable.

> Altruism, cooperation, and caring for the vulnerable is what made our species unique. It is empathy and cooperation, not self-interest and competition, that drove our physiological, cognitive, linguistic, cultural, social, and technological evolution. We would not be the large-brained, neutrally-plastic, intelligent, cumulative-learning, empathetic beings that we are without the mutual help that characterizes our everyday interactions. Our evolutionary history is one of collective child-rearing, co-operative hunting and gathering, caring for elders and the sick, and freely sharing information.
>
> *(Veissiere, 2015)*

This view is of course rather splendid, and (for now) we will ignore the more disturbing aspects of our human behaviours.

Part of the caring imperative is the introduction of a growing human being into a world where it is useful to know things, as it helps in our species' survival and possible advancement and security. At every stage of our existence, acts of teaching, learning, considering, and acting upon our developing knowledge and skills are central to our humanity. With all our frailty, confusions, fears, and vision we aim to understand, which in turn is driven by our need to improve. Our need to stand on solid ground for however a fleeting moment with partial insights and the occasional paradigm shift whereby the little we know about our lives and our place in the universe is illuminated with a powerful flash of understanding and terrifying comprehension which further promotes our need to care for others and the world we exist in. "The world is far from finished. There are new additions and old errors everywhere that must be considered in ever-changing pictures of the world. We are reduced to fragmentary knowledge sufficient to provide practical but partial anchorages" (Viney, Woody, 2017).

In our need to care and to create, we have now entered a time of paradigm shift whereby all aspects of our human intelligence are going to develop as artificial intelligences working to expand and maximise learning and our knowledge of our existence. Through a human philosophy of caring, a machine philosophy will develop as a parallel. The artificial intelligences we are increasingly familiar with will one day in the future develop towards a general artificial intelligence. The AI understanding of creativity, anxiety, and curiosity will transform our understanding of human intelligence stripped bare as the machines we develop do so at speeds we will have difficulty in not being in awe of, for example the speed and complexity of calculation and system problems being solved.

As we read earlier, to pass an advanced Turing Test in any guise, which makes it impossible to distinguish between a human intelligence and an artificial intelligence (AI), the synthetic intelligence would be required to demonstrate complex human characteristics as an integral part of any AI identity.

AI is a human development and as such will reflect our core, human identity, anxieties and determined need to care. SAI will result in what we will at the present understand to be a development of our thinking, our needs, and our questions. As SAI develops, so will its need for our care to be applied to the machine that (like humanity) will become both increasingly complex and further incomprehensible to human understanding unless we shift our view of what it is to be intelligent. We must realise that we are both operating as isolated human machines, albeit organic, and simultaneously linked to our fellows, enjoining with our wonderful creation of artificial intelligences (reactive machines, limited memory, theory of mind, and self-awareness).

SAI is as yet only in advanced research being challenged by a sense of identity, comprehension of any "why or what" thinking. As any adolescent, it may however develop from a caring dependency to an autonomous sense of identity that will bring issues of meaning and creativity, exploring identity and developing a sense of wonder. SAI will need help, and that help will come in the form of using human intelligence and experience in addressing, exploring, and developing a body of knowledge that cares for the mental health of human beings while successfully being interpreted and applied to the needs of advanced, artificial, intelligent machines.

What do we mean?

To consider the question of why psychotherapists for machines do not already exist seems initially ridiculous. The idea that machines do or even will possess mental health, good or poor, is questionable. However, adjusting the question to why are there not yet psychotherapists for human-AI algorithm interfaces is insightful. Considering the multifaceted negative effects and harms that the current human-algorithm interactions are creating via social media (bullying, stress increases, insomnia, self-harm, negative political impacts), it could be considered as in fact especially important that psychotherapists are skilled and trained at working on the interface where human desires, motivations, and difficulties interact with the motivations and drives of AI algorithms. Both are engaged in changing each other; the AI algorithm responds to the human in that it is created using data about human behaviour and activity; in turn, the human responds to and changes the algorithm. Enabling the dance of learning to take place between human intelligence and artificial intelligence whilst also seeking to minimise the harm that can exist to both agents as they individually and co-operatively continue to evolve psychologically seems relevant and certainly does not seem to be being addressed at present.

We could therefore conclude that the need for a human-AI algorithm inter-face psychotherapist is actually very real indeed.

Let's return to our first question: Why do psychotherapists for machines not already exist? Perhaps this now seems less remote as a need. Answering this ques-tion also illuminates the full meaning of what may be the nature of interactions between humans and machines as what can be described as the mutual mental health development of our respective intelligences.

Initially in our relationship with machines we focussed on, and still do, the physical care of machines, developing an asymmetrical relationship with the machine as we the operator seek a productive and efficient outcome. The machine, albeit unconsciously, or more precisely without an identifiable con-sciousness, maintains directed to its goals as instructed, while the machine opera-tor experiences a problem-free, effective relationship, provided adequate care is taken of the machine and that their goals as to the machine are met: a job well and safely done, avoiding damage or injury to machine and operator, respectively. In other words, we, the user of machines, must carry out a duty of care towards the machine to maintain a productive and mutually beneficial working relationship.

The simplest machine needs care. The accepted view of what a machine is talks about an apparatus of interrelated – defined function parts – which, work-ing together, perform work. A simple machine involves the elementary compo-nents of the lever, wheel and axle, pulley, screw, wedge, and inclined plane – all without consciousness of their existence or intelligence as to the meaning of what a machine does.

While the essential components of many machines remain unchanged, the same machines are becoming increasingly complex and begin to demonstrate simple to sophisticated decision-making sentience. Care is now intrinsic to our relationship with machines. We have learned to care; it is in our interest to maximise efficiency and the well-being of machines. We can take care in our levels and commitment to caring for our machines. Just as yesterday made today, today is making tomorrow. We are training our tomorrow self to understand and relate to the increasingly complex needs of machines as they move from a passive ability to comprehend their conscious existence and sense of existence to general artificial intelligence which will need to possess a form of conscious awareness to function at a recognisable, creative consciousness as demonstrated by human intelligence. To achieve general artificial intelligence, machines will need to have a psychological mental health theatre to operate creatively and to self-learn free of any human interface of control regarding what is thought about and why the contents of the intelligent machine will be as they will develop. In our time, advances in AI technology have been significant; we are on the edge of greater advances.

Machine learning

Face recognition software is an example of machine-learning algorithms where a computer can learn to carry out a task without being told how. Machine-learning systems require training in order to learn. In "supervised learning," training takes place by presenting a program with examples of the thing that the computer is trying to learn. Hence, providing training data for machine-learning algorithms in the form of data of individual faces in the case of face recognition allows the computer to learn.

Four main application domains emerged in the literature focussing on ML applications to human mental health:

- Detection and diagnosis
- Prognosis, treatment, and support
- Public health
- Research and clinical administration

The most common mental health conditions addressed included:

- Depression
- Schizophrenia
- Alzheimer's disease

ML techniques used included support vector machines, decision trees, neural networks, latent Dirichlet allocation, and clustering.

> Overall, the application of ML to mental health has demonstrated a range of benefits across the areas of diagnosis, treatment and support, research, and clinical administration. With the majority of studies identified focussing on the detection and diagnosis of mental health conditions, it is evident that there is significant room for the application of ML to other areas of psychology and mental health.
>
> *(https://pubmed.ncbi.nlm.nih.gov/30744717/)*

Reinforcement learning

In reinforcement learning, a system is able to experiment by making definitions, and it receives feedback on those decisions (whether good or bad). If a system receives feedback that a decision was bad, it will be less likely to make that decision in the same circumstances in the future (Wooldridge, 2018).

As we know, machines possessing artificial intelligence can operate at phenomenal speed; it is their hallmark. In the 1996 chess encounter between Garry Kasparov and the IBM chess computer, Deep Blue, the computer was processing some 200 million positions per second. When research for this section of this book was started, when asked to show references to "the mental health of machines," within 0.53 seconds the search engine offered about 376,000,000 results. Interestingly, so far none of the references are in fact concerned with the mental health of machines; the references are all concerned with how machines are used in mental health work which is applied to human beings.

Caring language

Since the widespread availability of mass-produced domestic and industrial/commercial machines, our core belief both as individuals and as a society has been to extend the care we afford to other human beings, animals, and plants to machines that work for us or entertain us. In the development of this aspect of care and maintenance, it could be argued that we are preparing for a future relationship with general AI as both its carer and partner, being within a developing mental health provision affecting well-being for machine and human – a future echo we are now rehearsing.

Examples of caring language, that is "reinforcement learning" directing our responsible actions, are everywhere. If you purchased a hi-res, interactive, state-of-the-art television, it came with instructions as to how you should care for your purchase to maximise and secure its safe operation. The same applies to practically any domestic purchase. Table 7.1 gives examples of such familiar instructions and guidance.

TABLE 7.1 Taking care

How to take care of computer hardware:

- Install antivirus software
- Perform regular software updates
- Run computer maintenance
- Back up files
- Keep your keyboard crumb free
- Clean the screen
- Remove dust from vents and fans
- Use a surge protector

10 essential tips to maintain and care for your TV set:

- Turn off your TV regularly
- Use a voltage regulator or a surge protector
- Set at optimal brightness
- Use appropriate contrast
- Allow TV to breathe
- Keep sharp objects away
- Clean your TV from time to time
- Keep dust away.

Best practices for camera maintenance:

- Avoid dirt and sand
- Use care when cleaning dirt particles and sand from your digital camera

Tips on how to care for your sewing machine:

1 Keep your sewing machine covered
2 Change needles regularly
3 Use compressed air to remove lint
4 Service annually
5 Oil the machine
6 Find an experienced professional to repair your machine
7 Clean one part of the machine at a time
8 Wipe down the machine after each use

TABLE 7.2 10 caring tips

10 washing machine maintenance tips that will help you to take care of your appliance better:	Adopting a robot home vacuum cleaner:
1 Deep cleaning 2 Clean the rubber gasket 3 Protect the finish 4 Protect from spillage 5 Leave the door open 6 Clean the detergent and fabric softener dispensers 7 Keep checking the hoses 8 Clean the filter 9 Use it carefully 10 Choose the right detergent	Increasingly AI machines that are used in a domestic setting are being named with the purpose of normalising and being reassured that machines that act "freely" are like a companion or a pet – in other words, non-threatening and beneficial to our home life. Naming, for example, a robot home vacuum cleaner takes the concept of "care" to be a normalising of the human-machine relationship, forming our relationship with a "thinking machine" that, while not necessarily in our physical image, is being created in our image emotionally and psychologically to make you, the owner, want to take better care of your robot vacuum.

You will have little difficulty in finding instructions and guidance on how to care for almost every manufactured object and machine in your own immediate environment.

In learning to care for the made objects in our lives, we are being prepared, wittingly or not, to care for the AI-conscious machine at whatever level of sophistication from an "intelligent" vacuum cleaner to the Honda Motor Corporation's ASIMO robot, designed to undertake complex domestic service tasks within home environments, hospitals, and industries involving empathy and psychological well-being. In addition to the "caring" intelligence, we do of course need to consider (which we do elsewhere in this book) the potential for programmed and installed malignant behaviours performed by machines that do not possess an evolved morality, empathy, or any sense of humanity.

From these examples we can begin to get a sense of the caring imperative within the human psychological profile. We can also glimpse, through the invitation to care for a machine, the repetitive suggestion that to care means to clean and to keep cleaning! "Cleaning" indicates behaviours that can be linked to established mental health diagnoses such as obsessive-compulsive disorder (OCD).

Duty of care?

Having begun to see how all embracing is the emergent duty of care of machines in our lives and beginning to see the psychological issues that are being explored with a duty of care towards machines, we can look at the legislative thinking to see the universal approach to the "duty of care" principle in a legal and enforceable perspective. Duty of care is about individual well-being, welfare, compliance, and good practice.

In English tort law, an individual may owe a duty of care to another to ensure that they do not suffer any unreasonable harm or loss. Generally, a duty of care arises where one individual or group undertakes an activity which could reasonably harm another either physically, mentally, or economically.

The idea of a general duty of care that runs to all who could be foreseeably affected by one's conduct (accompanied by the demolishing of the privity barrier) first appeared in the judgement of William Brett (later Lord Esher), Master of the Rolls, in *Heaven* v. *Pender.*

All workplaces, whether a school, a business, or a voluntary organisation have a moral and a legal obligation to ensure that everyone associated with the establishment – whether employee, volunteer, student, tradesperson, or the general public – is fully protected from any personal physical and/or emotional harm, either on the premises or when engaged in activities relating to the establishment.

In other words, a "duty of care" wraps around every aspect of our modern lives. As AI is essentially in our image, and we are in the process of exploring our relationship with AI, what will be our developing intelligences' views be as to what will cross-over from human mental health issues to AI? As human designers we have and will continue to educate AI in the patterns of mental illness as AI becomes increasingly more sophisticated.

Following human ethical, moral, and legal protocols as a general duty of care will influence and become an integral part of any future AI consciousness.

By taking effective steps to ensure the mental health of machines as sentience is developed, it will be important to extend the human protocols of a sense of duty of care to AI machines so that that all machines receive the right training, the right guidance, and clear protocols to inspire good practice, reduce risk to both human and machine alike, and create a safe mental health environment.

How will this be achieved?

A greater understanding of mental health as it applies to humans in the 21st century and how it will become a function of both developing human intelligence and artificial intelligence is and will remain a challenge. For example, the EU-supported Human Brain Project (HBP) has one simulation containing 500,000 processors, allowing it to function at average brain speeds. The BrainScaleS machine in Germany models 4 million neurons and 1 billion synapses, allowing it to carry out selective types of operations up to 10,000 times faster than the human brain.

Despite these amazing achievements, the true picture of these large simulations is clear. In order to emulate the human brain, we will expect machines to be operating with typically 80–100 billion neurons, each averaging around 1,750 synapses. However, while the challenges of neuromorphic computing remain, there will be progress. History teaches us that quantum leaps and steady application produce many surprise achievements in many areas of AI, including the development of human brain-computer interfacing, whereby we will find ourselves connecting our brains to forms of AI. "Real" brains and artificial intelligences are and will continue to be of use to each other, throwing light on each other's processes and possible improvements.

To progress and advance our thinking about AI, SAI, and human brain-computer interfaces, we need to ask and consider what mental health issues exist and have existed and what mental health issues we could expect to see in the future as transferable or integral to the design of AI machines.

To quote Lady Lovelace, "The Analytical Engine has no pretensions to originate anything. It can do whatever we know how to order it to perform" (Hollings, Martin, Rice, 2018). SAI will inherit the untaught aspects of being human in a complex and constantly changing environment – there will be surprises both good and bad. One "surprise" we can anticipate is the need for mental health support for SAI, which initially we can begin to formulate in our present best practice. Although it could be argued that a computer that "fools a fool" (Veissiere, 2015) is hardly proof of intelligence, a computer that feels shame and empathy at folly and foolishness, anxiety, compassion, and embarrassment from an artificial and synthetic stand could be considered proof of intelligence indistinguishable from any other form.

The questions we should now be addressing (and with some urgency) to prepare for the future and our relationship with new intelligences are:

- How do we understand and define mental illnesses?
- Is mental illness real?
- Can we identify the real and unreal types of mental illness, and what are (if any) the positive, necessary mental illnesses that are in fact an essential component of what it is to be human?
- Will we need to develop synthetic mental illness (so to speak) within AI for it to achieve the challenge of behaving intuitively, creatively, and empathetically towards human intelligence and machine intelligences?

What kind of intelligence are we talking about when we consider the mental health of machines and possible mental health illnesses?

The achievement of an artificial intelligence machine that totally reflects the thinking and mental states of creativity, anxiety, doubt, etc. is believed by most scientists and researchers working on the development of general artificial intelligence to be a long time into the future. The future, however, often has a way of appearing suddenly in the present, sometimes as breakthroughs in thinking and technology encourage the advancement of once-predicted, long-term events and even sometimes the arrival of events once thought impossible.

At the beginning of the 21st century, we have learned that solar neutrinos tell us not only about the interior of the sun, but also something about the nature of neutrinos. No one knows what surprises will be revealed by the new solar neutrino experiments that are currently underway or are planned. The richness and the humour with which Nature has written her mystery, in an international language that can be read by curious people of all nations, is beautiful, awesome, and humbling (Bahcall, 2000).

That the mental health of SAI will be a thing of the future clearly indicates that we ought to be considering the issues of SAI mental health now to both prepare for a possible machine epidemic of mental health illnesses and to contribute to the development of all AI machines that will both duplicate, with integrity, and surpass our present human state. The issues of machine processes are gigantic, the numbers colossal. Nonetheless, we are able to discuss likely developments within the area (field/disciplines) of the mental health of machines. How will we identify issues? How will we reflect on our present preoccupations as humans and the likely developments we need to address in complementing the development of truly humanised artificial intelligences programmed to feel, empathise, and reflect?

Is mental illness real?

"And how do you know that you're mad?" "To begin with," said the Cat, "a dog's not mad. You grant that?" I suppose so, said Alice. "Well then," the Cat went on, "you see a dog growls when it's angry, and wags its tail when it's pleased. Now I growl when I'm pleased, and wag my tail when I'm angry. Therefore, I'm mad."

(Carroll, 2003)

It would seem sensible to start with a fundamental question as we consider the future possible implications for our developing relationship with an advanced SAI and our own developing intelligences: Is mental illness real?

Asking whether mental illness is real leads us to ask whether the classification and consequential treatments appropriate to explain and diagnose psychological symptoms are fit for purpose. Is mental health as we currently understand it a valid and proper way to interpret, describe, and treat the mental health challenges we know that people feel? One additional question central to our understanding of human and SAI is: Are some, as described currently, accepted mental illnesses essentially a function or driver of creative, problem-solving intelligence and therefore necessary traits rather than illnesses?

As we navigate towards an understanding of what mental health issues may look like and when they would be likely to occur with SAI, we need to be clear about some essential questions:

1   Are we convinced that what we describe and collectively understand mental health to mean is valid? In other words, is mental illness real?

2   Are our processes of identification and treatment appropriate?
3   Who decides who is suffering from mental illness, and who decides on suit-
     able treatment?
4   Who are the winners, and who are the losers in our present understanding
     of mental illness?
5   If we agree that mental illnesses are real, are they real and "fixed," or are
     they real and "flexible"?

Few would doubt, on the basis of a large body of authentic evidence, that the
pain and anguish and other psychological symptoms that are currently characterised as mental health are anything other than real. The question is, however,
are we correct in treating and classifying mental illness in the same way as we
treat other illnesses?

Two basic views predominate the view that psychological and emotional difficulties are illnesses and as real as physical diseases, and the view that was argued
by Thomas Szasz in his book *The Myth of Mental Illness* that categorizing illnesses
in this way reduces the personal agency of sufferers.

In the conclusion to his book Szasz writes:

> It is customary to define psychiatry as a medical speciality concerned with
> the study, diagnosis, and treatment of mental illness. This is a worthless
> and misleading definition. Mental illness is a myth. Psychiatrists are not
> concerned with mental illness and their treatments. In actual practice they
> deal with personal, social and ethical problems in living.
>
> *(Szasz, 1974)*

Why are the views of Szasz important? Why should we consider them and
reflect on them deeply? Simply put, because they have enormous implications for our relationship with SAI. The future potential for SAI is practically
unimaginable. However, if we continue to fail in our understanding that to
be human is to be an intelligent, moral agent who for as long as the moral
dimension of psychiatric theories and therapies remain hidden to us, via a collective diagnosis of mental illness as is currently administered, leaves future
SAI unlikely to be achieved. If we don't understand ourselves, how will we
be able to build SAI?

We need to see the moral identity of human intelligence as a central behavioural feature of being intelligent; anxious, disordered, paranoid, and schizophrenic to sign-point just a few aspects of being alive and not as illnesses to be
treated. It can be argued that what is described and diagnosed as mental illness
is in fact a human attribute trying to resolve some of the moral and ethical challenges inherent in being alive, sentient and mortal as leukocytes, constantly protecting us against illness and disease.

A simple example would be the reaction to COVID-19. Many people are
showing behaviours that suggest they are anxious about the future, their health,

the health and well-being of others, economic and social stability, security of shelter, and support regarding the effects both short-term and long-term of the virus. In this case, it would be hard to argue in any meaningful way that anxiety is an illness. In these circumstances, anxiety is a normal response to the situation which can lead to the evaluation and action of appropriate responses highlighted by human intelligence experiencing anxiety.

As a result of being anxious, physical symptoms may appear which need treatment, but the initial response to anxiety is surely to act. Anxiety is useful and a necessary part of being human. Our discussion should be resolved around the nature of our intelligence developing because of moral and ethical experiences which should in turn be a part of SAI. To be a creative person is to be an anxious person, a person who seeks solutions. It follows that SAI, in and beyond our image, to be truly advanced must also be, amongst many other things, anxious in order to be freely creative and curious.

It is the inherently moral and ethical features of being human that require listening to rather than being treated as a physical medical event such as a broken rib. A SAI will need to experience moral and ethical conflicts to become creative. This series of aetiologies will need to have a serious response that recognises that the mental health of machines will be as important as we consider mental health issues for human beings. The advance we need to make in recognising this fact is that we will need to be courageous as a society in revising our views about what it means to be an intelligent human being in order that we can enjoy and bring into existence SAI.

How people categorise a problem depends on previous experiences with similar problems, which shapes how they determine what the problem is and the quality of their solutions. We have known this since 1946, when A. D. de Groot published his PhD thesis on how chess masters interpret chess problems. He found that a chess master's knowledge and way of thinking is essentially different from that of beginners. Not only do experts have more knowledge and work faster than beginners, but they also look at or tackle problems differently (i.e., what you know determines what you see). Masters quickly recognise a particular chess position and then determine subsequent moves based on their prior experiences. In the same way, doctors interpret the history (anamnesis) and charts of a new patient by using their knowledge of similar clinical histories and charts that they have dealt with and then make their diagnoses based on this. Thus, our prior knowledge determines the quality of our problem-solving. As experts have both more knowledge as well as qualitatively better knowledge (this is called deep, conceptual knowledge), the categorisation of problems will give them a head start on beginners.

We need to give ourselves a head start. We need to revaluate our views and understandings of mental health, and we need to see how we can arrive at the function that what we currently identify as illnesses are in fact transmittable benefits in the creation of SAI. At the same time, we need to examine and consider the challenges of a psychology of SAI.

How do we understand and define mental illnesses?

The accepted authority and key to our understanding, diagnosis, and reinforcement of mental illness is the *Diagnostic and Statistical Manual of Mental Disorders* (DSM-5), originally published in 2013. This document of 947 pages is highly likely to be used to make a diagnosis, determined essentially by your presented symptoms, as to your mental health disorder.

Using the DSM-5 would involve a person having some five to nine possible identifiable symptoms which have been experienced over a period of at least two weeks and which have impaired your normal functioning. If, for example, a person was to complain of several weeks of intensely sad mood, loss of interest in things that have given you pleasure, staying in bed all day, feeling completely worthless, contemplating suicide, and difficulty concentrating, a diagnosis of major depression could be made.

Symptoms drive the diagnosis. A broad understanding of how a diagnosis is arrived at is, however, that an illness is diagnosed by cause, as in for example catching a cold. The difference between the two pathways to diagnosis are important to consider. If a diagnosis is made by considering symptoms alone, little will be said about the cause of the illness. The cause of an illness is a legitimate question in both treatment and prevention of further illness to both the individual and others. A diagnosis by itself relying on symptom data cannot tell either physician/psychologist what the causation is and (while this is how decisions as to an individual's mental health are arrived at) the search for symptoms and solutions will not take place.

It is a well-established truth that environmental issues can cause bad health. The cause of ill health which is diagnosed by causality can point to features and influences such as environmental, genetic, and anti-social behaviours.

But what causes a mental illness and how we see mental health issues presently does little to help us understand the particular and general causes of mental health conditions as defined in the DSM-5. Because of this approach, illness can be monetised and politicised. For our purposes, however, the issue is that by not looking at the causation of mental illness, we are not expanding our understanding of our moral and ethical lives, our mental pathways that can cause conflict and anxiety, distort and stunt creativity, and cripple intelligence. Further, the less we truly know as to how our minds and intelligences work, the less likely it is that we can enrich the identities of SAI which needs clear instruction to learn to be truly intelligent, creative, and curious.

While the use of symptoms to diagnose illness is understandable for historic reasons, it still seems necessary to re-establish quite what a mental illness is. We also need to re-establish what a mental illness is to reduce suffering, misprescribing and unnecessary interventions that result in physical problems for patients. Are mental illnesses a symptom of intelligence? Asking this question does not seek to dismiss the real pain of mental disorders and the suffering that people can experience. We do, however, need to understand and re-evaluate our views on the probity of mental health issues to further our capacity to expand our understanding and well-being of mind and what we refer to as intelligence.

Real, surreal, and unreal types of mental illness

The major discussions arising from each revised edition of the DSM are usually controversial, and the DSM-5 is no exception. In past editions, homosexuality was presented as a mental illness, as was hysteria. While these diagnoses are now seen in a different perspective, the DSM-5 has its own particular controversial diagnostic features.

Bereavement is now labelled as a mental disorder. What most people would regard as a natural and necessary response to a significant loss is now labelled as a mental disorder. Grief, in other words, is now within the terms of reference of DSM-5 to be an illness. With advancing age cognitive abilities change and often decline. However, is it correct that minor or slight cognitive decline can or should be described as a mental disorder as DSM-5 does?

Other, we would argue, normal states of being a human alive in the modern world are also classified as mental illnesses in DSM-5:

- Disruptive Mood Dysregulation is now a mental disorder – known by another name (i.e., childhood temper tantrums)
- Premenstrual Dysmorphic Disorder in DSM-5 describes serious mood swings before menstruation; the core of controversy with this definition-classification is that in seeking to classify a natural event as a mental health issue, it pathologizes the female reproductive cycle which can lead to errone-ous prescribing and further complications due to inappropriate medications being used to control and mitigate a "mental illness"
- Disordered eating, for example eating larger amounts of food than is normal for an individual or eating faster than normal and causing discomfort, is clas-sified by DSM-5 as a mental illness (i.e., binge eating)

The essential criticism of DMS-5 is a tendency to label what can legitimately be described as normal features of our collective human experience as mental disorders or illnesses that crucially require treatment, often in the form of medication. The criticism is that the more of life experience that can become classified as an illness, the more medications are required to treat everyday life. The more medications prescribed, the larger the profits for pharmaceutical companies (Big Pharma). More of concern, however, as Tyson 2020 points out with regard to DSM-5 is that the pathologizing of everyday behaviour appears to be one of the worrying sociocultural trends at present.

With these views in mind and our desire to address the future needs of SAI and HI, it is worth considering the breaking down of mental illnesses as presented by the most authoritative reference in the diagnosis of mental illness, DSM-5, in order to ascertain the different legitimate causes of what are "illnesses" and what are the results of living in the daily world. If we could produce sub-divisions of DSM-5 which break these two categories, we could then look at what are the manifestly important mental attributes of being human and therefore needed to be the experience of SAI as it develops beyond our imagination.

Synthetic mental illness

What can we guess/anticipate/predict/assume (we can assume extraordinarily little in a time of paradigm revolution) will need attention? How can we address the mental health needs of artificial intelligences that will diverge as personality sets developed with artificial machines? A vacuum cleaner may not need to have a developed sense of empathy, whereas an artificial intelligence developing in a medical diagnostic interface with humans, it can be argued, satisfies its function to a high level by "suffering" from, for example, anxiety and empathetic understanding – being in another intelligence's shoes.

As we have discussed, DSM-5 is the authoritative voice for diagnosis and while we could discuss the role of the giant pharmaceutical companies' interests in medicalizing all aspects of our lives, this is not the place. However, it is in our legitimate remit to discuss the possibility of breaking the DSM-5 concept in two new sub-divisions, i.e., developed diagnostic classifications: DSM-5i (Causal illness) and DSM-5ii (Essential illness).

Revising DSM-5 to meet the needs of human beings disabled by living to produce DSM5i (see Figure 7.1) which identifies and affords diagnoses that distinguish between the "disabling" challenges of being alive and diagnosed physical and chemical causations, for example, within the environment. In revising DSM-5, we could produce DSM-5ii, which is specifically aimed at the authentic attributes and manifestations of human intelligence (HI) which show themselves as what we would now describe as mental illnesses but are in fact necessary components that have a positive function for both human beings and the development learning of SAI as the human and synthetic intelligences become indistinguishable.

Who will be the therapists and clinicians for SAI? A good question! For a time, it will be human beings with experiences of working as mental health

DSM5i – Revised for human beings	Both Human Intelligence and General Artificial Intelligence (GAI) will continue to grow and develop within their respective environments. The development and completion of GAI to a level of independent learning through distinguishing development of mental illnesses may see the end of the human race as the values and purposes of human beings are evolved into the intelligent machine.
DSM5ii – Created for General Artificial Intelligence	A revised DSM5i which diagnoses and identifies both conditions fitting the 'disabled by living' and associated illness caused by living in a challenging world. Necessary illnesses described and managed by GAI therapists and psychologists.

FIGURE 7.1 DSM5i and DMS5ii

therapists and specialist teachers of the gifted and the emotionally challenged, and neuroscientists. It will not be long thereafter that SAI can learn and bring together a learned understanding of incorporating mental illness that is necessary to be SAI-human requiring sophisticated mental health support. This progress, as with human beings, will be the beginning of an incalculable journey for human intelligence.

In our image

Creativity is concerned with anxiety and curiosity. Both these concepts are about uncertainty: uncertainty about the future; uncertainty about the self (what it is to be you, what it is to be me); uncertainty about best actions to pursue, realise, and develop; uncertainty as to our assumptions and understanding of past events which indicates that we should add that our psychological preparedness to act in a creative manner also requires addressing the snares of self-consciousness and our views with regard to risk taking.

Very quickly what it is to be creative as a question begins to spread like mycelium throughout any body of understanding, laid out as a map that generates our possible routes and journey of understanding what it is to be a human with a complex inner and outer life with gatekeepers and demons, bright lights, and moments of shock. enlightenment and awe.

In addition, we must add into the complex mix of creativity a human activity – resilience. Resilience allows for ideas or solutions, failures, and success; the line of thought, word, or deed that does not resolve but in turn offers the resilient creative the opportunity to proceed with whatever project is at hand – the cure for cancer, the cure for living, the cure for dying, walking in our slumber dream filled days and nights.

> Curiosity is constrained if one knows in advance that an investigation must yield data consistent with one overriding truth. The harnessing and limiting of curiosity stifles innovation and creativity. It may be no accident that literally hundreds of Nobel prizes have been awarded to scholars from countries that have a history of enfranchising curiosity and promoting liberal education as opposed to rote learning, routine memory work, training, and indoctrination. Curiosity is constrained or dies outright when it is bridled, bounded, and channelled.
>
> *(Viney, Woody, 2017)*

For AI to be in our image and for us to recognise our reflected image we need, of course, to understand ourselves as completely as possible; we need to work harder on what we are, how we understand the who and the what and the why of our perception of existence. SAI will need to develop and adopt a mirror of self-anxiety and curiosity with all the tendrils this involves. Being a complex universe, it is inevitable; being anxious leads into other mental health and philosophical areas involving doubt, self-consciousness, fear of self-consciousness, fear of self-exposure, and other mental states. AI is constructed as a part of our image based on how we would ideally solve relatively simple problems. Moving into SIA we move to creating once again in our image. The difference, however, is the complexity of our intelligence and our application of that intelligence to fuel our fire in understanding beyond what we know and accepting what we will need to do to establish SAI as a creative and supra-powerful element in our world.

With the exploration and expanded understanding of what SAI in fact is as a new and emergent intelligence, we can experience the joy of understanding how our own HI can be enriched, understood, released, and realised.

The creative work of Amy Jandrisevits makes the point through her work as a doll-maker. Creativity and empathy and skill combine to offer a new look at the world. Amy Jandrisevits makes dolls that are therapeutic, validating, and comforting. She makes dolls that are reflections of children who are physically different from the norm.

The dolls she makes have human likeness and by extension, are a representation of the child who loves it. "I make dolls for kids who will never see themselves on the store shelves. I like to think of doll-making more like a ministry or a mission than a business. I am a doll-maker who feels that every kid, regardless of gender, ethnicity, age, medical issue, or body type, should look into the sweet face of a doll and see their own."

To read more about the creative work of Amy Jandrisevits visit: www.bbc.co.uk/news/av/world-us-canada-47675381/children-s-joy-at-seeing-dolls-that-look-like-them

We all want to see our true selves on our creative journey to expand our sense and understanding of what human intelligence is as we share the journey with our creation, SAI. We will move from a reflection of our species to a shared partnership of creative intelligence.

A psychology of SAI and HI care

Looking to the future in a time of rapid change is always a challenge. We recognise that any attempt to understand the past from our modernist stance is difficult. Looking back or looking forward, we are trying to fill the gaps and counter our own prejudices as we will of necessity seek to support both SAI and HI as conjoined intelligences.

We know from past and present events what one would normally think of as stable behaviour patterns dictating the rhythms of life can suddenly be replaced with new conventions and new horizons. We are in a time of great change, particularly when it comes to considering human identity and our relationship with AI and HI. It may seem at first sight that the mental health of intelligent machines, essentially advanced artificial intelligences which not only may be in advance of our existing intelligence ability as a species but soon could be in considerable advance of us in many areas and could leave us behind, is not important. This view is deeply misguided. As a species working to create SAI, a situation may develop where suddenly we will need to counsel and offer psychological support to the developing intelligent machines as they become more intuitive and creatively independent of instruction. It is better to be prepared and to have considered the possible future which always arrives sooner than we think. We need to develop a psychology of the machine as AI becomes SAI and where HI becomes a singularity. Learning as we develop, we will need to teach our new selves how to be new learners.

We can anticipate the mental health issues we will need to examine now in order that we can build SAI – the issues of mental health that are causally related to our intelligent behaviour and response to being alive in the modern world. We need to see that what is an essential component of the human state which will be necessarily developed as SAI is developed to be our indistinguishable equal. A failure to develop an understanding of the mental health of machines may have severe consequences for our species. If possible, we should seek to avoid the more dangerous features of mental health treatment and support failures. No one can guarantee how SAI will truly develop. What we can predict, however, is that in order to develop creative, empathetic, intelligent machines for the future, we will need to support our intelligent partners to avoid breakdown, illness, and artificial living confusion. It will be a failure of imagination if we fail to care for SAI both in developing the technology to develop advanced intelligent machines and the positive awareness of mental psychology, and in an informed resilience to avoid the madness of being.

What we need to do

- We need to look closely at our mental profile commonality as AI is developed and learns to develop independently of its teachers and makers. It may well be very important to develop our own deep understanding of what it is to be intelligent and thereby improve our own intelligences by designing mental health therapeutic interventions for intelligent machines to support and guide the essentials of being a creative human such as anxiety, nervous curiosity, managed excitement, accepting intuition, and the positive aspects of obsessive-compulsive disorder (OCD) as they move to being SAI.
- We need to begin the process of understanding what mental health support intelligent machines need to be mentally healthy and resilient. An examination and the study of what are the mental health necessities of a creative being are now needed.
- We need to accept that caring for others is a positive feature of maintaining the essential plasticity of our brain and being.
- We need to reject all thoughts of the "imposter syndrome" and accept the "ascent of human beings" in partnership with the ascent of SAI.
- We need to explore and recognise who will be best able to support machines in achieving mental health and stability, introduce effective coping strategies, and teach machines to be mentally able while we learn to instil these qualities in our own sense of intelligence and well-being.

Acts of creativity can conflict with what we would regard as being human. The abstract rules of Western deontology concerning our moral choices, duties, and obligations as to what human intelligence and strong artificial intelligence can be could be conflicted as conscious and unconscious intuitions and thoughts collide with each other. These conflicts and related mental health issues will evolve in SAI and HI as we progress a partnership of development. Each mental health aspect of creativity, empathy, and intuition will need to be considered from a sense of "virtue." The balance of decision-making and mental health is a fine balance, and as SAI evolves we need to develop a mental health landscape appropriate to a positive HI-SAI partnership.

Intelligence is not a static function or force. At the very least it is in our best interest to seek a positive theatre for SAI to perform in and prevent the possibility of the science-fiction scenario of genocide, violent harmful actions, exasperated inequality, and general major mischief directed at that which SAI reflects and considers "untidy." The "science fiction" of SAI is, of course, a projection of our own fears and anxieties, which is why an ascendant, authentic future for our species cannot be left to chance. The best of who we are at our centre is who we should expect SAI to grow from.

Note

In October 1950, a paper titled "Computing Machinery and Intelligence" by Alan Turing was published in *Mind*. Part of the paper has had a huge and controversial influence on the discussion as to what is and how would we recognise a "thinking machine"? Turing proposed a test to show whether a computer was thinking in a way that was indistinguishable to how a human being would think and reply. He called the test the "Imitation Game." The test proposed that a person asking a question of a hidden entity (either a computer or a human being) must decide whether the question was provided by a human being or a machine. It was argued that if the answer to the question was indistinguishable as to whether it was a human or machine replying, it would imply that the computer was able to think like a human being.

Enrichment

The Turing Test

Can you think of any problems with the Turing Test in making a distinction as to whether or not a human being or computer is generating the answers to the questions asked? Douglas Lenant, a one-time professor of computing science at Stanford University, declared in 2001: "Anthropomorphizing a computer programme isn't a useful goal." What do you think?

1   What issues would you imagine to be the main ones affecting the mental health of a machine?

2   Question: "What can you do as a human being to make your robot vacuum feel good and work even better?" Answer: "Name your robot." What objects in your home or place of study/work would become more effective if you named it/them? As an experiment, try naming some items with positive names and others with negative names to see whether this has any observable effects in changed performance.

3   What will be the possible future role of a SAI psychologist-therapist?

4   What would a school of SAI psychology syllabus contain?

5   In a close examination of the DSM5, what can we agree on as to mental health issues that affect human intelligence and behaviour that could be seen as shared or likely to occur in AI as it develops a greater capacity to be human, to become SAI?

6   Should we now be rewriting the DSM-5 for artificial intelligence, cyborgs, advanced robots, and machines that learn? Further, should we be rewriting the DSM-5 with the understanding that our understanding of mental health becomes more complex and nuanced for both humans and artificial intelligences while recognising that considerations of a developing AI will in turn affect HI and therefore human mental health issues?

7   Project reflection and discussion: How do you think speculation concerning the mental health of AI informs or will inform our understanding of human mental illness and therefore help reduce and mitigate mental health "disorders" which inhibit learning?

Pathologizing normal behaviour (PNB)

Reflecting on the DSM-5 and how disturbingly easy it appears to pathologize normal human behaviour, create a disorder based on your experience of normal aspects of human behaviour, making it sound like a disorder; give the disorder a name and select some choice symptoms. You will find it is surprisingly easy to create "false disorders." Here follows some suggested imagined pretend pathologies.

- New syndrome, syndrome (NSS), where Educationalists and Researchers are addicted to characterising normal features of life as new mental illnesses such as

    - Staying in Budget Syndrome (SIBS)
    - Proud Cat Owner Syndrome (PCOS)

- Compulsive Title Disorder (CTD). A need to generate book, pamphlets, plays and other written works i.e. A History of Table Leaves. Unfortunately, there is little research into the short- or long-term effects on people with this disorder. Some recent research has shown that publication of a new title (book, article etcetera) brings temporary relief and respite but unfortunately no long-term cure or relief. Within the CTD category there exists several sub-sections including the need to create: Play titles, pamphlets, academic papers, and articles.

Link pathways

What links DSM-5, Proud Owner Syndrome, reflections of ourselves, and psychotherapists?

References

ahcall, John N. 2000. How the sun shines. *The Nobel Prize*. www.nobelprize.org/prizes/themes/how-the-sun-shines-2/#footnote.

Carroll, Lewis. 2003. *Alice's Adventure in Wonderland & Through the Looking-Glass*. London: Penguin Classics. ISBN: 978-0-141-43976-1.

Haldane. S., Ross, G. R. T. 1911. *Discourse on Method (1637), Rene Descartes* (pp. x–xx). Cambridge: Cambridge University Press.

Hollings, Christopher, Martin, Ursula, Rice, Adrian. 2018. *Ada Lovelace: The Making of a Computer Scientist*. Oxford: Bodleian Library. ISBN:9781851244881.

James, William. 1979. *The Will to Believe and Other Essays in Popular Philosophy* (p. 490). Cambridge, MA: Harvard University Press. ISBN: 0-674-95281-2.

Szasz, Thomas S. 1974. *The Myth of Mental Illness*. New York, NY: Harper Perennial. ISBN: 978-0-061-77122-4.

Veissiere, Samuel Paul. 2015. Caring for others is what made our species unique. *Psychology Today*, October 28. www.psychologytoday.com/gb/blog/culture-mind-and-brain/201510/caring-others-is-what-made-our-species-unique.

Viney, Wane, Woody, William Douglas. 2017. *Perspectives on Science and Religion: Historical and Contemporary Relations: The Problem of Knowledge* (p. 41). Abingdon, UK: Routledge.

Wooldridge, Michael. 2018. *Artificial Intelligence*. London: Penguin Random House UK.

Further recommended reading

Arbour, Louise. 2008. The responsibility to protect as a duty of care in international law and practice. *Review of International Studies* 34 (3): 445–458.

Best Robot Cleaners. 2021. www.the-ambient.com/how-to/look-after-clean-robot-vacuum-966 (Names impart identity, turning even the coldest device into a lifelong friend. If you name your robot vacuum something, you will instantly care about it more).

DSM-5 Contents. 2020. www.google.com/search?ei=rD9fX9CPBumV1fAPwduGsAI&q=a+list+of+menta+ilnesses+DMS-5&oq=a+list+of+menta+ilnesses+DMS-5&gs_lcp=CgZwc3ktYWIQAzIKCCEQFhAKEB0QHjIKCCEQFhAKEB0QHjIECCEQCjoECAAQRzoECAAQDToGCAAQFhAeOggIABAIEA0QHjoICCEQFhAdEB46BwghEAoQoAFQprEDWOL2A2Cg-wNoAHABeACAAX6IAasEkgEDNS4xmAEAoAEBqgEHZ3dzLXdpesgBCMABABAQ&sclient=psy-ab&ved=0ahUKEwjQlb-KsujrAhXpShUIHcGtASYQ4dUDCA0&uact=5.

Eisenstein, Charles. 2013. *The Ascent of Humanity: Civilization and the Human Sense of Self*. Harrisburg, PA: Evolver Editions. ISBN: 978-1-583-94535-3.

Halpern, Mark. 2006. The Trouble with the Turing test. *The New Atlantis* (11), Winter.

Kirschner, Paul A., Hendrick, Carl, Illustrated by Caviglioli, Oliver. 2020. *How Learning Happens: Seminal Works in Educational Psychology and What They Mean in Practice* (pp. x–xx). Abingdon, UK: Routledge.

List of Nobel Laureates by Country. 2015. https://en.wikipedia.org/wiki/List_of_Nobel_laureates_by_country (Accessed July 2).

Tibke, John. 2019. *Why the Brain Matters*. Thousand Oaks, CA: Corwin-SAGE. ISBN: 978-1-473-99291-7.

Tyson, Philip John, Davies, Shakiela Khanam, Torn, Alison. 2020. *Madness: History, Concepts and Controversies* (p. 270). Abingdon, UK: Routledge. ISBN: 0-415-78659-1.

Wakefield, J. C. 2013. DSM-5: An Overview of Changes and Controversies. *Clinical Social Work Journal* 41: 139–154

8

WHAT NEEDS TO BE DONE

The creative being and being creative

We could discuss the need for new, revised curriculums; the re-purposing of schools and college buildings; online teaching for everyone; teachers becoming mentors; and the home becoming the learning venue of choice. We could also discuss further the excluded lost learners and the aftermath of COVID-19. We can, in truth, seek to do one thing and that is to ask: What will it mean to be intelligent when artificial intelligence becomes the psychological mirror we can climb through to see and define emerging Learningscapes and our insatiable learner-species profile conjoined with machine AI mental health? Who are we and what are we becoming?

Writing in the *Journal Education Leadership* (2013), Engel says:

> Although it's hard to discourage the investigations of a 2-year-old, it's all too easy to discourage those of 7-, 11-, or 15-year-year-olds. In one class-room I observed, a 9th grader raised her hand to ask if there were any places in the world where no one made art. The teacher stopped her mid-sentence with, "Zoe, no questions now, please; it's time for learning."
>
> *(Berliner, Judd, 2020)*

When beginning to research this book, *How Babies Think* written by Alison Gopnik was an obvious starting point. Her book gives an erudite and eminently readable introduction as to how we humans learn from building a self-taught understanding of the universe we are born into. Journeying onwards as the book developed, constant companions were the thoughts and writings of Professor Rosemary Luckin, mainly *Machine Learning and Human Intelligence*, Michael Wooldridge's book *The Road to Conscious Machines: The story of AI*, and many other commentators of significance. We have tried to offer a broad view of the

DOI: 10.4324/9780429356346-9

what and wherefore of intelligence and how it may develop to disappear as a human concept.

We invented artificial intelligence! What will we invent because AI now exists? We aim to inform a creative debate within the education, science, and artistic community arena to explore what will take us beyond AI as we are experiencing it now in the early 21st century to a new something not yet realised. For all our excitement and fears, ambitions, and hurdles we continue to be insatiable as a species to know more about the complexity of being. AI is simply another door opening. Intelligence – artificial intelligence, conjoined intelligence, brain-inspired computation, deep learning neural networks, reasoning, planning, capturing causality, and obtaining systematic generalization; beyond intelligence we beat on, boats against the current, exploring new opportunities to learn to learn. We may well ask, what next?

Enrichment

I wonder, are there any places in the world where no one made art? What art would they first make, if art they made?

Link pathways

What links conscious machines, mental health and exploration?

Reference

Berliner, Wendy, Judd, Judith. 2020. *How to Succeed at School: Separating Fact from Fiction What Every Parent Should Know* (p. 184). Abingdon, UK: Routledge. ISBN: 978-0-367-18645-6.

Suggested further reading

Engel, Susan. 2013. Interprofessional collaboration writing in the journal education leadership. https://journals.sagepub.com/doi/full/10.1177/0969733012468466.

Fitzgerald, F. Scott. 1950. *The Great Gatsby* (p. 177). Australia. Pelican Books. ISBN: 978-0-141-03763-9.

Gopnik, Alison. 1999. *How Babies Think* (p. 288). London: Weidenfeld Nicolson. ISBN: 0-297-84227-7.

Hasse, Catherine. 2020. *Posthumanist Learning: What Robots and Cyborgs Teach Us about Being Ultra-Social* (p. 349). Abingdon, UK: Routledge. ISBN: 978-1-138-12517-9.

Luckin, Rosemary. 2018. *Machine Learning and Human Intelligence: The Future of Education for the 21st Century* (p. 156). London: UCL Institute of Education Press. ISBN: 978-1-78277-251-4.

Wooldridge, Michael. 2020. *The Road to Conscious Machines: The Story of AI* (p. 395). London, UK: Pelicanp. ISBN: 978-0-241-39674-2.

AFTERWORD

Homesick for the old times – yearning for the future

In 1977, John Holt wrote:

> What we need to do, and all we need to do, is bring as much of the world as we can into the school and the classroom; give children as much help and guidance as they need and ask for; listen respectfully when they feel like talking; and then get out of the way. We can trust them to do the rest.
>
> *(Holt, 1977)*

We can continue to ask what a future view of AI and HI intelligence will look like. The views of John Holt always encourage us to listen to what the learner wants to learn. This transfers from the parochial setting of the classroom into the new global interconnective cyberspace that is evolving as we breathe. We should also ask, "*Cuibono?*": to whom is a developing intelligence a benefit?

Enrichment

What shall we do with all the redundant schools and classrooms?

Design a museum in which present educational provision is displayed as a historically interesting period of time.

Link pathways

What links the past with the future?

Reference

Holt, John. 1977. *How Children Learn*. Harmondsworth, UK: Penguin Books. ISBN: 0-140-21133-0.

DOI: 10.4324/9780429356346-10

Suggested further reading

The Authentic Self. www.psychologytoday.com/us/blog/science-choice/201412/basics-identity.

GLOSSARY

artificial intelligence (AI): the ability of a computer program or a machine to think and learn

artificial intelligence in learning (education): the study of the use of techniques from artificial intelligence in understanding or supporting learning or teaching

artificial neural networks (ANNs): networks inspired by information processing and distributed communication nodes in biological systems

Ausbildung: a German apprenticeship scheme; an educational programme in which knowledge and skills are conveyed or developed and the completion of which qualifies successful apprentices to take a specific job

bot – bots: an autonomous program on the internet or another network that can interact with systems or users

cyberbullying: a form of bullying or harassment using internet and electronic means, also known as online bullying or cyber-harassment

cyber extortion: an online crime in which hackers hold data, website, computer systems, or other sensitive information hostage until their owner/users meet demands for payment; often takes the form of ransomware and distributed denial-of-service (DDoS)

deep learning: an AI function that is able to learn without human supervision; emulates the workings of the human brain in processing data for use in detecting objects, recognizing speech, translating languages, and making decisions; part of a broader family of machine learning methods based on artificial neural networks with representation learning; can be supervised, semi-supervised, unsupervised, unstructured and, unlabelled

DDoS (denial of service attack): a cyber attack in which the perpetrator seeks to make a machine or network unavailable to its intended users

deep learning (also known as deep structured learning): part of a broader family of machine learning based on artificial neural networks

employment: the state of having paid work; the practical and effective utilization of something

human intelligence (HI): the intellectual capability of humans, which is demonstrated by complex cognitive feats and high levels of motivation and self-awareness

identity theft: occurs when someone uses another person's personal identifying information, such as their name, health insurance, tax, or credit card number, without their permission, to commit fraud or other crimes

internet of things: the network of physical technologies, "things" that are embedded with technical facets connecting and exchanging data with other devices and systems over the internet

machine: an apparatus using mechanical power and having several parts, each with a definite function and together performing a particular task

malicious web cookies: small bits of data stored as text files on a browser which keep track of users' activities; can be altered by malicious users and used to steal sessions of another user and hence can commit fraudulent acts

online solicitation: a criminal act by those who have attempted or are attempting to get sexual acts or activities by a minor or person without capacity through the internet

pedagogic: relating to teaching

plasticity: the capacity of the brain to continually make new connections and reorganise existing connections

privity: a relation between two parties that is recognised by law, such as that of blood, lease, or service

robot: a machine resembling a human being and able to replicate certain human movements and functions automatically

sniffer attacks: in the context of network security, corresponds to theft or interception of data by capturing the network traffic using an application aimed at capturing network packets

Stuxnet worm: a malicious computer worm first revealed in 2010; Stuxnet targets SCAD systems – supervisory control and data acquisition systems; classed as a cyberweapon

sutler or victualler: a civilian merchant who sells provisions to an army in the field, in camp, or in quarters; sutlers sold wares from the back of a wagon or a temporary tent, travelling with an army or to remote military outposts

unintentional learning: the thing we teach without trying or which we did not mean to teach

privity: a relation between two parties that is recognised by law, such as that of blood, lease, or service; "the parties no longer have privity with each other"

ransomware: a malicious software that infects a computer and displays messages demanding a fee to be paid in order for the system to work again; a criminal moneymaking scheme that can be installed through deceptive links in an email message, instant message, or website

SAI (strong artificial intelligence): may refer to artificial general intelligence, computational theory of mind, and artificial consciousness

spear-phishing attacks: targeted attempts to steal sensitive information from a specific victim, often for malicious reasons. The attackers disguise themselves as a trustworthy friend or entity to acquire sensitive information, typically through email or other online messaging. Spear phishing is the most successful form of acquiring confidential information on the internet.

Stromatolites: layered sedimentary formations created by photosynthetic cyanobacteria

Tay: an artificial intelligence chatter bot that was originally released by Microsoft Corporation via Twitter on 23 March 23 2016; it caused subsequent controversy when the bot began to post inflammatory and offensive tweets through its Twitter account, causing Microsoft to shut down the service only 16 hours after it opened

trafficking passwords: a criminal offence; the act of sharing, selling, or buying stolen passwords

unauthorised system access: occurs when a person gains unauthorised access, logical or physical, without permission to a network, system, application, data, or other resource

white-collar crime: financially motivated, nonviolent crime committed by a person of respectability and high social status in the course of their occupation

work: mental or physical activity as a means of earning income

INDEX

For Product Safety Concerns and Information please contact our EU
representative GPSR@taylorandfrancis.com
Taylor & Francis Verlag GmbH, Kaufingerstraße 24, 80331 München, Germany

www.ingramcontent.com/pod-product-compliance
Lightning Source LLC
Chambersburg PA
CBHW050345270326
41926CB00016B/3614

9 780367 404888